Hip Santa Cruz 3

*First-person Accounts of
the Hip Culture of Santa Cruz
in the 1960s, 1970s, and 1980s*

*Edited by Ralph H. Abraham
with the assistance of
Rick Gladstone, Kate Bowland, Paul Lee,
Fred McPherson, Don Monkerud,
Ed Penniman, and T.Mike Walker*

*Epigraph Books
Rhinebeck, New York*

For information contact:
Epigraph Publishing Service
22 East Market Street, Suite 304
Rhinebeck, New York 12572
www.epigraphPS.com

Book Design by Deb Shayne

ISBN 978-1-948796-50-7
Library of Congress Control Number: 2018964166

Bulk purchase discounts for educational or promotional purposes are available. Contact the publisher for more information.

CONTENTS

PREFACE

In the 1960s, Santa Cruz was a fountainhead of Hip culture. When I arrived in 1968 to join the new university, UCSC, the creative time was nearly over. By 1980, it seemed to me it had been such a miracle that its birth should be recorded. So I created the Santa Cruz Hip History Project in 2002, collecting oral histories and photographs in a website:
   http://www.ralph-abraham/org/1960s.

Original Concept, Volume #1.

The book *Hip Santa Cruz* published in June, 2016, was a compact summary of the 14 years accumulation of material from that website that was most relevant to the creation of the Hip culture of Santa Cruz. From 1964 to 1968, we followed the stories of some of the main characters of the Hip miracle in Santa Cruz, including 11 men and 2 women.

The book was presented to the Santa Cruz community in a reading and reunion at the Blitzer Gallery on August 6, 2016. Immediately there was a volunteering of additional stories, including several women, and stories into the 1970s. So I decided to create a sequel volume, *Hip Santa Cruz 2.*

New Concept, Volume #2.

In this second volume, I expanded the time-frame of the first volume, 1964-1968, up through the 1970s. My idea was to connect the decline of Hip culture with the ascent of the women's movement. Further, I wanted a balance of the genders consistent with the emerging equality of women and men, and here 50-50 was achieved. I ordered the chapters, as in the first volume, according to the approximate arrival date of the author in Santa Cruz.

In fact, the prime motive for this second volume was to balance the voices in the book according to gender, and to foreground the cultural transformation to Hip Women that occurred in the early 1970s.

New Concept, Volume #3.

The second volume was presented in a book launch event at the Santa Cruz Museum of Art and History on March 4, 2018. Once again there was a flood of offers of additional stories and interviews, so the idea of this third volume was born.

This time we again extended the time frame to follow the further evolution of the threads derived from the Hip Culture of the 1960s into the 1970s, and on into the 1980s. New threads have been included, such as music and the environmental movement. And several members of our community have stepped forward to assist me in the editing.

Acknowledgements

I am very grateful to all the contributors and supporters of the Santa Cruz Hip History Project, and especially to my co-editors: Rick Gladstone, Kate Bowland, Paul Lee, Fred McPherson, Don Monkerud, Ed Penniman, and T.Mike Walker. Also I am deeply indebted to Becky Leuning for heroic typing of all the interviews, to Nada Miljkovic for two interviews she contributed to the second volume, and to Hiroko Tojo, Deb Shayne and Bruce Damer for logistic support.

Special Thanks

Special thanks to Paul Lee, my friend since my earliest days at UCSC, who has been an emotional support, and also partner in editing for content and typos, throughout this project. He and I are the only ones, up to now, who have repeatedly read every page of this book.

Finally, deep gratitude to Fred McPherson, also my friend since earliest days here, who has helped this project all along the way. Very sadly he passed away, just two days before this volume was completed.

--Ralph Abraham, Santa Crua, November 10, 2018

Postscript

Hip Santa Cruz has brought to the surface the memory of the Santa Cruz of the 1960s and the spiritual spill into the '70s when the psychedelic ferment was actualized in various institutional sets; the music scene, so obviously a barometer of the times; the nonprofit scene and the hip entrepreneurship it represented; and most symbolic of all the birthing scene and the midwife revolution that made Santa Cruz a center of the national transformations of humane and personalized birthing. Remember Dolores Kreuger who had to re-introduce touching to the practice of nursing.

We are in turn touched by the extension of this sympathy and solicitude as it was manifested in our midst in so many ways. All celebrative of the spirit that was Hip Santa Cruz.

--Paul Lee

Ralph and Paul, getting into trouble.
Crown College UCSC, September 1968.
Photo by Caroline Blakemore.

MEMORIAL GALLERY
Our passed pioneers

\

Ron Boise, 1931-1966

Photo from BoiseLifeWorks.info

Tom Scribner, 1899-1982

Gusti Nina Graboi, 1918-1999

With Ralph Abraham at Cafe Zinho, 1988

Elizabeth Gips, d. 2001
Photo by Don Monkerud

Ken Kesey, 1935-2001
Ken Kesey with Paula Anima Fry Bevirt Holtz
(in a second exposure) to the right, who provided the photo.
At the Kesey farm in Oregon, 1967.

Peter Troxell, 1938-2004
Photo courtesy of George Stavis

S.D. Batish, 1914-2006; Shanta Batish, 1928-2017

Photo courtesy of the Batish Family

Al DiLudovico, 1926-2007

With Patti and Bob Ludlow in the Catalyst

Barbara Vogl, 1924-2009

Robert Hall, 1923-2009

Photo courtesy of Robin Hall

Leon Tabory, 1926-2009
Peter Demma, 1937-2015

Scott Kennedy, 1948-2011

Photo by Don Monkerud

Joseph Lysowski, 1939-2016

Fred McPherson, d. 2018

Photo courtesy of Nancy Macy

The Barn, 1966-1969

Photo courtesy of Holly Harman

Oganookie, 1970-1973

Drumhead by Terry King
Photo courtesy of Laura Littlefield

CHRONOLOGY

Here is a brief chronology of some the main events of the time. To the items from the PREFACE of the preceding volume, *Hip Santa Cruz 2*, I have added a few new items, in bold, which are covered in the present text.

- **1930s, Swing bands in Capitola, Beach street (Ken)**
- **1940s, Nine jazz clubs opened on Beach street (Ken)**
- **1953, Willie Mae Thornton on Beach street (Ed)**
- **1954, Two jazz clubs opened in Capitola (Ken)**
- **1956. Rock & Roll banned in Santa Cruz (Rick).**
- **1957, Dukes of R&R organised (Ed)**
- **1958 --------**
1. The Sticky Wicket, a cafe and gallery on Cathcart Street, was said to be the first Hip hangout. Later it moved to Aptos.
2. **The Dukes of R&R formed (Rick Alan).**
3. **Bridge Mountain created (Holly Harmen).**
4. **Began teaching childbirth education (Celeste)**
- **1959. Early years of Cabrillo (Roberta Bristol)**
- **1960**. Ken Kesey moved from the Wallace Stegner writing program at Stanford to La Honda and began house parties, along with LSD, fluorescent paintings, strobe lights, and music. Later, the house band became the Grateful Dead.
- **1961**. Peter Demma, discharged from military service, moved to Palo Alto, met Ken Kesey and Neal Cassady.
- **1962 --------**
1. Leon Tabory, psychiatrist, moved into Neal Cassady's house in Los Gatos, and opened an office in Santa Cruz.
2. Kesey published *One Flew Over the Cuckoo's Nest*.

3. Santa Cruz chapter of the ACLU formed.
4. **Cabrillo moved to large campus (Roberta Bristol)**
- **1963**. Peter, while running a bookstore in San Diego, visited Big Sur. In the hot baths with Ron Bevirt a plan was hatched to open a bookstore in Santa Cruz called the Hip Pocket Bookstore. The sign was to be made by Ron Boise, a sculptor living in Big Sur in a bread truck. A set of his works called the Kama Sutra sculptures was then showing at the Sticky Wicket.
- **1964**. Beginning of the golden years. --------

0. **April 17, Site dedication of UCSC (Herb)**
1. Ken Kesey published *Sometimes a Great Notion*, formed the Merry Pranksters. The bus Further took them to New York for a Kesey book event. Neal, Ron Bevirt, Lee Quarnstrom, Stewart Brand, Ed McClanahan. and others were on the trip.
2. Peter and Ron Bevirt opened the Hip Pocket Bookstore on September 13 in the St. George Hotel. The Ron Boise sign and two nude sculptures (covered by a sheet) were on hand. Norman Lezin, the mayor of Santa Cruz, had agreed to unveil the sculptures at the opening, which was busted by the police.
3. Later, Neal and Leon used to hang out and help out at the bookstore. Neal suggested the bookstore have free speech night every friday. Leon started them off, speaking about marijuana.
4. Leon hears Eric "Big Daddy" Nord was opening the Loft, a cafe at a barn in Scotts Valley. Leon went there, met Cathy, they married.

- **1965** -----
1. November 21, Wavy Gravy's Lysergic A GO GO in LA, with light show by Del Close. (See www.rollingstone. com/music/news/acid-tests-turn-50-wavy-gravy-merry-

prankster-ken-babbs-look-back-20151130.)

2. November 27, the first Acid Test, in Soquel, near Santa Cruz.
3. UCSC opened in the Fall.
4. The Hip Pocket Bookstore closed. Ron Lau purchased the books.

- **1966** --------

1. Bookshop Santa Cruz opened by Ron Lau.
2. In the summer, the Barn opened in Scotts Valley by Leon. It featured dances similar to the acid tests, with fluorescent wall paintings by Joe Lysowski and Pat Bisconti. Great artists such as Janis Joplin and Country Joe performed there. A local band performed on musical sculptures created by Ron Boise. Light shows created by Joe were among the first in the US.
3. Paul Lee (philosopher, founding editor of The Psychedelic Review) joined UCSC.
4. In the Fall, the Catalyst Coffee House and Delicatessen, run by Al And Patti DiLudovico, opened in the St. George Hotel next to the Bookshop.
5. **Trips Festival in San Francisco (Paula)**
6. **The Jefferson Airplane played a benefit for the "Miller for Congress" campaign at the Civic Auditorium (Rick)**

- **1967** --------

1. Jefferson Airplane played in Santa Cruz.
2. Hippies moved into the Holiday Cabins in Ben Lomond. (See Holly Harman, *Inside a Hippie Commune*, 2015, for the full story.)
3. 1000 Alba Road community created by Raven Lang and Ken Kinzie.
4. Methuselah I, summer camp at UCSC.
5. Alan Chadwick arrives at UCSC.

6. Start of the Chadwick Garden (Paul)
7. **Summer, the Redwood Ripsaw (started by Tom Scribner, Rick Gladstone, John Tuck, John Sanchez, Carol Staudacher - and Paul Lee was also at the first org. meeting) began publication. It was the first "alternative press" published in Santa Cruz (Rick)**
- **1968 -----**
1. Spring, I visited UCSC and the Barn, and decided to join UCSC.
2. Fall, I arrived with family. Moved into a 24-room Victorian mansion at 724 California Street.
3. Fall, The Kite (cafe) opened at UCSC.
- **1969 -----**
1. The Barn closed.
2. The Catalyst closed.
3. Jack Kerouac died.
4. I got into trouble at UCSC for political actions, along with Paul Lee.
5. Odyssey Records opened (Rich Bullock) with the Occult Shop (Lew Fein).
6. Logos Books and Records opened (John Livingston).
7. Fritjof Capra's epiphany.
8. **November, the Free Spaghetti Dinner, the original local alternative newspaper to which all subsequent alternative weeklies can trace their roots, began publication at the Blaine Street Family Collective (Rick)**
- **1970. The end of the golden years --------**
1. February 26. In the local alternative newspaper, *The Free Spaghetti Dinner*, I wrote in my regular column "Scientific Advice on the Politics of Life," under my pseudonym, Dr. Abraham Clearquill: "Last Fall I felt that the emerging community in Santa Cruz was at a

watershed, and that a development of some importance to the world was possible. Now I am convinced that this opportunity has passed, and the old structure is being recreated." (Thanks to Rick Gladstone, founding editor of the FSD, for recalling this.)

2. June, we vacated the Victorian mansion. (Ralph)
3. The decline of Hip, and ascent of the Women's Movement.
4. Santa Cruz Birth Center started (Raven Lang).
5. **Warmth created by Don McCaslin (T.Mike).**
6. **First ecology course at UCSC (Fred).**
7. **Oganookie arrived in Brookdale (Jack).**
8. **Fall, Krishna Cafe opened (Ralph)**
9. **Jazz instruction began at Cabrillo (Ken)**
10. **Start of the USA (Paul)**
11. **Start of the Whole Earth Restaurant (Herb)**

- **1971** --------
1. Women's dances began in San Lorenzo valley.
2. **Oganookie first appearance, UCSC (Jack).**
3. **Community on Last Chance Road (Paula).**
4. **Raven started the Birth Center (Celeste)**

- **1972** --------
1. **Beginning of action to stop SLV development (Fred).**
2. **The Birth Book published (Celeste}**
3. **Tandy Beal came to Cabrillo (Roberta Phillips)**
4. **Don McCaslin began Warmth (Ken)**
5. **Start of the William James Association (Paul)**

- **1973** --------
1. **Save the San Lorenzo Valley Association formed Fred)**
2. **Oganookie ended (Jack)**

- **1974** --------
1. SC Birth Center busted (Kate Bowland).
2. **Emergence of the Hanuman Foundation (Roberta**

McPherson)

3. **Nurse Midwife Practice Act passed**
4. **Hanuman Tape Library formed. (Paula)**
- **1975, Theater program began at Cabrillo (Ken)**
- **1976, Start California Conservation Corps (Paul)**
- **1977, Kuumbwa opened (Ken)**
- **1978 -----**

1. Institute of Feminine Arts created (Raven Lang)
2. **Mount Madonna opened (Paula)**
3. **Start of the Valley Women's Club (Nancy)**

Part 1
THE WOMEN'S MOVEMENT

Chapter 1. Kate Bowland, Interviews

I believe that Santa Cruz, for women artists and poets has been our Paris. There was so much happening here for creative women and these first person accounts are a continuation of the Hip Santa Cruz project. Being hip for women is different than for men. Often we don't give ourselves the respect we seek from others, from men, from the patriarchy. We down play the importance of very things that make us unique as females. The cycles of fertility, the ability to carry life within and give birth. So often our work primarily involves creating, sustaining and celebrating life.

I interviewed four women from a long list of women whose stories are remarkable. I regret that I was unable to cover everyone, especially the poets and writers. There are many women I consider to be heroes, who rarely come to public notice until their obits are published. Then you realize how much they did in their lives. Our grandchildren will take for granted things that it took us a life time to change. These women's paths may or may not have crossed, but they were on the same boat riding the same waves of consciousness and feminism. They dedicated their life's work to better the lives of women and all people.

Heroes, these women are. Some are little known and seldom seen outside their intimate circles. In the arts, health care, the world of dance, movement and yoga they have helped to connect people with each other and supported people to go deep within and listen to their minds and bodies. They created a special community. It is often difficult for women to get their bearing in a world that often does not give them the acknowledgement, credit or take their work seriously.

Roberta Bristol began teaching at Cabrillo College in 1959 and had a special talent for connecting people and creating community through movement and dance.

Celeste Phillips stood at a bedside watching a birth in 1956 and knew in her gut that babies and mothers belonged together from first breath and worked to create family centered care in all the 50 states.

Coeleen Kiebert shed her Midwestern world and came to Santa Cruz to be an artist and teach art as a process.

Paula Holtz was 16 years old when she joined the Merry Pranksters. She married Ron Bevirt and inspired by her homebirth of Joe Ben she went on to become a nurse midwife and a PhD psychologist.

Paula Holtz

Paula Holtz: I'd be happy to share my story with you. Part of my story is that I have been influenced in a deep way by some very powerful storytellers in my life. I was born in October of 1948, and I grew up in Santa Cruz. When I was in grade school, my parents owned a beautiful 100-acre ranch up Rodeo Gulch Road. That property had spectacular views of the Monterey Bay, meadows, redwoods and livestock. That experience of nature and place in Santa Cruz County really influenced my interest in and involvement with the "back to the land movement" of the late 1960s and 1070s.

In grade school, I became friends with a girl named Laurel Naman. Laurel was my best friend in junior high and high school. Santa Cruz at the time was a very different place than it is now, or has been for the last 54 years. It was a small town in the '50s and '60s. The town of Santa Cruz had a total population of about twenty five thousand people. It was a politically conservative place, and there were a lot of retired people, and summer homes here. In the winter months there were a lot of unoccupied vacation homes in Santa Cruz, and in the San Lorenzo Valley. People from the San Joaquin Valley and other places came to Santa Cruz in the summer to get out of the heat and be near the beach and Santa Cruz mountains. Santa Cruz was also not ethnically, racially or religiously diverse. In second grade I was at Bayview School, and there was a girl who was considered kind of unusual because she was Jewish. The culture in Santa Cruz at the time when I was growing up, and also when I was in high school, had a racist, sexist, and ethnocentric flavor.

KB: We had the Ku Klux Klan here.

PH: You got it. My friend Laurel's parents, Gladys and Dr. Marvin Naman were very liberal. Marvin was a founding member and a pediatrician at the Santa Cruz Medical Clinic that is now the Palo Alto Medical Foundation. He and Gladys were the parents of six kids. Laurel was the oldest. Gladys made an art form of homemaking and raising her children. She sewed, cooked amazingly and gardened. It was really a very special experience to watch how she made an art form of homemaking and raising her children. The Namans were also very well educated and prioritized giving that kind of education to their children. Their kids learned to sew, play instruments, garden, do all of those kinds of things. The Namans encouraged Laurel and me to express ourselves, to talk about our ideas, our beliefs, including our political beliefs. Gladys and Marvin were involved in the local ACLU and later, Marvin was involved in starting the Catalyst.

In my sophomore year of high school, the Beatles performed on the Ed Sullivan show, in February of 1964. As students at Soquel High we were enjoying the Beatles and the words to their songs that emerged into songs that really had to do with love, life and belonging. In the late summer of 1965, on August 31st I saw the Beatles perform at the Cow Palace, and it was a wonderful experience. That same summer, when I was between my junior and senior year of high school, I met and became friends with Bill Laudner, who lived down the street from me on 7th Avenue. He was also from Santa Cruz and in his early 20s. He surfed and played guitar with Paul Kantner at the Sticky Wicket, a Beatnik place in Aptos. Paul Kantner later became a part of the Jefferson Airplane. Bill became the road manager of the Airplane. Also, that summer I read the book, Summerhill: A Radical Approach to Child Rearing by A. S. Neill. The book was in the Naman's library. A. S. Neil had a school called Summerhill in the United Kingdom. The educational methods were very progressive, and really focused on what the interests of the students were, and self-directed learning. I shared my enthusiasm for the book with the Namans and they told me they understood there was a book of photos of Summerhill. Because I was interested in attending a school like Summerhill I went to the Hip Pocket Bookstore to order the book.

Ron Bevirt, who owned the store, took my order. A couple weeks later, when the book came in, he called me to tell me it had arrived. When I went to pick it up he asked me out on a date. I was 16 years old and he was 25. When he picked me up to take me to dinner several weeks later, he was wearing a three-piece suit and sandals. His hair was the length that the Beatles was at that time, which was considered long hair and radical at that time.

KB: Over the earlobes.

PH: Over the earlobes, you got it. We went out to dinner and had a lovely time together. We went on to date and do things together over the next few years. Ron Bevirt has also been called Hassler. At the time he was a part of a group called the Merry Pranksters. He had been nicknamed the Equipment Hassler on the Further bus trip in 1964. He was given that name for a number of reasons. One of them was that he would hassle the problems with the equipment, like the cameras or the equipment related to the film being made about the trip. He also took many still photos of the trip. That trip was memorialized in Tom Wolfe's book The Electric Kool-Aid Acid Test published in 1968 and the movie Magic Trip released in 2011 which includes actual footage and photos taken on the bus trip. Hassler took me to Ken Kesey's home in La Honda that fall. That was when I first met Ken Kesey. There was a party going on there and Bob Dylan songs were blaring on the outdoor audio system and people were working on painting the Further bus. It was quite an amazing scene. Another time that fall Hassler and I attended a party at Eden West, a nudist colony and community in Pescadero. We danced to the Beatles music ecstatically. I fell in love with Hassler. My experience was that he was a thoughtful, educated, and a kind man. He had gotten a bachelor's degree from Washington University in Saint Louis, Missouri. He then attended three years of law school before he dropped out. and then he joined the military. In college he was part of the ROTC. So when he dropped out of law school he became a lieutenant in the army and was stationed at Fort Ord, a US Army post in Monterey County, California. There he met Gurney Norman, who was also a lieutenant. Gurney was an author and writer who knew Ken Kesey and other authors and writers like Larry McMurtry, Wendell Berry and Bob Stone, who had attended Stanford University's creative writing program as Wallace Stegner Fellows, studying under Stegner in a seminar. Through his relationship with Gurney, Ron went to Perry Lane, in Palo Alto, where Ken Kesey was living at that time. Ken Kesey later moved to La Honda. So that's how Ron became a part of that group of people, the Merry Pranksters.

Hassler at the time I met him was a very down-to-earth man. He could make things happen. He was also a student of yoga. He had met a man named Cliff who was a Native American man who had learned about yoga and yoga philosophy in Burma. Cliff had a farm in Placerville, California where Hassler went and lived and worked off and on over the next two years. In the fall of 1966, Hassler handed me, at the Hip Pocket Bookstore, his copy of the book, How to Know God: The Yoga Aphorisms of Patanjali authored by Swami Prabhavananda and Christopher Isherwood. Patanjali was an Indian sage and was said to have written the yoga sutras, around 400 BC. They are concise aphorisms that outline the whole philosophy of yoga. So I first had the sutras in my hand when I was 16. Yoga philosophy and the teachings of the ancient sage Patanjali have over the decades become a central part of my life.

The Merry Pranksters at the time that I first met them, in the fall of 1965 were beginning to do the Acid Tests. There were two of the Hip Pocket Bookstore employees that were part of the Merry Pranksters: Ken Babbs and Gretchen Fetchin' – that was her Prankster name. Her real name was Paula Sundsten. Babbs and Gretch had rented a place in Soquel which they called "the Spread" where they lived and where the first Acid Test was held. On January 21-23, 1966 I went to the Trips Festival at Longshoreman's Hall in San Francisco. This was an Acid Test that had in part been organized by Ken Kesey, Ron Bevirt and Stewart Brand. The Grateful Dead and Big Brother and the Holding Company performed. There was music, dancing, strobe lights, day glow paint and free access to LSD, which was legal at the time. On March 19 of 1966 I went to the Pico Acid Test in Los Angeles. The Grateful Dead played, and I remember they played Midnight Hour for probably an hour. They just kept playing it and playing it and playing it and we were all dancing and dancing. These experiences were really life-changing for me. The Pranksters used LSD for consciousness expansion at that time. They really, really believed that LSD was going to change the world.

KB: It did.

PH: The psychedelic experience can open what Aldous Huxley called "The Doors of Perception" in his 1954 book; a book I read in 1966. The experience can help us access a greater degree of awareness and allow us to see life through a wider lens. It certainly did this for me and many others including the 6000 people who attended the Trips Festival, an event that is credited with being the start of the hippie counterculture. So the fall of 1965 and the winter/spring of 1966 was when I began hanging out with what I can now think of as the psychedelic intelligentsia. I was a senior at Soquel High School, and I remember I had these leather loafers that I had painted with day glow paint. Looking back I realize that wearing those shoes to school was a radical statement. At the time high school girls were not supposed to wear pants to school. We always wore dresses and we wore girdles, garter belts and stockings under our dresses.

KB: Right.

PH: The lyrics of a popular song at the time was "Love and marriage go together like a horse and carriage". In fact it was culturally not ok for teenage girls and women to have sex before marriage. I was having sex before marriage and this was certainly radical at the time. Somehow, I had learned about birth control pills, so I went to a male OB/GYN who worked at the Santa Cruz Medical Clinic, and got birth control pills. He expressed his criticism of me for having sex before marriage but prescribed the pills anyway.

KB: That was the revolution.

PH: Yes, and the availability of effective methods of contraception has been a revolution for women since that time.

After I graduated from high school in June of 1966, that summer I lived in San Francisco, in the Haight-Ashbury.

KB: I was there.

PH: Mm-hmm. I lived in a house on the panhandle and –

KB: I lived on the park, between 8th and 9th and Lincoln Way.

PH: I had gone to the Haight-Ashbury with Hassler the winter before, and met Janis Joplin, who was not a part of Big Brother and the Holding Company then. She came in and was wearing all these clothes from free bins and smelled like patchouli. She was very open and talkative and fun. Because I knew Bill Laudner, who had become the road manager of the Jefferson Airplane, during the summer of 1966, I spent time with members of the Jefferson Airplane and watched them rehearse. The Airplane were not then famous and honestly neither were the Grateful Dead. They were both local bands that people really enjoyed and who played publicly, but it was before the Summer of Love in 1967. The Haight-Ashbury wasn't a famous place at that point.

KB: Right. It was an affordable place to live.

PH: Yeah, exactly. People were smoking marijuana and using LSD. However, it was more on the level of consciousness expansion and not so much about getting stoned. I had been accepted to the University of California Santa Cruz, UCSC, for the fall of 1966. UCSC and Cowell College had opened only the year before in 1965. I was admitted to Stevenson College at UCSC for the fall of 1966 the second year of UCSC and the first year that Stevenson opened. So the summer between graduating from high school and beginning college, I spent time with Hassler and friends in the Haight Ashbury.

At the end of the summer I went to see the Beatles with the Pranksters at Candlestick Park on August 29th of 1966. That was the Beatles last live performance.

That summer of 1966, Ken Kesey was a fugitive. He had been arrested for possession of marijuana at his place in La Honda and then fled to Mexico. The Pranksters, on Further bus, followed Ken to Mexico. And while there, Gretchen had her first baby, Mouse, a little girl.

KB: And where did she have it?

PH: She had her baby at a Mexican hospital in1966. When the Pranksters came back from Mexico, Kesey came back with them from Mexico. While he was still a fugitive, they did an Acid Test at San Francisco State. It was called the Whatever It Is Festival, and it happened on September 30th through October 2nd of 1966. There were lots of people there who took LSD. Ken Kesey told stories to the crowd over the radio because he was still a fugitive. A little later the Pranksters began living in a warehouse on Harriet Street, South of Market, in San Francisco. The Further bus was parked inside the warehouse.

Even though I had started college at UCSC, at the end of September, I spent a fair amount of time up there in the warehouse. Neal Cassady was there throwing a hammer and talking his nonstop narrative. When I would come in I would be added to his narrative, "here comes Paula Fry she's now a college student . . .". I had become friends with Ken Kesey. He and Ron Hassler Bevirt, were organizing the Acid Test Graduation which was to be held at the Winterland Ballroom, and the Grateful Dead were going to play. One day I was with Ken Kesey. He was still a fugitive. We went into the basement of a house, and the then-manager of the Grateful Dead was there. He told Kesey that the Grateful Dead were not going to play for the Acid Test Graduation because they did not want to be associated with LSD.

KB: [laughter]

PH: They were not then famous, and the culture was such that they were worried about being associated with LSD, which on October 6, 1966 had been declared an illegal drug in California. So the band that played at the Acid Test Graduation was called the Anonymous Artists of America. The Anonymous Artists of America were a group of people who were living in Los Altos, California. Many of them had been Stanford students, and they played ad-lib, improvisational music. While they were living in Los Altos, Richard Alpert, now known as Ram Dass, had come from the East Coast and was living there at the house where members of the Anonymous Artists were living. Richard Alpert helped to launch the band. The slogan for the Acid Test Graduation was, "Cleanliness is next." In the big warehouse where the Acid Test Graduation took place, there was a huge painted sign that said, "Cleanliness is next." And the gist of it was that we could be clean from drugs and still expand our consciousness. What was starting to happen in the Haight-Ashbury and certainly during the next year, in '67, was that the counterculture scene was deteriorating, and people were using drugs to get stoned.

So, the Acid Test Graduation occurred on Halloween of 1966. It was an amazing event and I received a diploma for having "passed the acid test". Maybe a week or two prior, Tom Wolfe showed up at the warehouse in his dapper three piece suit. Tom Wolfe was an author from New York. He had come to check out what was going on with Ken Kesey and the Merry Pranksters. And he subsequently published a book about the Merry Pranksters called Electric Kool-Aid Acid Test.

The Acid Test Graduation occurred when I was in my first quarter at UCSC. I was a biology major. When I was a sophomore in high school, for some unknown reason, I remember saying that I wanted to be an Ob-Gyn when I grew up. Of course I knew Dr. Marvin Naman. I don't know how much of an influence that had on me, but just out of the blue, it was, I want to be Ob-Gyn. That was why I had chosen to be a biology major at UCSC.

That fall I also spent some time hanging out at the Spread where Kesey was living with Babbs and Gretch and others of the Pranksters. Hassler had sold the Hip Pocket Bookstore to Ron Lau who had changed the store's name to Bookshop Santa Cruz. Hassler would come and go from the Spread to Cliff's farm in Placerville. All of these activities with the Pranksters were of course a huge distraction for me in my college studies.

In early spring of 1967 Babbs and Gretch left the spread and stayed with me at a house I rented in Felton when I decided to move out of the dorms at UCSC. I learned from them and Ken Kesey that there was an event coming up on March 16 in Houston, Texas. Ken, as the author of One Flew Over the Cuckoos Nest and Sometimes a Great Notion, had been invited to speak at Brown College, Rice University. So the Pranksters were planning on going on the Further bus to Houston. After two quarters at UCSC, during spring break, I decided to drop out as a college student. Life with the Pranksters seemed much more interesting. Kesey had made a deal with me; he would pick me up at the Greyhound bus station in Amarillo, Texas. I trusted him enough that I caught a plane and went to the bus station and he and Pranksters picked me up on the Further bus. Neal Cassady was driving the bus. I then traveled back to California and then Oregon with them.

Ken Kesey was raised in Eugene, Oregon. He had a younger brother, Chuck. His dad was in the creamery business, and his brother Chuck had gone to Oregon State in creamery science. Chuck had a creamery called the Springfield Creamery, and was married. He and his wife, Sue, ran the creamery. While they lived in Springfield near Eugene, they also owned a really beautiful farm nearby in Pleasant Hill. The farm had a big barn on it and some other outbuildings. Ken Kesey, no longer a fugitive, was anticipating going to jail for six months for possession of marijuana beginning in the summer of 1967. He had sold his home in La Honda and his wife Faye and his three children, Zane, Shannon and Jed had moved to his brother's farm. The Pranksters, some of whom were from Oregon like Michael Hagen and George Walker, also moved to the farm.

Because Kesey was anticipating going to jail, before he went he wanted to take another trip. So after we arrived back from Texas on the Further bus, he and I took a driving trip together for several weeks through the western United States. We started the trip in Santa Cruz. It was then that I first met Richard Alpert, now known as Ram Dass. He was living in Los Altos at the time, with the Anonymous Artists. He and Kesey had made a date to get together. Richard Alpert had come to Santa Cruz because there was someone he knew whose son had had a psychotic episode, who was in his early twenties. Richard Alpert came over from Los Altos to talk to this young man and give the family some help. Richard Alpert was a clinical psychologist who had taught at Harvard and was a colleague of Timothy Leary. The two of them had authored the book, The Psychedelic Experience: A Manual Based on the Tibetan Book of the Dead. I had read this book prior to meeting him. After that meeting Ken Kesey and I drove to Yosemite, to southern Utah, and ultimately to Jackson Hole, Wyoming where he had a friend. On the way back we went to Salt Lake City, and then drove to Springfield, Oregon. That driving trip with Kesey was life changing for me. He and I spent hours together talking. I heard stories about Kesey's life.

For example he told me the Indian character in Cuckoo's Nest came to him as a Peyote vision. Importantly I learned about my intellect and the life of the mind. After returning Ken Kesey went to jail at the Sheriff's Honor Camp in the Santa Cruz Mountains above Palo Alto in the summer of 1967 for possession of marijuana. I visited him there a few times. That summer I moved to Chuck's farm in Pleasant Hill and lived there with the other Pranksters.

One of the things that happened on Chuck Kesey's farm, that later became Ken's farm, was that there were some renovations done to the barn so people could live in it, and there was a kitchen and some cabins built. So in a sense the Pranksters started going back to the land, in the beginning of a back-to-the-land era. Like the Merry Pranksters, after the Summer of Love in 1967, the Anonymous Artists of America boarded their psychedelic bus and set off for southern Colorado, to Gardner and Redwing, where they ultimately bought land and also, like the Pranksters, lived the essence of the American back-to-the-land movement. At that time those of us who were involved in that movement were interested in nutrition, sustainability, organic food, growing your own food, raising livestock and building things.

Chuck Kesey, who had the Springfield Creamery, came to those of us who were helping with raising the baby calves in the early spring of 1968. These were dairy calves who were taken from their mothers when they were one-day old. Chuck explained to us that he had learned about what is now called probiotics during his creamery science education at Oregon State. He had an idea that feeding the calves milk that had the bacteria lactobacillus acidophilus and bifidus in it would increase the survival rate of the calves. So he began culturing this milk at Springfield Creamery to feed to the baby calves and we fed them with it. Because of this the survival rate of the calves we were raising was very good. Later Chuck and the Springfield Creamery went on to culture yogurt with Acidophilus and Bifudus, a product called Nancy's Yogurt. Nancy was a secretary that worked at the Springfield Creamery. So Chuck Kesey was a real pioneer of the probiotic movement from 1967.

In the fall of 1967 Gretch became pregnant with her second child. Gretch had given birth to her first child Mouse in a Mexican hospital as we talked about before, and now she was pregnant again, Gretch decided she wasn't going to go to a hospital to give birth. She said, "If I can have a baby in a Mexican hospital, I can have a baby at home."

KB: That's a good quote.

PH: So she went to the public health folks and learned about how to prepare. I was living in the barn with George Walker, who was one of the Pranksters, and my friend Jenny Scott. Gretch assigned George, Jenny and I the job of helping if there was a need for transport to a hospital during her labor and the birth. In case there was an emergency, the plan was to load Gretch into the Bam Truck, a carryall truck with a mattress in the back, and go to the hospital. One night, in the middle of the night, we were awakened and told that Gretch was in labor. Babbs and Gretch had built a little one room cabin down by the pond, behind the barn. It had a little child's bed built on the wall for Mouse. I went down to their cabin. You couldn't really tell Gretch was in labor. She was lying on her side. She was breathing quietly. It was hard to tell when she was having contractions. After about half an hour, she said to Babbs who was to deliver the baby, "Babbs, can you see its head yet?" He said no, and then, with the next contraction, she turned over onto her back in a semi-inclined position, the baby's head began to show, crowned, and the baby delivered in one contraction.

KB: Wow.

PH: The baby just slid out into Babb's hands. Just as that happened, with that contraction, Mouse woke up, sat up in bed, and as the baby's head was delivered, said, "ooooooo" .

KB: How old was she?

PH: Less than 2. It was dawn. That was the first birth I witnessed in my life. It was so peaceful and sweet.

KB: Wow, that's a great story.

PH: Later that spring, I heard that Hassler was at our friend Lee Quarnstrom's house on Zayante Road in Felton. Because I had been in love with Hassler for quite some time, I decided to leave Kesey's farm and go see Hassler. We spent some weeks together at Lee's house and then decided to get married.

KB: How old were you then?

PH: I was 19. We were married on June 12th of 1968 in the quarry at UCSC, by Paul Lee.

KB: Wow.

PH: And my friend Laurel Naman attended the ceremony with Paul's, young daughter. . After we got married, we decided to go to St. Louis, Missouri, because Hassler, was from O'Fallon, Illinois, which is east of St. Louis across the Mississippi River. His family, generations back, had been farmers. His dad was a very dedicated man and worked for a company and had moved to St. Louis, and Ron in part grew up in St. Louis. His parents had bought a little farm in a little town west of St. Louis called Villa Ridge. Because we were moving in the direction of being back-to-the-land folks Ron wanted to go check out the farm. We lived there for about nine months. Hassler got a job teaching elementary school during that time. I was learning to weave and I also knew how to sew. George Walker came to visit us there. The Pranksters had a certain psychedelic style to clothing, so I was sewing and making clothes with bright colors and striped sleeves.

The culture of the Saint Louis area was, in the end, just too conservative for us. So we left the Saint Louis area to go back to Eugene, Oregon and to Kesey's farm. That summer Wavy Gravy came with three buses carrying people from the Hog Farm to Kesey's farm. They were on their way to the Woodstock festival that happened August 15 through August 18, 1969. I had been to the Hog Farm in southern California the summer of 1966 and knew Wavy from that time. George Walker, Hassler and I had purchased a bus. We were fixing the bus up with a plan to also go to Woodstock; but in the end decided not to go. So we were there at Kesey's farm until the fall of 1969. Then we moved back to Santa Cruz and rented a house in Zayante with George Walker. We wanted to look for land.

Our friends, the Anonymous Artists of America, had moved to Gardner, Colorado, which is on the eastern slope the Sangre de Christo Mountains in Southern Colorado in the Huerfano River Valley. As I mentioned before, they were part of the back-to-the-land movement. In the spring of 1970 Hassler and I decided to move to Gardner, Colorado. We drove our big bus and a truck to Gardner and then rented an old adobe farmhouse near this little town called Red Wing that was near Gardner. Hassler got a job as a ranch hand at the Singing River Ranch in Redwing. I gardened, had goats that I milked, and canned fruit. The area was very rural and it was sparsely populated with about 500 people, mostly Texans and Mexicans. Outside of Gardner, Libre had started. Libre was a huge commune. Most of the people at Libre, were from the East Coast. The Gardner area in the late 1960s and early 1970s was being overrun with back-to-the-land counterculture folks. This was also the time that Stephen Gaskin and his group left San Francisco and went to Tennessee.

KB: I call it the diaspora, where we left San Francisco and

planted little pods of psychedelic consciousness.

PH: Exactly. And so we lived in Colorado for about a year. My experience of the area was it was a deeply spiritual place; it felt like there were fairies behind every bush. We looked for land in various places in Colorado and George Walker came to visit us because he wanted to buy land with us.

KB: Yep. I was doing the same thing.

PH: We looked and didn't really find anything and so we returned to Santa Cruz, with our goats in the bus. We returned in part because George Walker had purchased a 65-foot yacht called the Flying Cloud, and it was docked in Honolulu. He wanted us to come to help him work on the boat. David Crosby, of the Crosby, Stills, Nash and Young Band, had also purchased a yacht. George Walker and David Crosby talked about the Psychedelic Armada. The thought still was that LSD was going to change the world. After finding a home for our goats in the Bonny Doon area of Santa Cruz County we went to Hawaii, to Honolulu, to work on the boat. We were in Honolulu for a couple months. When we got back from Honolulu, Stewart Brand, who had started the Whole Earth Catalog, had asked Ken Kesey, Hassler and Paul Krassner, who did one of the first counterculture magazines called The Realist in New York City, to edit the Last Supplement to the Whole Earth Catalog. The Last Whole Earth Catalog, published in 1971 was at the time the biggest seller Random House, the publisher, had every had. The editorial focus of the Whole Earth Catalog was on self-sufficiency, ecology, alternative education, "do it yourself" (DIY) and holism and featured the slogan "access to tools". So we came back from Honolulu and worked on The Last Supplement to The Whole Earth Catalog. I authored, as Paula Bevirt, an article about acidophilus and lactobacillus bifidus in The Last Supplement to the Whole Earth Catalog.

KB: Is it on the web?

PH: Yes, The Last Supplement to the Whole Earth Catalog, was archived by The Realist on the web.

KB: How wonderful.

PH: And it really had a lot of how-to stuff in it, you know.

KB: I remember. I wish I wouldn't have let mine go.

PH: Yeah.

KB: A treasure trove of ...

PH: for the back-to-the-land people.

KB: Absolutely.

PH: After that, Hassler and I and Paul Krassner moved to a house on a cliff above the ocean in La Selva Beach, in Santa Cruz County. Paul had founded, edited and contributed to the Realist magazine. He was also the founder of the Youth International Party (Yippies) in 1967. In 1968 the Yippies had protested at the Democratic National Convention demanding an immediate end to the war in Viet Nam. Paul has described the Yippies as "an organic coalition of psychedelic hippies and political activists". Paul is quite an amazing man and was, ironically as a male, the first "feminist" that I knew. It is certainly true that many men in the sixties were sexist.

KB: Yeah, they were raised by men in the forties and fifties.

PH: They were not necessarily disrespectful of women, but they thought a woman's place was in the home and their purpose was to have babies and raise families.

KB: Because we know, '68 kind of marked the rise of consciousness. The Feminine Mystic was written in '65 and consciousness-raising groups were starting to happen.

PH: Right. So we were living in La Selva Beach with Paul Krassner in the summer of 1971. While living in La Selva, Hassler and I continued to look for land. And we found a piece of land, 150 acres, up Last Chance Road in the Swanton area of northern Santa Cruz County. Gurney Norman and his partner Chloe Scott who were friends of ours wanted to buy land with us. Gurney had written and just published a mini novel in The Last Whole Earth Catalog called "Divine Right's Trip". The story was about an archetypal counter-culture hero, Divine Right, and appeared "episodically" as a series of sidebars on right-hand pages of The Last Whole Earth Catalog. The Whole Earth Catalog was established as a non-profit organization. But because Divine Right's Trip was a novel within the catalog Gurney received a royalty from Random House and had some money. We bought this 150 acre property that had these beautiful mountain meadows looking down the Waddell Basin to the ocean. It was an old homestead, and without electricity or telephone.

KB: Or water?

PH: No, it had a spring. And in fact, Last Chance Road got its name from that spring, because the spring on our property was the last chance to get water for the horse-cart wagons that were going into the hills, before cars. We bought that property in the fall of 1971. Paul Lee and Hassler agreed that we would provide kind of a back-to-the-land educational experience for people that Paul referred. In the summer of 1972, Gurney and Chloe decided they wanted to sell their share of the land, and so what Hassler and I did was to gather together four other people as partners in the land. Three of them had been students at UCSC and had done training with Alan Chadwick in biodynamic horticulture at the Garden at UCSC.

In the winter of 1972, I intentionally got pregnant and decided to give birth at home, which was three and a half miles down a dirt road behind a locked gate. I made that decision because if I had chosen to give birth at the hospital at the time, I would have had to lay flat on my back, had an episioproctotomy, an incision from my vagina through to my rectum, and had my baby taken away immediately to the nursery.

KB: Yep.

PH: I didn't want to have that happen to me and my baby at birth. Because of my experience watching Gretch give birth, I felt safe having my baby at home. While I was pregnant I looked into my options for who would attend me when I gave birth. I actually came to the Birth Center on Escalona Dr.

KB: My house, you know.

PH: Yes, your house. I talked to women there, and asked a few questions. One of my questions was,"How do you tell how far along a woman is in labor?". I was told, "Well, we don't do pelvic exams because of the risk of infection". My intuition told me the midwives didn't do pelvic exams because they don't know how to. So what I did instead was I found an emergency room doctor named Barbara Gabert, M.D. who agreed to attend me. Also, Kitty Lakos agreed to come as well as Donna Lyke, who was a registered nurse and our childbirth instructor, who later became the first Ob/GYN nurse practitioner in Santa Cruz County. I went into labor close to midnight the night of Labor Day, September 3, 1973. I had a short labor and a pretty easy time laboring. Because we were three and a half miles down a dirt road and behind a locked gate, we sent one of our land partners out to call Barbara, Kitty and Donna on the phone in the phone booth by the Last Chance Road gate by what was then The Big Creek Pottery School. When Barbara, Kitty and Donna arrived I was calmly breathing through contractions.

KB: You had a great example before you.

PH: Exactly. And I was managing just fine. Barbara examined me and told me I was completely dilated. JoeBen was born five minutes later, after a five minute second stage, near dawn.

KB: Amazing. It's a great story; because I was doing births

out there in the '70s. I just want to ask a question. One of the things that I noticed in those years when I was doing births was, many times women when they were in labor would say, "Oh, I'm getting that psychedelic feeling." "Oh, this is like a rush," you know. And the whole language came from higher consciousness. So did you experience any of that familiarity when you were in labor?

PH: Yes. I did, and also a kind of opening of the heart, you know, just a real sense of being held by the Universe. It was a very empowering experience. I was lucky in the sense that it was a really straightforward labor, and also JoeBen was an avid breast feeder right away. Giving birth to JoeBen was an amazingly significant experience in my life. In the years following that, I became interested in being able to provide services for women that weren't available to me when I was pregnant and gave birth to JoeBen.

During that time in the early days at Last Chance we were friends with Ram Dass.

KB: When you had the baby you were friends with Ram Dass?

PH: Yes. As I mentioned earlier I had first met Ram Dass when he was Richard Alpert, in the spring of 1967 in Santa Cruz when I was with Ken Kesey. That was right before Richard Alpert went to India where he met his guru, Neem Karoli Baba and his teacher Baba Hari Dass. When he came back from India and began teaching through public speaking in 1969 he had changed his name to Baba Ram Dass. Hassler and I had many friends in common with Ram Dass, the Anonymous Artists, Paul Krassner, Dean Quarnstrom who was Lee's brother. So we became friends with him. When he came back from India, he told as many stories about Baba Hari Dass, his teacher, as he did about his guru, Neem Karoli Baba. He talked about this Himalayan yogi who had been silent for many, many years (in fact Baba Hari Dass had been silent since 1952) and drank two glasses of milk a day. Baba Hari Dass was Ram Dass's teacher when Ram Dass was in India. During that time Ram Dass had also taken a vow of silence. Baba Hari Dass would come in the room Ram Das was staying in and would write little aphorisms on his chalkboard. An example I remember was, "A snake knows heart". Ram Dass told the story that when he was on the airplane coming back to the United States, somebody had given him a book about Ashtanga yoga, the school of yoga described in The Yoga Sutras of Patanjali that I mentioned earlier. In his story Ram Dass described that as he was reading this book about Ashtanga yoga, he realized that Baba Hari Dass through writing these little aphorisms on the chalkboard had taught him Ashtanga yoga. Ram Dass called this form of teaching maiutic teaching. This method of teaching involves a dialogue of asking and answering questions. Ram Dass described how Baba Hari Dass taught him just one step ahead of where he was so the learning seemed to come from inside. The Lama Foundation, in 1970, had published a book by Ram Dass entitled From Bindu to Ojas, that was later revised and published as Be Here Now. It was published in the form of what was called the book in the box. There were a number of small books inside the box. During the time when JoeBen was an infant and small child, Ram Dass would come to Santa Cruz, we would get together with him and he would give talks to large audiences at the Civic Auditorium in Santa Cruz.

In 1971, Baba Hari Dass came to the United States. He was sponsored by a woman named Ruth Horsting, also known as Ma Renu. Ma was a professor at UC Davis in Art. She was the first tenured female art professor at UC Davis. At Davis she had students who had gone and met Baba Hari Dass in India. Ma Renu had a home in Davis, she had a summer home at the Sea Ranch in Sonoma County, and she had a house on Leonard Street in Santa Cruz. Baba Hari Dass would come to Santa Cruz and do darshan at the Leonard Street house. He was also invited and attended and taught via his chalkboard, through questions and answers, at a religious studies class at UCSC. The class was taught by S. Paul Kashap. Baba Hari Dass moved with Ma Renu to Bonny Doon in Santa Cruz County in 1974. Ma Renu had retired from her job as an art professor at UC Davis and devoted the rest of her life to the study of yoga and service to orphaned and destitute children. Baba Hari Dass, also known as Baba-ji, taught his students the importance of developing positive qualities through selfless service and the practice of Ashtanga yoga with the aim of attaining peace.

After Baba-ji moved to Santa Cruz County he instructed his students, many of whom had been or were UCSC students, to look for land. In 1976, they found the land that is now Mount Madonna Center. His students then went through the process of getting permits to build, and in 1978 Mount Madonna Center officially opened. Before Mount Madonna Center opened Baba-ji did weekly Satsang for years at Natural Bridges School on the West side of Santa Cruz that I attended. His students also taught yoga classes in the early 1970s at Cabrillo College and UCSC. His students, under his direction, founded the Hanuman Fellowship in 1973 and the Sri Rama Foundation in 1972. Sri Rama was founded to support the development of Sri Ram Ashram for destitute children located in Shyampur, near Haridwar, India through the publication of Baba-ji's writings. Under Baba-ji's direction his students through Hanuman Fellowship also started Gateways Books, a non-profit spiritual bookstore, that opened on the Pacific Garden Mall in downtown Santa Cruz in 1978. Gateways Books was open for 32 years in Santa Cruz. The

Hanuman Fellowship, under Baba-ji's direction also founded and sponsors the Pacific Cultural Center and Ashtanga Yoga Institute a community yoga center in the Seabright neighborhood of Santa Cruz.

The seventies was also a time when there was a whole emergence of kind of ecumenical spirituality in Santa Cruz County. The Dalai Lama was actually at the UCSC campus in the 1979. The event was down in the meadow below the East Field House. The meadow was packed with people.

KB: Yeah, I remember that really well.

PH: Mm-hmm. And of course, Allen Ginsberg was a Buddhist and shared Buddhist philosophy. I had met and spent time with Allen Ginsberg in 1967. He had influenced his good friend Neal Cassidy who frequently mentioned "karma" in his narrative monologues. In fact one of the slogans painted on the ceiling of the Further bus, above the driver's seat, was "Nothing Lasts" a philosophical statement about impermanence that is central to Buddhist teachings.

In 1974, because Ram Dass was lecturing and teaching all over the United States and people wanted to get access to his talks, the Hanuman Tape Library was established in Santa Cruz. Stephen Levine, who later became very well known for working with death and dying and authored many books, lived in Santa Cruz and taught Vipassana meditation classes at the Hanuman Tape Library on the west side of town. I attended these classes when I was 26 years old. In other words there was this whole spiritual renaissance in Santa Cruz, from the late '60s into the '70s.

KB: Right up 'til now.

PH: Yes, right up 'til now. And Baba Hari Dass has been very much a part of that renaissance, both in known ways and in unknown ways. He has influenced many, many people, and taught classical yoga and weekly classes about the Yoga

Sutras of Patanjali, and the Bhagavad Gita from the early seventies at the Leonard Street House until he retired from teaching in 2013. As I mentioned, I first had the sutras in my hands when I was 16. One time in Yoga Sutra class I asked Baba-ji a question about Sutra 1:47 that describes the state of nirvichara samadhi (enlightenment related to one-pointed concentration). I asked, "Baba-ji what is that state like?" In response he wrote on his chalkboard: "Compassion automatically flows."

In other words, I think there were a number of cultural transformations that occurred in Santa Cruz because of the counter culture, or the hip culture. Certainly, the racist culture transformed because of the involvement of people like Marvin Naman and the ACLU and the Civil Rights Movement. In addition, the very narrow Christian view of the 1960s was expanded into an ecumenical view that really, all religions have the same fundamental base. As the Beatles said, Love is all you need.

KB: Yeah. Love and compassion.

PH: Yeah, I really see how the events of the 1960s and 1970s have changed our culture in amazing ways in Santa Cruz and that has spilled over to other places as well. One of the ways, of course, is with the sense of women empowering themselves. In my life, because of my experience watching Gretch give birth in 1968 I was enabled to chose not to become a victim of the medical system of obstetrics in 1973. In that year and for decades before that women were routinely given analgesics, pain relievers, like scopolamine, which is an amnesic. With this drug on board women weren't able to participate in the second stage of labor and to push their babies out. Because of that, many babies were born by forceps deliveries. I've heard women tell stories of waking up alone in the hallway on a gurney outside the delivery room after their baby was born.

Because of the amnesiac effect of the drug they'd been given they couldn't remember having given birth and their baby had been taken away to the nursery

These stories are in sharp contrast to my empowering home birth experience giving birth to JoeBen. After his birth and after witnessing Gretch give birth to her son, I began to feel that it was very important for women to be able to choose to give birth in the hospital. However, I believed the environment needed to be safe, women needed to be supported to give birth naturally if possible, their partners/husbands and other family members should be able to be in attendance, and the labor and birth should not be medically intervened on as long as the labor and birth were going along in a normal fashion. In the years following my son's birth I actually was at a few home births and decided I wanted to go back to school and become a registered nurse. So I enrolled at Cabrillo College and started back to school and took the prerequisite courses in 1976. I began the nursing program in 1977 and completed it in 1979. After completing the program I got a job as a labor and delivery nurse at Dominican Hospital and was a part of a specialty educational program for labor and delivery nurses taught by Carolyn Fisher, RN and Celeste Phillips, RN. The training emphasized natural and family centered childbirth. After completing that program I took a job at the birth center at Community Hospital of Santa Cruz, which offered a more family centered approach. I worked there for two years. Then I decided I was going to go back to school and applied at University of California at Davis and became a family nurse practitioner (FNP). I was especially interested in maternal child health. Because of this right after I completed my FNP training I started a program at Stanford called the Women's Health Care Training Project, and became a nurse-midwife. As a part of my education as a nurse-midwife, I worked clinically at the then Santa Cruz Medical Clinic, with Larry Lenz M.D. an OB-Gyn who was very supportive of the idea of using OB-Gyn nurse practitioners and nurse-midwives. Because of this he later supported me in applying for hospital privileges as a nurse-midwife at Dominican and Community Hospitals. My first job as a nurse-midwife was in Mountain View. I worked for an OB-Gyn named Gert Pakorny M.D.. He, very progressively, had founded an out-hospital birthing center across the street from El Camino Hospital. I worked with him as solo nurse-midwife, on call 24/7. I did between five and twelve births a month at this out-of-hospital birth center, and worked four ten-hour clinical days a week. It was like midwifery boot camp. And after a year, I insisted that I have a partner, and a woman, who had just graduated from Yale's three-year program that allows you to become a registered nurse and then a mid-level practitioner nurse-midwife, Elizabeth Yanaga, CNM, joined me in practice.

KB: She's really a good friend of mine now. We really connected very deeply, we spent a long time together. I had lunch with her yesterday. She's fabulous.

PH: Yeah, she's a wonderful woman. So Elizabeth and I worked together for a period of time. Then, Larry Lenz, M.D. invited me to come back to the Santa Cruz Medical Clinic to see patients prenatally and do women's health care. I continued to work to get hospital privileges. It took three and a half years for me to get privileges. The woman who helped start the Nurse Midwifery program at UCSF, Rosemary Mann, CNM, MSN, JD, PhD had become the director of the Women's Health Care Training Project at Stanford. She had become an attorney after she was a nurse-midwife. Rosemary advised me to communicate with lawyers at the Federal Trade Commission. She told me the Federal Trade Commission was looking for a test case related to a nurse-midwife and hospital privileges.

KB: Were they a government agency?

PH: The Federal Trade Commission is a federal governmental agency. So I contacted the Federal Trade Commission and the female attorney that I talked to said, "I'm not supposed to give you this advice, but what you need to do is find an attorney that specializes in antitrust". And so I found an attorney in San Francisco named Pat Cutler, JD. I talked to her on the phone and she instructed me to write a letter to her explaining all the details of the process that I had been through so far with trying to obtain privileges. I did write that letter, a 20 page document. Part of what had happened was first the idea was presented to the doctors at the Santa Cruz Medical Clinic. It took a year to get the Santa Cruz Medical Clinic's permission for me to apply for privileges at the local hospitals because many of the doctors weren't aware that nurse-midwifery was legal at that time. This was in 1984. So, after they learned that nurse-midwifery was legal in the State of California, the Medical clinic decided to support my application for privileges. Then the idea of nurse-midwifery hospital privileges was presented to the OB-Gyn Committee a couple times at Dominican Hospital. Some of the obstetricians were against the idea of having nurse-midwives. In the first go-round the OB/GYN Committee at Dominican Hospital refused to allow privileges. I had written, as I said, a very detailed description of all the events that had gone on with respect to my getting privileges. When I called Patricia Cutler, the antitrust attorney to tell her I'd written the letter, I was told she wasn't there. They said she was ill. Eventually I did reach her and she agreed to take the case. Some months later I found out that she had been home on bedrest because she was early in pregnancy and was bleeding and spotting because she had a placenta previa, a low lying placenta. What I want to emphasize here is the synchronicity. I just happened to find Patricia Cutler, an antitrust attorney, and she just happened to be pregnant, and then she decided to take the case. What are the odds? Pat wrote two demand letters, after doing a lot of legal research. One was submitted to Dominican Hospital and one was submitted to Community Hospital. I had applied at both those hospitals. After receiving the letters, the attorneys for the hospitals told the OB-Gyn committees that they had to allow protocols to be written and allow nurse-midwives to apply for privileges because they would lose the case if it went to court.

KB: When was this?

PH: Patricia Cutler wrote the demand letters in 1986. One of the things that had happened in the series of events that took place before Patricia wrote the letters was that one of the obstetricians had made the argument in writing that nurse-midwives should not be allowed privileges because of the increased morbidity and mortality. There was actually research at the time that showed that even with high-risk pregnancy, the morbidity and mortality with nurse-midwifery deliveries was equal to and in some cases lower than that of OB-Gyn's.

KB: Right.

PH: The other point this same obstetrician made was that given the fact that family doctors were doing deliveries, there were not enough pregnant women to support the OB-Gyns who were already in practice in Santa Cruz. That statement was considered a restraint of trade statement. Basically the documentation that argued against allowing nurse-midwives privileges from the OB-Gyn Committee included untrue assumptions and suggested restraint of trade. And so the attorneys advised the OB-Gyn committees that they needed to allow me to have hospital privileges. Ultimately, I did gain privileges and also wrote the protocol for nurse-midwives.

In the year prior to my receiving privileges, because we didn't know if I was going to get privileges, I was hired by Drs. Tony Damore and Sid Sogalow, both obstetricians in Los Gatos, and was the first nurse-midwife at Los Gatos Community Hospital to gain privileges. But I didn't have to fight for that, because Drs. Tony Damore and Sid Sogalow were some of the only obstetricians working there at the time and they wanted nurse-midwives. So I left my job at the Santa Cruz Medical clinic and delivered babies at Los Gatos Community Hospital. And then, six months after I started doing that, I received privileges in Santa Cruz, and Tony and Sid were amazed. They had told me when I applied to work for them it was never going to happen at Dominican and Community Hospitals, but six months later it did. I started working as a nurse-midwife doing deliveries at Community and Dominican Hospitals in 1987, with Larry Lenz, M.D., Howard Salvay, M.D., and Bud Dickerson, M.D. as my back up obstetricians. And so, my goal as a nurse-midwife doing hospital births, was to be able to provide women safe, family-centered care. Also to be present during labor and birth and support and not intervene unless needed, but to make sure that things stayed safe. One of the things that I also did was to teach childbirth education classes that anyone could attend. The focus was labor pain management methodologies that utilized body centered visualization and breathing practices. I also taught prenatal yoga classes with Tripura Sundari, who was also a student of Baba Hari Dass, at Pacific Cultural Center. We worked to create a culture of awareness around the personal meaning of being pregnant, childbearing, giving birth, mothering and understanding what it was to become a mother. We used to sing and chant in prenatal yoga class. At that time I was on call 24/7. And working clinically two or four days a week, and I did deliveries at both Dominican and

Community Hospitals. In the time that I was doing births at Community and Dominican Hospitals, my C-section rate was five percent. As I mentioned I wrote the first protocols and it said that nurse-midwives were to be in the hospital once the person was in active labor, which is four centimeters dilated. I was also able to do vaginal births after cesarean, VBAC.

I felt called at the time to pursue getting hospital privileges and feel grateful for the synchronous events that enabled me to do so. There are many nurse-midwives who now have privileges and deliver at the hospitals. In fact I have heard that a third of all the deliveries are being done by nurse-midwives. But unfortunately, because of the way the nursing practice act is written, nurse-midwives are really under the thumbs of the obstetricians.

KB: We lost again.

PH: Yes. And to some extent what that means is that families and child-bearing women and babies lost again. Now the cesarean section rate is above 33 percent and the epidural rate I've heard is something like 60 to 70 percent, which increases morbidity and mortality. In addition women lose the experience of feeling empowered.

In 1992, I decided I wanted to go back to school and get a Ph.D. in clinical psychology. My interest was prompted by my experience with my patients and the psychological and spiritual dimensions and experiences they had in the course of childbearing. There was no way I could be in school and be on call in a private nurse-midwifery practice so I left the job at the Santa Cruz Medical Clinic. I then took a job at Kaiser, and I was one of the first group of nurse-midwives doing deliveries at Santa Teresa Hospital. I did go back to school, and eventually got my PhD as a clinical psychologist. While still in school, after I left Kaiser, I managed the prenatal clinics for the County of Santa Cruz, working with the medically indigent. I also began working as a psychiatric, mental health nurse practitioner at the County of Santa Cruz. Later after completing my Ph,D, I worked at UCSC as a psychiatric mental health nurse practitioner and psychologist in Psychiatry and the Counseling and Psychological Services department. I am now semi-retired and work part time in a private psychotherapy practice as a clinical psychologist.

There has been a lot of synchronicity related to events in my life. The term synchronicity was coined by Carl Jung and refers to events that are meaningful coincidences that occur with no causal relationship. One of the most important of these events was being brought to Santa Cruz when I was three weeks old and then growing up and living in Santa Cruz for most of my life. Because I grew up in Santa Cruz I met Ron Hassler Bevirt. Gretch told me a story after Hassler and I got married. Remember Hassler asked me out on a date when the picture book of Summerhill arrived in the fall of 1965. Gretch told me when she and Babbs were working at the Hip Pocket Bookstore during that time, there were was a big Prankster event at Asilomar that fall. Hassler told Gretch and Babbs he wasn't going to the event. So Gretch asked Hassler, "Hey, how come you're not going to this event?" and he said, "I'm going to take the girl out to dinner that I'm going to marry."

KB: And you were 16.

PH: I was 16.

KB: And you married at 19. And he knew it.

PH: Yes.

KB: When did you marry Jonathan Holtz?

PH: I married Jonathan in 1985. But we have been together since 1977. JoeBen was 4 at the time. Part of the reason that I left the marriage with Ron Bevirt, with Hassler, was because he really believed that women should stay home and be mothers, and wasn't that supportive of me going back to school. So while he is a good man and good father, it didn't work any longer for me to be in the relationship with him. Jonathan is five years younger than I am, and went to UCSC for his undergraduate education at Kresge College. Kresge College was a place where the Human Growth and Potential movement was really coming into full bloom in the 1970s because of faculty like Michael Kahn Ph.D. who practiced Zazen and was in the Psychology Department and was a central faculty at Kresge College at UCSC. I met Jonathan at an anatomy class at Cabrillo when I was doing my prerequisite courses for the nursing program there. He was taking the course because, although he'd been a premed major at UCSC he wanted to become a physical therapist. The next year, in 1978, he was admitted into Stanford's physical therapy program. In the anatomy class I experienced that Jonathan was not challenged by my intelligence and in his core was a feminist. Over the years he has supported me through all of the education I've done: registered nursing, family nurse practitioner training, nurse-midwifery training and getting a Ph.D in clinical psychology. He also supported me doing nurse-midwifery and being on call 24/7. Most importantly, he supported my parenting my son JoeBen and has been a committed and devoted step-father to him. His presence in my life has been an amazing gift and healing in my life that I am deeply grateful for.

Another series of synchronous events in my life was related to my having had the book How to Know God: The Yoga Aphorisms of Patanjali in my hands when I was 16. A later synchronous event that was related to this was when Ram Dass first came back from India. Because I had met him as Richard Alpert, with Kesey, I could recognize that he was a changed man. It was one of the most faith inspiring experiences of my life, because like I said, the motto at the

Acid Test Graduation was Cleanliness is Next. And he had moved on from the psychedelics to the spiritual. I was hanging out with the psychedelic intelligentsia at the time, and in some ways their lives were a mess. Like I mentioned earlier Ram Dass told as many stories about his teacher Baba Hari Dass as he did his guru Neem Karoli Baba. I didn't have to go anywhere to find my guru. Baba-ji came to Santa Cruz and I have now been his student and a student of yoga practice and philosophy for decades.

Because I grew up and lived in Santa Cruz, I was lucky enough to see the Beatles perform twice. George Harrison, who was also deeply influenced by yoga philosophy in his life, in the lyrics of the song Brainwashed, that is in his last album, of the same title released in 2002 almost a year after his death, sang "The soul does not love. It is love itself. It does not exist it is existence itself. It does not know. It is knowledge itself". How to Know God, page 130". This quote was taken by George Harrison from the book How to Know God: The Yoga Aphorisms of Patanjali that I had in my hands when I was 16.

So the many experiences I've had in Santa Cruz, including those I had in the 1960s and 1970s have transformed me.

Ron Bevirt and Paula Bevirt.
Shortly after their wedding in 1968.

Photo courtesy of Paula Bevirt Holtz.

Coeleen Kiebert:
ART AND SPIRIT, CLAY IS THE WAY

In 1970 Coeleen Kiebert heard the west Coast calling and she listened. She had hit the glass ceiling at the University of Minnesota, after she pitched her plan to combine art and psychology and was told she could be a high school counselor. Her Midwestern life had come to an end. Her inner navigator guided her to California to do personal therapy with Janie Rhyne. She packed up and with her four children swerved west and drove to Santa Cruz.

A world traveler, her work is influenced by Asia and her many trips to China and Japan. She studied Japanese Traditional Arts at Oomoto School near Kyoto. Her bronze sculptures reside all around the county--on Pacific Avenue, at the Museum of Art and History, at UCSC on the Coeleen Kiebert Patio at Cowell College. Also at Cowell is the series of 5 sculptures called "Justice" in the Provost Garden.

She dared to ask "Why are there so few great or famous women artists." One of the very important aspects of her pioneer work in Santa Cruz was to address the psychology of women artists, in particular issues of development of ego strength, self confidence and self esteem. She had taught hundreds of women over five decades as well as doing her own work. She developed a way of working "side by side" with women, a partnership model that allows for experimentation and growth in their work.

Coeleen had just turned 86 years old when I interviewed in her Aptos studio on the cliff's edge high above the Pacific where she lives with her children and grand children in a rambling house with add on studios filled with art books, paintings, sculptures and plants. A sculpture garden over looking the Pacific Ocean was the rich back drop for the visit.

Coeleen: I had been attending the University of Minnesota, and one day I walked into the graduate school office and noticed that the dean's door was open. "Do you have a minute?" I asked. "I'm very frustrated. There is this movement going on called the Human Potential Movement." The dean didn't know what I was talking about. "Wait a minute." He went and brought back an assistant. "Listen to what she's saying." I explained what was going on in the movement and what I wanted to do with my studies was to combine psychology and art.

"Would you write a page about this?" he asked. I did and received a letter from him three days later which said, "Your message is all very interesting, but we really see you as a high school counselor, and that's it."

I stayed on, studying, trying to do the best I could. My friend who was a psychotherapist in Minneapolis knew about my problem, and one night he introduced me to Janie Rhyne. "I'm just going to leave you two alone. I can see you have a lot to talk about." He said.

Janie had recently moved out of the Haight-Ashbury when she realized that thirteen different people had a key to her apartment. She had a house in Pescadero California and was writing her book *Gestalt Art Experience*. I asked her if she would work with me, do Gestalt Art Therapy with me, and she agreed and invited me to stay with her and offered me her painting studio. I talked with my children and arranged for the teenage neighbor girls to take care of my four children for the two week sessions with Janie.

I painted all day while she wrote, and at night we would look at my paintings and she'd do Gestalt Therapy using my images.

Working with her process I realized there was a part of me, an inner spiritual place that I wanted to live from in order to thrive. I didn't think that it was likely to happen in Minneapolis. The culture to support it wasn't there. It was more likely to happen out here in California. I went home and thought seriously about my choices, came back out job hunting and stopped to visit Janie in Santa Cruz on my way to San Diego.

"You have good timing. I'm on my way to lunch with Frank Barron up at UCSC today. Would you like to come with me? I don't know much about him, but he sounds interesting. Turned out Frank was interested in what I was interested in; psychology and art. He taught psychology, and had done an elegant study of the creative females at Mills College, with Ravenna Helson. He'd been at UC Berkeley, and before that he was one of the three or four men at Harvard that did the early LSD experiments. He had worked with Richard Alpert, who became Ram Dass, Timothy Leary, and John Lilly who did the work with the dolphins, and Lois Bateson and Gregory Bateson. This was about 1964-1970.

Gregory and Lois went to study the dolphins with John Lilly in San Diego, which sounded pretty exciting to me. I interviewed at UC San Diego, and they said they could offer me a teaching position and wanted me to finish my graduate work there. I called Janie and said, "I'm moving to San Diego, although it doesn't feel exactly right."

"I'm so glad you called. Frank thinks that you ought to come back up here to UCSC and do your graduate work here."

I came back to Santa Cruz and I interviewed with Frank, Ted Sarbin, Pavel Mackotka and David Marlowe, and that was it. I went home, told my kids we're moving to California, packed up, and sold my house. Both of my parents had died and I was divorced and was no longer anchored to Minneapolis. With the money from my house and a small inheritance I bought this house in Aptos. Because I was a woman, a single mother, the lender kept upping the amount they wanted for the down payment but somehow I worked it out. When I arrived at UCSC, I was informed that there was no teaching job for me; however,' when Frank learned of my work in Minnesota doing Organizational Development, consulting with hospitals and doing reorganization of the nurses he suggested I apply with the UCSC Extension Program. I was hired.

Two years later the man who I had worked with in Minnesota, David Jones, followed me out here. We married and together ran a consulting company together. I continued doing organizational development in hospitals, mainly El Camino Hospital in Mountain View and at Stanford and here at Dominican with then director Sister Josephine, raising self-esteem of the nurses and reorganizing around that issue.

It was very exciting for me at UCSC because my primary interest then and still is what happens psychologically when we're creating. Personally I had experienced one of those awful dry spells, and I worked my way through it. I was beginning to see there were stages that I went through when I was creating, and I felt a sense of personal empowerment from this realization. I was teaching art, and was excited to tell everybody about my insight. You've all got this process you go through, and everybody ought to understand it. When I talked about it people would respond, "Well that's what I do!" Many artists confirmed my insights. I believed that it made artists stronger when they knew this about themselves, and understood they're going through a process, especially when they felt like their work had dried up or hit a block.

Five phases of Creative process

There are five phases that I've identified, and the first one is making a **Statement of Intention**. This is what I'm going to do. Maslow said that you don't have to wait around to be hit all of a sudden by a great idea. You can create your life; you can set your life up so that these things happen. When you're going to create, you decide what it is you're going to do, which is what we do in my classes.

Then you go into the second stage, which is **Gathering**. You pull your materials together and your ideas together, and usually in that gathering there will be some point where you think, "Oh, I should have never taken this on, or I don't have it, or I've lost track of what I was going to do. Who am I to spend my time this way?" — all of that. And many people walk away from their creative process at that time.

Kate: At the gathering stage, because of self doubt?

Coeleen: Yes. But from C.G.Jung's point of view, this is the shadow coming in, you know, it's all part of it. And then it takes ego strength to hang in there through that. Because this doubt almost always precedes something really wonderful breaking through. And when that breakthrough comes through —there is a rush of creative energy.

This is stage three I call it **All of a Sudden**. It's an **Explosion**. You have stated your intention, gathered materials and ideas, and then there is an explosion. You lose track of consciousness. You lose track of time, of hunger, of being cold. It's just this thing that's happening and if it's two in the morning and it's going to take two more hours, that's what it's going to take. You're lost in it. And sometimes I feel like it takes all I've got to keep up with it, because I know it's bigger than me, or better than me, you know, if I can just keep up with it. And it has its own energy-- it's like an orgasm. Exactly like an orgasm, or just exactly like the birth of a child. It's something that's experienced all the time in other ways.

It happens and it has its own thing. When my students have that experience they start talking about their sculpture as she or he or even it, but it becomes another entity outside of them. Now those three stages have been identified by others way before me, but Frank thought that I was onto something more, because I identified two more stages.

The fourth is **Assimilation**, just being with it, really looking at it. Just being with what just happened. Write about it, draw it, play music to it, just look at it. Just see what happened. Journal about it. This, I call assimilation.

Kate: You know as a midwife my metaphors are always about birth — The woman in labor in transition sometimes will give up. She has gathered her coping skill and her energy, the energy's there, but sometimes she gives up. Giving up can either manifest "I can't do this!" a declaration, a loss of faith in herself, her ability to cope, or as an obstructed labor which requires medicine or surgery. I believe it's a spiritual crisis more than a physical one. She has to have the spiritual willingness to do it. It's the intention. A woman has to reset her intention and be willing to labor, feel the pain, transcend the passing pain, and gather her energy and do it. And of course the orgasm, the birth, is obvious. Then the assimilation after the birth, which is integrating the baby into her life, her family and the community.

Coeleen: Oh Kate, I'm just absolutely right there with you. Oh, I love the way you say that, about that. I knew, and I birthed four children, I knew that it was the same experience, but to hear you say it — and last night I heard on NPR a doctor talking about the importance of the bonding at the moment of birth, and that women aren't doing that, and babies are dying. And they think it's because of that. I remember the interviewer saying, "How many babies do you think would be saved a year?" He said about 55,000. If the mother brought the baby to her breast, to her body, immediately. This is just assimilation, it is amazing.

The fifth stage is **cognition**. You start to talk about it. You want somebody to come and see it. Look what happened! You want to show it. I believe we've ignored that, even though it kind of happens to artists who are able to show their work. Those two stages are really important in terms of developing that ego sense and that mastery over the process, taking care of assimilation and cognition and recognizing that they are inner processes, that you're not just running around responding to inspiration.

Assimilation, and cognition, sharing it with other people. And you know what happens in cognition? You'll hear someone say; Next time I think what I'm going to do is..., and they've made their statement of intention. You hear it all the time; "Well, I like it, but I think next time I'm going to..."

Kate: Yep. You start planning the next one.

Coeleen: Yeah, this is a contribution I made. I wrote a workbook about this process for teachers. Frank thought that I was onto something in terms of Maslow's thinking. You don't have to sit around and wait for it to happen. I knew that, before I moved out here. I knew it, I had tried to explain that to the UM dean of the graduate studies, I think he thought I was nuts. He said, "Well it's a very cogent argument, but." I pleaded, "Listen, I really think this is happening." He said "No!"

As artists we need to understand this is going on, and women are beginning to care about it because it helps them hang in there and trust their process.

These stages, assimilation and cognition folded right into the study Frank had done at Mills College, about the qualities of women who make it, both in a productive way and creative way. The older sisters seemed to be more productive, as well as more creative. The younger sisters tended to be creative but would get married, have kids, end up dropping their art work. What was that difference? His research added to my interest in ego strength. Working with an inner awareness of what it is that you're doing builds ego strength, which for women I thought was sorely needed at the time. It still is needed.

Kate: Could you explain what you mean by ego strength? Some women I talk to have a negative view of ego.

Coeleen: I am talking about a personal sense of self that allows you to be in the now, present in the moment, not future or past. The ability to trust yourself, your gut and your personal process.

Carol Christ explains it well in her book, *Diving Deep and Surfacing*, but let me tell you about my work with my church in Minneapolis. I had been very active in my church's arts program and I arranged a jazz mass with Paul Horn. I'd heard Paul's music and I bought his new record and I took it to the church retreat and played it. It knocked my socks off. The composer was Lalo Sekifrin, and it was new and really exciting. The next day I read in the Sunday paper that Paul

Horn was playing at our local jazz club in Minneapolis that night and said to my husband. "Get your boots on! We're going." We went down and listened to Paul play. After his gig I asked him, "Have you ever performed in church?" He'd never preformed in a church. He said we would need a couple dozen voices and several pieces from the symphonic orchestra. I went home, called my minister and we agreed to meet the next morning and set it up. Four months later it all came to pass— the Paul Horn Quintet, the symphony players and a dozen voices including myself performed.

"How did you get to where you are?" I asked Paul. He told me all about transcendental meditation and that he had done a lot of it. The men, they were all men who were into TM, thought that is a good thing, to drop the ego. I thought, "Well, listening to you, it's nice for you, Paul, but I don't think this is a good thing for women. The issues are different for women. Women shouldn't be trying to clear their minds and drop the ego. This is exactly the opposite thing that women should be doing today.

About this time, Carol Christ's book *Diving Deep and Surfacing* was published. She was a Divinity student at Yale and was one of two women in a class of a hundred males. There was a lot of talk about the pursuit of the holy grail, and she began to wonder, does this have anything to do with women's spiritual trips? She looked for data that would support her theory that women's spiritual quest was like the pursuit of the holy grail. She couldn't find anything; she researched the literature of great women leaders. She chose five women: Doris Lessing, Margaret Atwood, Nitozaltle Scharge, Adrienne Rich and, Kate Chopin. Carol Christ looked at the paths of these women in their life journeys, in their stories, and she recognized the very unique pattern for women, which was very different for men. Then she researched ego strength, and noted that women are born and raised to assist the egos of the males in our family, and that we're taught not to care about our own egos. The cultural assumption was that will get taken care of with whomever we marry. But all the time we actually help the male with his ego and with this script, it benefits us to keeping doing so.

In Kate Chopin's *The Awakening?*, the heroine breaks away from her family. She's in a traditional marriage in New Orleans in the early 1900s, and with other mothers she spends the summer with the children at the lake. Bored, she has an affair and leaves her family to live with the man with whom she fell in love. He turns out not at all interested in a committed relationship and in fact competes with her other children. She goes a bit mad, and she takes the long swim and drowns.

Kate Chopin is cautioning us. The protagonist made her move, but she didn't have the personal inner sense of herself, the ego strength to live it out. When her lover walked out on her, she didn't have the strength or the will to survive.

The issue of ego strength has been the basic tenets of my teaching. I believe that while the women who are working here in my studio, doing their art out of their own personal voice and imagery from their unconscious, they are at the same time developing their sense of self, their egos. They are getting stronger and stronger.

Kate: Don't you think it's just a function of age and wisdom?

Coeleen: I don't — it could be, of course. Ravenna Helson understood-- she was the one that did the Mills College study with Frank. She thought that it was really personality development, and in those days' psychologists didn't think that. They thought it was age, events in someone's life, that would cause people to change their personality toward the stronger core but, she didn't think that. She thought that these women were consciously working on it. They were really creative and productive people who knew what they were doing. I'm so fascinated with how consistent it is.

Kate: My mother was an artist and when we moved to Wyoming from Michigan she systematically smashed all 600 canning jars after emptying them. My father had grown up on a farm and loved growing and canning food. He loved filling the Michigan house's huge fruit cellar. The midden of broken jars made her feel liberated from that exhausting task. She wanted time to paint and paint she did.

Coeleen: Well, a similar story is when I graduated from high school I had good grades, and time came to start at the university. However, my father said that I would not go to the university, that I would go out and get a job and bring money home and help out like my older sister. My mother had always made all of our clothes and upholstery. Beautiful--works of art —I kept a few. If she wanted a dress, or a coat, she made it. Dad said, "Coeleen will go out and get a job just like her sister did." My sister never went to college.

One-night we all were sitting around the dinner table and Dad noticed Mother was dressed up and asked her, "Did you have your bridge club today?" and Mother said, "No, I got a job today." That was a big affront to a man's ego. A man is supposed to be able to support his family to the extent that the wife does not have to go to work.

He said, "Well, where did you get a job?" and she said, "At Amluxson's". Which was a high end import fabric store. "Well what are you going to be doing?" "I'm in the pattern department. "Would you start like next month?" he asked. I just loved what she said, "I'll start tomorrow, if you'll give me a ride to work. And Coeleen will go to the university." There was never another word about it, no argument. Quickly she became head of the pattern department, and moved on to be the head of Vogue's annual fashion show. That was the only discussion they would have around that whole subject. She got me out of there without an argument. My dad drove me to school many times, and became interested in what I was doing, he wanted to know what I was studying and what I was thinking. It wouldn't have happened if she hadn't stood up for me. Then later she said, "And I have Tuesdays off for Bridge Club." I think there's a lot of her in me.

Kate: Women's stories are so different than men's stories. 1968 is kind of the demarcation line of the beginning of big changes in this country. I'm reading this book, *1968*, by Mark Kurlansky — I was just focusing on the women rights and the women's movement that mushroomed in 1968. As you know, Betty Friedan had written *The Feminine Mystique* years before, and people had been reading it, and small groups had been forming, but they were all isolated. But '68, a whole bunch of things happened.

Coeleen: Yeah. That's about the time when I went to the dean. Let me go back to 1965, my marriage was falling apart, and I thought it was my fault. I thought if I could just be a better woman, I could save the marriage. So I went into B. Dalton book store and asked for a book about the feminine, or femininity. They took me over to the Good Housekeeping and cookbooks and home decorating. "No, that's not it." And one of the clerks said, "Oh, something just came in this morning. I think I know what you're talking about, and she came back with Friedan's, *Feminine Mystique*." I took it home and I read it.

Kate: Wow! You're one of the first women in the beginning of the second wave of feminism.

Coeleen: Yes, and I read that the University of Minnesota and Northwestern University were the only universities that had a Women's Studies program. I went over to the university and said, I want to do graduate work. Well, we don't have a graduate program yet.

In the meantime, my church had started sensitivity training groups, and a Transcendental meditation groups, the TM, the old Allen Watts National Training Laboratory TM groups, which was a pretty progressive thing for a church to do. This was the Episcopal and the Methodist Church together. I decided to start a group of women to talk about women's issues and I called about six or seven women. I was so scared. I remember saying, "I want us to just take about an hour and a half or two hours to just get together and try talking about something else other than what we usually talk about, which is —Children and husbands —and recipes and such. We can do it in the summer. I'll get a babysitter for our kids. You don't have to call me and tell me whether you're coming or not." I couldn't face the rejection. "Just show up if you want to."

About 15 women showed up. We didn't know what we were going to do. I thought this is too big a group. Betty Friedan didn't know this was happening in Minnesota as she'd written her book in '65. In fact, in June 1965 she was in Washington DC starting NOW. One of the women in our group called me in the fall and said, "There's this woman coming from Washington DC and they're starting an organization, and I'm going to go listen to her tonight. Do you want to go?" Four of us showed up and this woman said, "We're starting an organization called NOW, and there will be groups of women getting together." We said, "Oh, we're doing that now, you know, it's already happening." Over the course of the next four or five years women kept coming. By the time I left for California, 40 women had come through our consciousness-raising group. Those group meetings were really important in terms of getting me moving out of my marriage, moving out of Minnesota and on my way here to Santa Cruz."

Coeleen Kiebert   81

Early on at UCSC in one of my graduate classes two young women from Wellesley and Radcliffe who were doing their graduate work in Psych asked if I'd like to join a consciousness-raising group. We started one here in Santa Cruz and later Lois Batson, Margie Cottle, Natalie Rogers daughter of Carl Rogers, Ingrid May wife of Rollo May and Laura Manforth, came up to me and said, "We'd like to start a consciousness-raising group with Janie Rhyne," which we did. So there were two really strong groups started around 1971 and 1972.

Kate: That is when I joined a consciousness-raising group that changed my life. Out of our group came the seed energy for the Santa Cruz Women's Health Collective, a child care center and the midwifery movement. When did you start your art classes, where you were doing art?

Coeleen: I had been doing my art all along. My undergraduate degree was in Art, and Art Education. I wanted to do my graduate work in Psych and I was able to do what I wanted here at UCSC. However, after four years of graduate school, I began to doubt that, for a couple reasons. A graduate student from Berkeley, was studying self-esteem in men and women. She came to Santa Cruz and called for a meeting of all the women in graduate school, and 35 of us showed up in the old bookstore and Whole Earth Restaurant.

Her research showed that the self-esteem of men, goes up when they leave graduate school, but the self-esteem of women goes down by the time they leave. In fact, many women often left school before finishing. She asked how many of us were married, and two of us raised our hands out of 35 women. The women said, "You can't do it." You can't be in a relationship and be in graduate school at the same time. However, the men in graduate school often had wives or girlfriends who were researching the abstracts for them, typing up papers, getting their work out for them. Doing whatever needed to be done including all the house work. She asked how many of us had ever been invited to a professor's home for a meal or tea or coffee. No one. Nor had we been invited to do any research with them.

I began to miss the clay, and doing art when Janie Run showed me a book called *Finding One's Way with Clay*, by Paulus Sarandon. She gave me a copy of the book. Paulus, who had been a dancer in Westside Story for many, many years, had left dancing and got into clay. He was going to do a workshop at Big Creek Pottery Studio. I attended that workshop, and I realized, this is my tribe, these potters are my people. I came back to Frank, and said, "I've made a big mistake. I'm not a psychologist, I'm an artist." and I started to cry. He said, "Why are you crying? That's perfectly wonderful." And I said, "Well, that means that I have to leave you." and he said, "No, no you don't." And I said, "You know that the men here are bright-eyed and healthy and they run up and down the halls, they go anywhere they want, full, bushy heads of hair, and the women are skinny with long, stringy hair, creeping along the edges of the hallways, hoping that nobody will notice them." I said, "I don't want that to happen to me." and he said, "You're right. There is that difference." And so — I said, "Give me my Masters, I'm out of here, and that's what I did."

I began to believe — and I still do— that doing the art is where people grow, because you have so many problems in art you have to deal with, so many decisions to make, it's so hard to do, it's hard to hang in there. Sometimes I think there's more personal growth in the art-doing than there is in talk therapy. Some of the people in my classes are therapists who started to use art in their therapy practice, and they would come to class and say, you know, somebody last week did a collage. We talked about the images and issues we'd have never gotten to just talking. It really helped them.

Kate: I did art therapy with Lois Bateson, drawing it was powerful — insightful.

Coeleen: Lois and I did art together. I started a clay studio and Lois came and Gregory came with their daughter Nora. That was in '78 to '82 about. I started teaching classes while I was in graduate school in the 70s. I taught two classes "Art and Spirit" and "Clay as a Way" through UCSC Extension for 30 years. Some of those women are still in my classes today and some of them were in my early consciousness-raising groups. We used collage and clay and drawing doodles, because I think the ego development is in the doodles, is one's true mark. People use doodling to go through problem-solving, it relaxes the mind. Not only does it relax the mind, but it's a person's individual mark. Janie Rhyne gave her dissertation on those marks. She helped me with my doodles, because my doodles were very circular, and she knew that that's the beginning of the end of a civilization. I noticed in Carl Jung's drawings, he began to get transparency. I think that's probably the highest I've seen in a doodle, when it's transparent, then the mind is really —

Kate: You can see an images with something behind it?

Coeleen: Through it even, through it she works on that unknown place, unconscious, or mythological, and that's the difference, to be able to tolerate that, and when I was at the university, Pavel Mackotka was teaching and he did some experiments around ego strength and art, and he determined that it took ego strength to be able to tolerate abstract, to tolerate the abstract. Even in a cloud, there are people who are nervous with the abstract, and will turn it into an elephant or a bear or something, they have to have something concrete and have a lot of difficulty with abstract art. But if you can, if the mind can be free enough to be able to just take it for what it is, Pavel measured that, and got ego strength out of that. And so, I'm a believer.

Unbeknownst to me, Faye Crosby, the Cowell Provost, decided that I should be honored in some way. One day they told me that they had raised money in 2015 to name the patio outside of the Eloise Pickard Smith Gallery after me. The karmic justice in all of this is so incredible because I started out at Stevenson, not Cowell, working with my psychologist friends. One day I walked past the Cowell dining room and heard Mary Holmes giving a lecture. This place was packed. I went in and I listened and I thought, Wow, you know, she's something else. I went to Frank, and I said, "I think that maybe I should be working with Mary Holmes." And Frank said, "Oh, that would be a real red herring. No. You just stick to what you're doing." And I did. I followed his orders and I left with my MA. However, fortunately for me Mary and I became really good friends until the day she died. By coincidence, when Janie Rhyne said that day, I'm meeting somebody at UCSC, come along with me, Janey and Frank and I met at Cowell. Not at Stevenson. We met on that beautiful plaza looking out over Monterey Bay.

After that, with Faye's work the patio came alive. It had been a dead space. Nobody was ever there and nobody ever went into the Mary Holmes Gallery unless you had an opening or something. When I was up there just a couple months ago they had turned the gallery into a reading room, and the coffee shop opened up onto the Coeleen Kiebert Patio. It was loaded with students, and one of my sculptures stands in the patio, it is an abstract called China Rocks.

The other thing that I've found moving and am proud of is that five of my "Justice" sculptures stand in the Provost garden, thanks to Faye Crosby's instigation.

My son died in 1996 — he was killed in a mysterious way in Italy. I was trying so hard to find out how he died, why he died, what was going on, and trying to get justice for him. I was dealing with the Italian magistrate and the legal system there. At the time I was very naïve how the Italian system worked. I thought, if I created enough justice pieces I will get justice for my son. When he died I flew to Rome to see the magistrate and tried to get him to do something. There in the hall of justice was the image of Justice that we all know, standing blindfolded, with her scale and her sword. I looked up to her, prayed to her to be able to help us get through what we had before us. Over the next two to three years I started making Justice pieces, thinking, if I make enough of them, we'll get justice. I'll manifest justice. Well, that didn't happen. But I did end up making four or five very large pieces, in ceramic, of Justice, as she progressed from this kind of Mussolini kind of justice, this determined to get it, to the Justice who realized that it's all karma and that she has to let go of trying to get justice, that it will take care of itself in its own time, let karma work it through. I had to let go of it.

I had those pieces cast in bronze, and now the five of them are in the Cowell Provost's Garden. It is just amazing to me, thanks to Faye Crosby, that they're there. The new provost, Alan Christy, teaches different forms of social justice, so he has these in his garden, and he uses them with his students, as a way of talking about justice and the many ways that justice happens. The different outcomes... that we have to accept it or watch for it or look for it or even live without it. It amazes me that I have those pieces up there at Cowell on campus. Along with the China Rock at the Coeleen Kiebert Patio, I believe they my academic contribution to the arts.

I wish that Frank had lived long enough to see that the real honor was the naming of the patio. It is embraced by the

Eloise Pickard Smith Gallery and the Mary Holmes Fireside Library. It is such an honor to have my art displayed there, and that the plaque says "MADE POSSIBLE BY HER LOVING ADMIRERS". I think that is the height of it! That I would end up there, as an artist, as well as a psychologist. For that reason, I'm really proud.

I don't know why I understand creativity the way I do, but I do. It's a real gift to know what I know and recognize it the way I do. For decades I have balanced doing art and researching art at the same time. I have been researching those who work here with me, the women's creative process and their progress and continuously asking "What is the science behind the process of creating?" Like the doodle. It's going someplace, and there's growth there. I think my incentive to work with the mystery and to swim in these unknown waters, along with others, has been a true blessing.

Celeste Phillips:
Passionate Advocate for Mothers and Babies and
Family Centered Care

Some people are seldom seen in their own communities. As an artist and writer Celeste recognized as a young woman, knew in her gut that things had to change the way women were treated during childbirth. She knew that she had to have the tools to create humane compassionate care for women and babies.

Inspired by what she learned from the hippy mothers about the midwifery the model of care as practiced in home birth, she went on to spend decades working to transform hospitals to family center care all over the United States, Europe and China. She rode the waves of change. Her CV is 25 pages long. She is author of seven books and recipient of two lifetime achievement awards. This woman with a passion for compassionate care accomplished fundamental change in the way women are treated in childbirth all over the world. She is a Santa Cruz Living Treasure. She is a National Treasure.

Kate: A few months ago you gave a presentation at the Museum of Art and History that made the audience gasp. At 85 years old you stood there as living history, holding a bag with the word "Parlodel" printed on it. In your soft spoken authoritative way, you gave a short history of birth practices. You reached into the bag and pulled out two thick leather straps with metal buckles and began to buckle them on to your wrists as you explained that not only were your wrists strapped to the table when you gave birth but also your ankles.

As a nurse you told us that you applied the same

restraints to women in labor. You made it clear that this was compassionate care because women were given powerful mind-altering and amnesiac drugs routinely, causing them to be so out of their minds that they trashed about, so out of touch with reality that they needed to be protected from hurting themselves and their babies. So they were tied to the delivery bed with the leather straps. The young people in the audience gasped and were shocked to learn this part of birthing history. Women who in the past had desired pain free births instead ended up with no memory of the pain that caused them to writhe and cry out, nor any memory of having given birth. Next you pulled out the forceps that looked like giant spoons that were used to pull the baby out by its head. That was after an episiotomy was cut in the vagina. These practices were all routine. Next you explained Parlodel is a drug that was given without consent to some women right after birth to dry up their milk. It has the nasty side effects of dizziness and fainting and often women would fall. So new mothers were rendered unable to safely care for their babies. Babies that they didn't even remember they had given birth to. One man began shaking and rubbed the forceps' scars on his head.

Kate: Can you tell me your story?

Celeste: My story is a love story. I found the work I loved and the love of my life, my husband Roger early. At nineteen, when I attended my first birth I knew immediately that I wanted to spend my life working with women, babies and birth. Post WWII there were lots of babies being born and my first responsibility was to carry a newborn baby from delivery room to nursery. I loved those babies. Birth is where love begins. As long as you keep the mothers and babies together good things are going to happen. My vision was to create family-centered care. I knew that there were a lot of things about hospital birth that needed to be changed, especially after my own births. The biggest one in my mind was to keep the mothers and babies together. I had found my passion.

Kate: You were a woman with a vision and a mission.

Celeste: Yes, and my first job was as a maternity nurse in a New Orleans hospital where I met Roger, a pharmacist. We were married in New Orleans in 1954 and it was a very hard time for us. I was from Pennsylvania and Roger had grown up in Louisiana in the southern culture. It was the time of the civil rights movement and the freedom buses were coming south with activists. People were dying fighting for voting rights and integration.

Roger and I knew we wanted to have children and raise a family and I wanted to move someplace where I thought there would be less turmoil than in New Orleans. When he got a job offer at Horsnyder Drug store in Santa Cruz and we moved here in 1955. This was before Cabrillo College opened its Aptos campus and before UCSC. I got a maternity nursing job in Sisters Hospital across from the Dream Inn on West Cliff, it is a parking lot now. However, his only day off was Sunday and the nuns wanted me to work every Sunday. If we never saw each other it was going be difficult to start a family, so I quit.

My son was born in 1960 and I felt in my heart and gut that something was fundamentally wrong with how I was treated.

Kate: Can you tell me more about your birth experience?

Celeste: The labor room had three beds and Roger was only allowed in for a very short time, so he was in and out. I was alone most of the time. I used relaxation and breathing techniques from *Childbirth Without Fear* by Grantly Dick-Reed. We read it together. I was educated as best I could be. I thought that I was prepared. I did my breathing and Roger helped me with relaxation until we got to Dominican Hospital where we were separated. We had practiced together for weeks and then when I needed him the most he was not allowed to be with me. I refused an enema and drugs and most of the other hospital procedures. After the birth we were all separated--my baby Duncan was sent to the nursery and Roger was sent home.

After Duncan was born I felt something was missing, I felt empty, it was a horrible feeling. I was separated from my baby and my husband. My baby was taken to the nursery where the head nurse, Mrs. H called him "her baby". She ruled the nursery and called all the babies "her babies". I wanted to breast feed but I was only allowed to see him every four hours for the first three days. Nurses would say "Mrs. H wouldn't like that. Mrs. H had to give your baby formula". I knew in my gut that this was all wrong. My heart ached to be with my baby and my husband. Roger was so upset by the experience that when he called his mother he threw up.

It was a little better with my second birth but Roger was still not allowed to be with me for the birth.

Kate: Like many women who became childbirth activists your passion arose after a difficult birth experience with hospital policies and procedures.

Celeste: Yes, and I was inspired to become a teacher and change those practices. But, because my RN was from a hospital-based school it did not give college credits. In the 1960s I knew to be a teacher I would have to have at the least a master's degree and I concentrated on what I had to do to get those college degrees. This was the time of the hippies and the Beatles and drugs, sex and rock and roll. I did not participate in these happenings as I was the mother of two babies born two years apart. There is only so much time and energy and we were being very busy as a new family. Roger was incredible. Being a wife, a mother and a full time student would not have been possible without his love and support.

It was the time of the Viet Nam war and while I was at San Jose State I volunteered to be part of the medical group for the antiwar demonstrations. Police would ride around the campus on horses and they would use clubs on the students to get them to calm down or get out of the way or what-ever. The students would need emergency first aid for their injuries.

Kate: So you were supporting the protesters?

Celeste: Yes, but I was not one of the protesters, I was working from inside. I was helping people who had their heads hit with batons.

I graduated from San Jose State in 1970 with a bachelor's in nursing. That was a very busy ten years and I went immediately for the master's degree and completed it in 1972, and on to get a EdD.

It was the end of the 60s when I got active in changing things. I taught some of the first childbirth education classes in Santa Cruz in a church on Mission Street. I served on the boards of the International Childbirth Education Association (ICEA) and the Association of Women's Health, Obstetrics and Neonatal

Nursing(AWHONN). I didn't just sit on the board and eat cookies. I had a large influence over policies and wrote many. I created vision and action plans for hospitals and their staff to create family-centered care to keep the babies and mothers together.

Kate: I was living in San Francisco in the sixties and was part of the diaspora and was one of the hippies who came to Santa Cruz. At the time it was a sleepy retirement community with incredible natural beauty and affordable places to live. Many communes sprang up in rural areas and in town. With the hippies came the seeds of the environmental movement and back to nature. The women's movement helped to empower us as young women to trust ourselves, our instincts. As women we wanted to give birth naturally and breast feed our babies. It was impossible to do it in the hospital at the time and women decided to give birth at home with friends as their attendants. You were already involved teaching clinical maternity nursing at Cabrillo, and childbirth education. When did you become aware of the hippy culture and that homebirths were happening?

Celeste: I read some articles in the local weekly newspaper. There was an article about you at the spring fair with a booth and birth pictures. Word was out on the "underground" that women were having babies at home with lay midwives.

Kate: When I met you in 1972 the natural home birth movement was mushrooming all over the country. Can you tell me how you came to visit us?

Celeste: I heard about the midwives' meeting on Wednesdays and came to the Victorian house at 208 Escalona Drive where you held your free prenatal clinic. When I visited I saw many pregnant women in the living room and in the back yard. The group that you were working with, The Birth Center had more patients than Dominican Hospital where I was working and teaching maternity nursing.

That was rather threating to the medical establishment.

Kate: Yeah, we were doing 20 births a month and that was 20% of the births in the county at that time. Raven Lang had started the Birth Center in 1971 because doctors refused to see women for prenatal care who wanted a home birth. Raven called for an educational meeting and called it "The Birth Seminar" and she invited doctors and nurses, public health people and other professionals to have a conversation with the home birth community, and you invited Dr. Anzalone to the Dome?

Celeste: Yes, your group was busy. The world was changing very rapidly. At that time there was a lot of pressure on the establishment because of the Viet Nam War. There was a lot of pressure on the government, women were wanting more say, *Our Bodies Ourselves* had been published. Women were demanding husbands in birth room, natural birth, and breast feeding.

When the Birth Center collective of lay midwives called for the meeting at the Dome up at Alba Road in Ben Lomond, I thought that this was what Dr. Anzalone needs to see. He was chief of Obstetrics at Community hospital. He really was interested and he really cared about women during childbirth. I asked him to come to the **Birth Seminar** [3/25/1972] and by God he came—as well as several other hospital nurses. I looked across the dome and there he was, late as usual, because he always had patients. He walked across the dome to look at the pictures for Raven's *BIRTH BOOK* mounted on poster boards.

[Raven Lang had been attending home births and was in the process of writing the *Birth Book* published in the fall of 1972. It documented homebirth with accounts written by mothers, fathers and midwives. It included political ·

statements and instructions on how to do a home birth. It was the first such book and had national influence.]

I asked "What do you think of this?" The pictures were of women giving birth in different positions. They were graphic, shocking. I am sure it was pornographic to some people. There was a naked woman on the floor of an art studio on her hands and knees giving birth. I'd never seen a woman give birth on all fours. He had never seen a woman give birth on all fours.

"Well it makes sense." He said. "Anatomically it makes total sense. I can ask the next patient if she wants to try that." And he did. Dr. Anzalone and I went back and created single room care at Community Hospital with rooming in for babies, so babies stayed with their mothers. The changes came from a collegial relationship I had with a doctor willing to change things.

The **Birth Seminar** was phenomenal. Afterwards I thought so where do I fit?

I decided to study social change. Changes come from both external and internal sources. We need the people with the placards marching out in public, in the streets, out in front of institutions calling for whatever they want changed. We need the people to put the pressure on from many external sources, and we need people on the inside putting on the pressure. The Viet Nam war is a powerful example of how demonstrations influence people in power to end it. It could have gone on for years more. Without someone on the inside willing to change and putting pressure on, all the pressure from the outside is not going to work.

Over time I became recognized as an authority, and gained a certain measure of influence. I thought, I must know something or people wouldn't be seeking me out. They wanted to know what I knew. I concluded I was better working on the inside than working on the outside. I put the pressure on and it worked, it just plain old worked. I came to understand that there needs to be someone inside the hospital willing to take the risk to change.

At that time in Santa Cruz there were women teaching natural birth classes and lay midwives attending home births. However, there were no prenatal classes in the hospital to prepare women for hospital birth or tell them that they had choices, what the choices were and the evidence behind them. Issues like the benefits of support people in labor and delivery, of freedom of movement and rooming in with babies, of breastfeeding and bonding. I started prenatal birth classes for women and families and I tried to be as non threatening to the doctors as possible.

The bonding issue was especially threatening to all the physicians, when we would say that the babies needed to be with their mothers and not in the nursery. It was radical. I had to be very careful because my phone would ring here at my home and I would get scolded by a pediatrician who would say the babies would all die if they were not being taken care of by skilled knowledgeable people, meaning nurses. There were doctors who would scold me and even threaten me. They wanted to know exactly what I had said to the pregnant people in my classes. I knew my teaching was effective because women were asking not to be separated from their babies. I would tell the mothers "You know you have a choice of whether to have your baby with you or in the nursery."

Kate: One of the arguments pitched by the doctors was that babies would get chilled if placed in mother's arms immediately. You did research which was published in 1974 on that issue and demonstrated that placing a baby in a heated bed had no advantage over the mother's arms.

It was so ironic that mothers would be in the hospital with

the so called "qualified caretakers", the nurses, for three to five days and during that time new mothers were considered incompetent, but they were sent home with, minimal education, no care and no supervision!

Celeste: None of it made sense. One day I was digging in the garden and I had to go to work at 3pm at the hospital. There was a woman who lived right next to us and she also was in her garden that particular day. She was a mother of twins born preterm and they had to stay in the hospital, but she couldn't go into the nursery to hold her babies. Mothers were not allowed in the nursery. Here is the crazy part. I had dug in the dirt six feet from where she had dug in the dirt. I could come in to the hospital, scrub up to my elbows go into the nursery and I could hold her twins. I could be with her babies but she had to stand in the hallway looking in the window. It made me crazy, so I guess you know what I did. I said "Come on with me, this policy of not allowing you in the nursery makes no sense whatsoever."

I thought, "I don't need a doctor's order! Mothers belong with their babies and denying them admittance to the nursery is cruel. I didn't care if it was a hospital policy. I can't follow a policy that has no science, no evidence behind it."

I took her into the nursery, had her scrub and put on a clean gown. I had her sit down and I handed her babies to her to hold. It was the right thing to do. I felt it in my heart and in my gut.

I believe that without the meeting under the dome, without the births occurring at home we might still be struggling over these issues.

Cabrillo College Director of the Nursing Program 1981-1984

Kate: After the Birth Center Birth Bust,[1] when three of us were arrested and charged with the practice of medicine without a license, and the Nurse Midwife Practice Act passed in December 1974, I decided to go to nursing school and get my license.

In the beginning of my second year the Grand Jury investigated the Cabrillo RN program and due to many serious complaints the director was dismissed. Cabrillo was looking for a new director. I was one of the people who called you and begged you to take the job. My second year of nursing school was a great experience because you were the director. You were there to empower nurses and the nursing role and made it more palatable to me personally. Sorry to say, but I never wanted to be a nurse. I felt it was too subservient to doctors. I was a feminist and I wanted to practice as a midwife legally in California.

Celeste: Yes, and I took the job as director of nursing at Cabrillo. I did the job I was hired for and quite honestly it got boring. Near the end of my tenure we had a student, who was breast feeding a new baby and my colleagues said that she had to leave school. "What! she has to leave school because she wants to breast feed in class? Oh, here we go again!" and I felt like it wasn't my battle that time. I suggested she sit in the back of the room and be modest, which she did.

All the issues that tore that program apart were resolved and I needed to move on and do something else.

My Work with Dr. Fenwick

Celeste: It all came together when I met Dr. Fenwick at a conference in Long Beach on the Queen Mary where he was demonstrating the "Borning Bed" he had developed. He had

1   Golden Gate University Law Review Volume 9 Issue 2 Women's Law Forum Article 11 January 1978
Midwifery: A History of Statutory Suppression by Cynthia Watchorn

taken a hospital labor bed and with a blow touch cut it in two. He transformed it into a "birth bed." [Later marketed as the "Borning Bed]. Everybody was astounded. He cut out a U-shaped seat and added leg supports so a woman could birth sitting up or kneel on all fours and lean into that hollow. The bottom could be pulled away to enable the doctor to sit on a stool for the delivery. It was rather primitive and very heavy and hard to use.

There were some outspoken feminists who surrounded his bed saying that he just wanted to make money off of women's bodies and that was his only motivation. The women advised me not to get sucked in to his scheme. I thought that they didn't understand. They didn't know him, they had it all wrong.

I stepped up and spoke up, right there on the Queen Mary and said "You don't understand. It's not women who need this bed—it's the doctors who need them. If we are going to have women able to have their choice, then doctors have to be comfortable and have the tools that help them to do that."

He believed what I believed, he shared my values: that women needed choices. We became partners in a consulting practice helping hospitals transition to Family Centered Maternity Care (FCMC).

Dr. Loel Fenwick had grown up in South Africa and had been trained by professional Dutch midwives. He was shocked to see mothers tied down to the table and immediately understood why American women were having such a hard time birthing their babies.

He realized to make family centered care a reality doctors needed to be comfortable and the birthing bed could help get doctors to support the concept.

When we first converted labor rooms into birth rooms in this country we equipped them with all kinds of gadgets. The fancier the equipment was, the happier the doctors were. But that wasn't all we wanted. We wanted a safe birth, and it was not going to be safe if doctors were fighting us. They had to be comfortable and it had to work for them.

Dr. Fenwick realized that he needed to educate the hospital administrators and staff as to why a woman needed to be free to move and chose different positions like getting on all fours etc.

Celeste: Dr. Fenwick contacted me and asked if I would write self-learning modules to be used to train nurses and staff. I agreed and I wrote six modules they accredited for continuing education. They included the principles of non-separation of mothers and babies, physiologic labor support and the presence of support people for labor. Hospitals liked the modules because they could use them for training the nurses and doctors.

Dr. Fenwick called and asked me to do a nation-wide search for him, to find a Director of Professional Relations. I'd had a particularly boring day at Cabrillo, it was a very boring day. Yeah, it was a nice little office and there were pretty flowers outside the window, but it was a boring day and I knew there would be a lot more boring days.

I said "How about me, Loel?"

"Would you do this job?"

"Well I haven't thought about it before now. Lets' talk about what the job entails." I created the job and went all over the United States to more than 700 hospitals, and a lot of babies are with their mothers today because of that. Now, when I open the American Journal of Nursing 2018 or go on the web and look at the ads, they are for mother-baby nurses instead of labor or nursery nurses. I had known that day would come and I knew it would take twenty years—but it did come. I am so happy every time I see the ads for mother-baby nurses. That role did not exist when we started this work.

Kate: For years I would cut out the newspaper ads and save them. "Dominican opens single room maternity care." "Home-like atmosphere, home-like setting." They are still advertising home-like setting with midwifery care with the added benefits of the NICU, [the neonatal intensive care unit]. Home birth was the gold standard of care.

Celeste: Yes, and I know coming to the Birth Center and the meeting in the dome opened my eyes and inspired me. I believe that without the meeting under the dome, without the births occurring at home we might still be struggling over these issues.

Kate: How was it that you succeeded in your work to transform hospital practices.

Celeste: I always sought out allies, someone who was open and loved what they did and was willing to challenge the status quo, someone respected, with authority who could make decisions. Wherever I have gone I sought a partner who shared the same vision. I would seek them out and enlist them. However, sometimes I would connect with the chief of OB in some hospitals who did not value what I had to say or the changes I was advocating. They would do it just to get the pressure off, or because it would bring in more patients and revenue.

Kate: I find it very interesting that, as a woman, you adopted a partnership model from the start, which is different than the hierarchical, top down model.

Celeste: Yes, and I have to say it was almost always working with a male Doctor in a position of power within the organization. When I began to work, few women were in top positions. I have worked in every state and several European countries and China.

Kate: You've written seven books and received awards from the American Journal of Nursing for two of your books. The last book was translated into Chinese, and When Dr. Fenwick and you returned to China you said that 500 more hospitals had been converted to family centered care.

I know that you have received many awards, including two life time achievement awards. One award that blew my mind is from a national organization that honored you along with other great women in history, Martha Ballard, a 1700's midwife, Mary Breckenridge, a Nurse Midwife who started the Frontier School for midwives in Kentucky, Margaret Sanger, advocate for birth control, Maude Callen, a black Nurse Midwife who worked for 60 years in rural poor South Carolina—and you, Celeste Phillips.

At the beginning of this interview you showed me an architectural drawing of the **Birth Place**, a hospital in North Carolina designed with single room care for mother and babies, including a Neonatal Intensive Care Unit with a bed for the mother next to the baby's bed, so she could recover next to her infant. It was state of the art and served the rich and poor equally.

Celeste: This kind of care should be the standard of care everywhere. We shouldn't have to look at a map and put pins in it and then say this is a good place to birth. There actually are some very good places, good examples of excellent care, but when you think about it they should all be good places-- they should be everywhere.

The issues for women does not end with the birth of their babies. There are many issues that we worked hard for decades to change, to make health care better for women. These struggles are on going. Women are going to have to work hard to keep their choices about control over their bodies available to them. It has not been easy to change birth practices from the "strap them down and pull the baby out" days to family centered care. The cycles related to childbearing and reproduction and family planning are center to a woman's life. How a woman remembers her birth affects her self esteem, affects her entire life, her relationship with her family and all of our society. We need to continue to refine and improve maternity care. You can measure the height of a civilization by how they treat women in childbirth.

We need to recognize how important birth is.

Roberta Bristol: --
A World of Yoga, Dance, and Body Awareness

Roberta Bristol is a pioneer in the world of movement, including dance, yoga and the Mind-Body Connection. As one of Cabrillo College's first teachers she had the vision and the energy to create a community with the students. At the time of this interview in 2018 she is 94 and is still teaching yoga and meditation classes in her home. She is engaging, open minded and very curious about what young people are doing. Roberta often connects people she knows so that they may work together.

Roberta was teaching at Stockton College when she was recruited by Cabrillo's President Bob Swenson to teach at the new community college in Santa Cruz County in 1959.

Roberta: They needed somebody with broad experience, and wanted teachers with at least ten years of experience and a Master's Degree.

Looking back over 50 years I know that my life has been blessed. In 1959 when I arrived in Santa Cruz County Cabrillo College was just a dream, a thought. There were no facilities, no dressing rooms, no studios, no offices for the 10 faculty men and 3 women.

I was one of those women. I had many hats to wear. I was assistant dean of student activities in charge of recreation and bringing people together so the spirit of the college could begin. I was also a counselor and physical education teacher. I sort of acted like the Dean of Women.

Through my work with my students during that time I began to offer recreational activities. The first classes I taught were folk dance and social dance to encourage the students to partner with people and become interested in dancing together. I saw that the students were receptive and whole heartedly having fun together and making friends, even the shy ones.

The students came from various places in the county and as they came together they began to see each other as part of a new college, a new spirit and became excited and proud to be the start of something new. I saw at the time that I was waking up to the social values of rhythmic activity to help people come together. I changed from an enthusiastic physical education and sports teacher to one who worked for dance and proudly called myself a Movement Dance Educator. In 1962 we came to the mid-county Aptos campus. We chose this property on the hill when there was nothing here except the Swenson house on the ocean side of Soquel Drive. We built a dance studio and we were able to make a wonderful program because of the support from the administrators who said to us at that time: "You can innovate. You don't have to do traditional things. Do new things. Help the students to find a way to be confident in their being. If you can fill a class, you can teach it." I began to fill as many classes as I could with modern dance and other aspects of dance, with creative movement on more advanced levels.

All through the 1960s I was the only teacher in our department and the programs grew in many directions. I developed programs on weekends for children as well as evening classes for adults who wanted to exercise with rhythm and dance. I started several leadership programs for the students giving them skills so that they could work with children. I had a very successful ten years of running a co-ed recreation night. In the gym we would set up a co-ed volleyball game, the swimming pool was open; we had the dance room and the weight room open. Different leaders demonstrated techniques and helped students with these activities. It was really a wonderful boost in leadership training as well as for students getting a chance to know each other. Between three to five hundred people would come to these events, every week. I also taught movement classes using live drummers whenever possible, Jim Greiner was one of the drummers.

It kept getting better and better until at the end of the 60s I found that I personally needed a way to relax. I had been married to a faculty member for five years, but it didn't work out. It was a good experience, but I'm glad I got out of it. After our divorce in 1968 I took a sabbatical and went to Europe. When I returned I studied Yoga at Esalen with Joel Kramer. Joel promoted the idea of being whole and connecting the mind and the body together. He also didn't believe in gurus. He wanted to have everybody learn to listen to themselves. That's what yoga's about, you know, learning to trust yourself and to listen to your body during each movement in each moment as it is.

It is an interesting thing that anytime I found something new that worked for me I wanted to share it, wanted to teach about it. I learned by teaching it. I also learned by practice. In the end of the 60s I started a yoga class early in the morning at seven o'clock and a lot of working people came and it was amazing the number of people who came. It seemed that Santa Cruz knew more about yoga than I did. They flocked to these classes early, before they had to go to work. The yoga class grew an off-shoot and I called it the Body Awareness Class. It took a lot of insight to help students focus the mind in a mind-body unit, in a meditative state, and to tune in to an inner direction that came out of those practices.

That's what yoga's about, learning to trust yourself and to listen to each movement as it is. When I started teaching yoga classes at Cabrillo, I would bring Joel in for special weekend workshops and he was really good for attendance. At first yoga class was an extra activity that you couldn't get credit for it. But so many people came I was soon able to get it offered for credit in the regular class schedule. I was surprised how many working people came, not just young students. I was even introducing yoga to teachers at the University of California at Berkeley.

Kate: When you first brought yoga to Cabrillo, did you meet any resistance?

Roberta: Well I did, and I had to really understand it. There were certain academic-type people on the committee that would argue when you tried to get credit for a class, and I'd have to really explain in great detail and fight for it. I hate to think about it, but it really was a struggle, sometimes, to get credit for the classes. First I had to get our own department to believe in it. Then we would have to get the department to put a new class proposal forward, and then we had to get the whole college academic committee to approve it before it could go into the catalog. There were women and men together on the committees. The men didn't understand what yoga was about, but they could understand that it was similar to coaching and that you needed to have more time. They respected me and approved pretty much what I did. Today instead of just having one or two yoga classes, there are ten or twelve currently. It grew, and students wanted it, the community wanted it. Baba Hari Dass an Indian teacher had come to Santa Cruz in 1971 and began to teach Ashtanga yoga and in time with help from the community they bought land on Mount Madonna to create a center. I was one of the people who lobbied the Board of Supervisors to permit the project because I understood what yoga was about and able to explain that they were not a crazy cult. And that's a wonderful thing, you know.

One of the smartest things I ever did was lobby for longer class time for yoga. I could see that if you got people into yoga, they'd needed at least an hour and a half and maybe two. So I asked for double credit, for these longer classes, and we got the faculty to accept that. It became clear that two days a week wasn't enough and we expanded our schedule to four or five days a week, so people could take a class on Monday Wednesday and Friday, and then the same level class on Tuesday and Thursday. That way they could practice postures like Downward Dog every day and get the feeling of a class five days a week. It's the same as with a musician: You can't play your instrument just once or twice a week. You have to practice every day.

I was also really into body awareness and co-counseling to help student tune in to what their mind was thinking, and what they felt in their body. I was interested in massage and helping people through touch to become aware of their bodies, to tune in to what their body was telling them. This seemed to help people wake up to their own potential.

For many years, once a week, I hosted a vegetarian soup and salad dinner at my house, which was an open invitation for students who would do all the cooking. We would do movement and meditation or massage and the hot tub was open to all. Clothes were optional. In addition to that I worked a lot with freeing the natural voice and give body releases with foot and neck massage. Those became an important part of my teaching and I think I am more famous for those classes than anything else I taught or ever did.

Kate: Would you describe yourself as a feminist?

Roberta: I have never really done what I do as a feminist. I have worked with everybody, and a lot of it is because I've always been accepted equally in the jobs I've had. I've never had a feeling that men were paid more than the women, and I always had a way to do things I wanted. I've never been blocked despite the fact that I'm a woman, at least I don't think so. But anyway, the thing is that dance is a perfect place for women to learn and to excel, especially the performance. I'm sure that there's some women who would want to fight for the rights of women more than I do.

When we began to have enough money to hire additional teachers Helen Jackson and Wilma Marcus became a part of the team. They developed their work in more advanced skills in their performance and the jazz programs.

Our biggest change happened when Tandy Beal and Diana Linze Crosby came to our program and took it to a new level by adding performance skills.

Tandy began teaching the discipline of back stage organization, she understood how to present dance as an art form, as a choreographic form. She also does a lot with costumes in the way she uses materials in the shape of wings and extensions of bowls and stuff like that. She took a lot of what she does from Alan Nicolai, who was one of the greats, like Martha Graham. He was a real leader in developing dance for theatre, for instance, instead of just having the body as a shape on the floor, he would add extensions, so that you'd have wings and fly in the upper dimensions of the space.

Tandy is very creative in finding her own path, especially with combining circus and extraordinary movements with gymnastics and other sports. Tandy not only does very interesting theatre, but she is one of very few really high-level dancers who are interested in working with children. She has developed a core of teachers who go into the schools and give dance shows and invite the children to come in and perform with them. They call it "World Dance", and all sorts of wonderful things have come out of that. Maybe six or seven thousand children get to be exposed to performance, and learn what adult performances are all about. Tandy is known for her ability to work beautifully and positively with everyone. Everyone loved her work, and soon graduate students, people already trained in the basic skills of dance, started coming to Cabrillo's classes.

A woman by the name of Stephanie Delano, who writes plays and has become quite a performer herself, has developed both with me and with Tandy. As a result of all these talented people, Cabrillo started giving beautiful concerts using every student in Tandy's and Diana's class. They started the dance ensemble and traveled northern California as dance ambassadors, sharing our work with other schools and colleges.

There were many other teachers in the Santa Cruz community in yoga and dance, like African Dance classes at Louden Nelson, the 418 Dance Group and many others.

When good seeds are planted great blooms will come. When there is so much negativity as there is at this time in the world it is up to each of us to do what we can to stay embodied in positive practices as we grow older. We need to find a movement form that suits us. The gyms are offering dance and yoga and Asian culture has brought us tai chi and chi gung. All these things are important as we grow older.

Everybody has to have something to keep them moving. I, as an octogenarian, have a lot of fun in the water aerobic classes where we walk in water, but not on water. It is a wonderful thing to know that all those of you who have moved with me through these 50 years will carry on my work. Never under estimate the power of dance in Santa Cruz. My wish for all of you is to stay connected to dance and find a way to dance through the rest of your life.

For more information there is a great DVD put out by Cabrillo College Dance Dept. and Tandy Beal and Company that honors Roberta Bristol. "Prime Movers" Jan 15 2013 by IMPACT productions.

Part 2
THEATER

Chapter 2:
Ed Penniman, The Sticky Wicket Interviews

1959-1963. The Sticky Wicket was Santa Cruz' first Coffeehouse. It was an incubator for a cultural shift in a small coastal town that relied primarily on summer tourists northerly from Oakland, inland from Sacramento and South from San Louis Obispo. They flocked here from all over Northern California to enjoy the cooler nights, warm beaches and exciting boardwalk. Then on Labor Day the tourist season was finished, the tourists, like shorebirds migrated and we felt a sensory vacuum. The Roller Coaster was still, and the girls were gone. We locals would enjoy empty and pristine beaches; a quieter downtown, and with a sense of relief the town would go back to an off-season, ideal, quiet seaside community. The bucolic rhythm would return. We were relieved to have our town back.

Things started to change. In a little cubbyhole of a place on Cathcart Street in downtown Santa Cruz between Johnny's Bike and Sport Shop and Sam's Shoe repair, a Brit named Vic Jowers opened a small coffee shop and eatery. Or at least that is what the general population thought it was going to be. A cup of coffee was a dime, Shandy Gaff thirty five cents.

The first time I heard about it I was a teen and played there with a little musical combo. I remember seeing bamboo curtains and bamboo mat wall coverings, art on the walls, small wooden tables with candles and flowers, and a comfy couch with pillows, sound dampening carpets and shelves of intellectual books, periodicals, newspapers, and magazines as well as esoteric materials to read. It was different, it was unique, and it was the dawning of a cultural paradigm shift for a younger generation in Santa Cruz.

For this historical endeavor I have contacted and interviewed a few people, with delight, who were then and now my friends who worked there or frequented "The Wicket" as we locals called it. As with any historical enterprise there are still some people that could add more to this story and I'm sorry I missed you. But they, like me, are on the "B" side of life's song with the tune possibly ending at any time like musical chairs! I have endeavored to reveal the personality of the owner through friends who were working or interacting with Vic and his wife Sidney Jowers. We saw the original location move to Aptos near Cabrillo, and first handedly experienced the Wicket evolve into an incubator for experimentation of music, art, healthy food, poetry, and theater all of which was glued together by the wit, intellect and unique character of this mostly appreciated, sometimes misunderstood, but never dismissed fellow.

Bill Tara

Ed Penniman: Well it's certainly nice to reconnect after all these years, I must say.

Bill Tara: Yeah!

EP: So you still have the same twinkle in your eyes, same smile, so that's all good.

BT: Thank you so much. I try to keep it there. [laughing]

EP: Good! Let me just give you a brief background, unless you already understand where I'm going with this.

BT: I think so. I understand that you're taking one chapter in the book, *Hip Santa Cruz*, and on the Sticky Wicket. I was thinking the other day, I was trying to remember how I first went there, and I think it was probably because it had a proximity to Cabrillo, when I saw it, because I remembered the name. I had to go look up the name, when I saw it downtown, I thought, "Sticky Wicket, what the hell is that?" and I looked it up in a dictionary. It's a British cricket term, and then I saw this name there, and so I popped in, and I fell in love with the place immediately. That I do remember. Santa Cruz in those days didn't seem like it was any kind of a cultural oasis. Part of what went on at the Sticky Wicket was really new for me, and it was something that I wanted. When I was in high school, I used to take my car and drive up to San Francisco and stroll around in North Beach and enjoy some of the coffeehouses there, and I was looking for that kind of cultural input.

EP: I would agree that Santa Cruz was an empty pallet, a clean slate at that time, and I'm wondering what influenced you to go to San Francisco? Was it Dolores Abrams? Was she a big influence in your early life?

BT: No, not Dolores, actually Isabel Pepper, who was the drama teacher at Santa Cruz High School. She was somewhat influential, but I have to say, I was just doing a lot of reading. I got busted in history class reading Allen Ginsburg.

EP: Okay.

BT: That teacher, I don't know if you remember Mrs. Nash? Charmin Nash – well actually, I had an interesting conversation with her at the Sticky Wicket many years later. She was out there having lunch.

And we had a little laugh about her busting me. And she took it away, and so when I went to see her after class, "I don't mind you reading poetry, but this is trash." I said, I don't know, I think it's interesting. I was reading a lot of Beat literature. And then, also, you mentioned Bill Hunt.

BT: I knew his brother Jimmer, and was a friend of his and hung out with him, and we lived fairly close together for a period of time, below Branciforte Elementary School, down in the flats. His family had a home there, and that's where I got turned on to folk music. And Bill Hunt had some records there, Weavers and Leadbelly and stuff like that, and I had never heard music like that before.

I heard that music and I thought that stuff is really great, there is content to it. But for me, I never really got into the whole rock-n-roll thing, It's great to dance to and all of that, but it didn't do anything for me. Going to San Francisco, I'd hear a little bit of folk music and go to City Lights Books. So when I went to the Sticky Wicket, there it was. There were books, there was art, there was music, there was a fair amount of eccentricity. Because I really got along well with Vic. I just thought he was a riot, and he hired me to wash dishes, and one thing led to another.

EP: Well, what was your relationship with Vic? How would you characterize him?

BT: He was boisterous, he was funny, he was witty, he could be really devastating. I heard him insult people very badly who didn't know they were being insulted.

EP: Oh, you'd love that. I love that too. Those are the most revealing kind. If they say thanks at the end it's even better.

BT: When he would get in his cups he was really masterful at that. He was a very smart guy, I really liked him, I appreciated his wit because a lot of people didn't get that. They got the boisterous part of him but he was very witty, obviously very cultured guy. He always came across with that Cockney persona. I really loved that about him. And he was a pretty open guy. If you got into a conversation with him, he would go wherever you wanted to go with it. He employed me for quite a period of time. I used to go out there in the early morning and clean the place. So I was a dishwasher in the evening and I was a janitor in the morning. And in the evening, when I was washing dishes, sometimes I would have to close things down, because he was really beyond it. He had a terrible problem sometimes with controlling his drink, and I would have to take the money out of the cash register and count it up, take him downstairs and sit him on the couch and hide the money, and it's kind of sad, because, really you could see it undermining him. My father had a problem with alcohol, it was sad to see anybody going down that route and with Vic even perhaps more so. My dad turned it all around, for himself and that was really good, but I didn't know Vic past when I left Santa Cruz,. I left Santa Cruz in '64 I guess.

EP: Right. Sixty-four would be right in there. Let me ask you a little ancillary question here. Did Sidney, being a costume designer, engage you at any level to direct you or encourage you to take on the theatrical aspects that germinated then?

BT: Sidney was a little bit of a mystery to me. I was a little leery of Sidney because she was really a bright box and I think that she was a physicist, if I'm not mistaken. I don't know if I'm just pulling that out of thin air or that's a proper memory, but she was a very, very bright woman. And she and Vic, after I came back – I did a season of summer stock in New Hampshire, in the summer of '61. And when I came back, I got involved. They had talked about theatre several times, and they came to me one day and said, Would you like to direct a play? I'd done a summer's acting, and I had told them that I really wanted to direct. That was what I really wanted. That was my aspiration.

EP: What a wonderful opportunity. They engaged all your positive intrests.

BT: I couldn't believe it. And they said, Well we're going to build this theatre next door, and Bob Hughes is going to do the music. We want to do theatre too,. Tell us what you want to direct. And I was so arrogant, naive, the first thing that came out of my mouth was, *Waiting for Godot*, and they both cracked up laughing.

EP: That's funny that you should say that, because when I was talking to Jim Hunt, Jimmer, he started laughing before he even said anything. And he said, I remember Bill Tara as Godot. I guess you played the lead role in it. And he started laughing and said for him it was hilarious.

BT: Well, it was really something. Because you can't even get permission to do that play now. It's that much of a part of the whole history of modern theatre. And they laughed, but they asked theatrical questions, they said, what do you think it's about? How do you see it? and I told them, and they said, Fantastic! Get some actors together and you can do it. And yeah, that was that. And it was an incredible experience, and I was just so thankful to them for that. They trusted me to do that. And then with some other people I did a couple of one acts there, and they were completely supportive always. But I think everything is okay. They actually bought me a beautiful director's chair with my name on the back. This is what they were all about.

EP: I love that sensibility, don't you?

BT: I was just a kid and it was like having this beautiful chair and they set it up in the Wicket and had a party to the chair.

EP: That alone was theatrical. Can you describe to me a little bit about the theater, physically – the construction, where it was located, maybe who put it together, what your involvement was with that?

BT: I can't remember who put it together. I mean it was very simple. It was a raked stage, like the old Shakesperian spaces, so it had a bit of a slope to it down towards where the audience would be. So the carpenter team – I want to think maybe that Ed Wood, who was a sculptor, had something to do with the construction of it, but I'm not certain about that. But the construction of that was really fast, it was just 2x4s and plywood, and they jury-rigged some lighting in it, and a very shallow stage, so it was a very primitive situation. They just put bamboo fencing around the outside and some tables and some braziers to keep people warm at night. I think it was maybe October or November even, when they started doing stuff there, so it wasn't warm. But it worked like a charm. It was fun because it was very intimate, and the amount of culture that came off of that stage was pretty incredible. I mean when you think about it, you Moller, Stravinsky. Vic did the Soldier's Tale and that teacher from Cabrillo, Hamilton he did the narration of it.

EP: Was he British as well?

BT: No. And that was funny, because I was doing practice with him, or taking classes from him. And later I think he became very active with the music, putting together the whole music festival at Cabrillo.

EP I see.

BT: He was my teacher at Cabrillo and he knew who I was. I was taking his classes and I was directing him in one of the masterpiece performances.

EP: Story of your life.

BT: It was because it was very cool, they were fantastic people. That little piece of music that I sent you, by the way, that was the handout from Lou Harrison, and we had a Christmas party there one year, and they made these little music sheets out for everybody, and passed them out and then directed this little piece of music that all has to do with – inventive sound

EP: I loved that. I totally got that when I saw that. That was so simple, but yet so cohesive. I'm sure it was a lot of fun to do. I remember it was really experimental, and of course Jimmer had some comments about Lou Harrison which were fun, because he was a self-starter, self-directed, had a sense of what he wanted to do with his interests, and certainly did.

BT: Well Lou, you're talking about Lou Harrison? Yeah, he

was a genius, a Da Vinci. I mean he translated Shakespeare into Esperanto; he won competitions at this Spoleto Music Festival in Italy. The Ford Foundation, many other foundations, supported Lou and his work is performed all over the world now. He's an acknowledged classical composer of this century.

EP: Yes, absolutely. How did he come to start frequenting the Wicket? Do you recall?

BT: I think – I'm not certain of the history of that, but I know that Robert Hughes showed up first, for me, anyway. I remember Robert Hughes rented a house next door to the Wicket, the other side of where the theater would be and Robert Hughes of course did studying with Lou Harrison, and I didn't see Lou for quite a while. He was a little bit of a mysterious figure. I heard of him, and then he started coming in every once in a while. And of course, he was so outrageously gay that a lot of people, really were set back by it. But he was a very nice guy, and here is a fun story. He invited me to clean his house. He was going on vacation, and he said, Vic told me that you're the janitor here in the morning. I said yeah, and he said, I want you to come and clean my house while I'm gone. I'm going on a trip somewhere. And I said okay, and he told me where it was and he gave me keys. I spent a day in there. I didn't do a bit of cleaning. That house was phenomenal. He had a harpsichord that he made himself, following the design of a harpsichord that was used by Mozart originally or something like that. He had all this incredible Aladdin's Cave of books and a massive collections of erotica.

EP: Of course.

BT: He had all of this stuff in there.

EP: A different world, entirely.

BT: I didn't have much to do with him, but I always thought he was certainly a very interesting guy, if nothing else. He was funny because a couple of times he came in and there were some surfers that worked there. Doug Haut. He was a big muscly guy. And I remember Lou Harrison came in there one night and he started flirting with him. He just didn't know what to do. We all thought it was so hilarious. He was just playing it.

EP: Well I have to inject something here. You know, the Santa Cruz experience with a gay couple, which of course was very closed, were the window dressers for Leask's Department Stores, all throughout the '50s. Remember Whip and Rick? And they had a little house out on 7th Avenue, it was real cute, that they had built together. And they were a couple. At the department store every year they had these phenomenal animated Christmas decorations. As I remember one year in the main display window on Pacific Avenue they had Santa Claus and a couple of elves naked in a bathtub. I thought it was just phenomenal and an elf is scrubbing his back I think I was 12, so in the years my visual memory may have been "enhanced." The display was really fun and imaginative. But anyway, that was one kind of early and fun experience with gay people.

BT: That was one of the things about the Sticky Wicket too. Because I'd been in theater and I'd been in at least one professional company. I was more familiar with gay culture, that the Sticky Wicket was the only place in Santa Cruz I can ever remember seeing gay men, and gay women too, showing up and being themselves.

EP: Yeah, exactly. It's one of the reasons why Pride in San Francisco has been so popular is that all the guys can get together and have a terrific time and just celebrate. Why don't you continue with the theatrical productions that went on there at the Wicket, and then I want you to segue into your awareness of natural foods and how that kind of piqued your interest and so think about that on a subconscious level as we're finishing up with the other.

BT: The theater was very homegrown, that's for sure, and everybody that was involved in it were people that hung out at the Sticky Wicket. That's where everything was cast from. It wasn't like we put notices out anywhere. It was, if you look at the cast list that I was working with, Ed Miller was a sculptor, and Richard Gee was a poet, and Wayne Monk was a lineman, a telephone lineman. And of course Gene Hamilton was this professor up at the college. And I remember him showing up. He heard that I was doing *Waiting for Godot*, and when I read the play, the only part that I thought would be Hell to cast and a joke would be casting Lucky, because there's a scene, which is about, I don't know, 10 pages long, which is all the character of Lucky, right? And who do I know that could do that scene – and it's all nonsensical stuff, but it has a poetic rhythm to it, and I thought, god, the only person I could think of was a speech teacher. So I go up to Gene Hamilton and said, I'm a little embarrassed asking you, but I'm going to do a production of *Waiting for Godot*, are you familiar with it? And he said, Oh yeah, and I said, because you get to play Lucky. And he said, Oh my god, yes, that would be so much fun! There you go. As I said before, there was just so much support for that. If Vic had any money available to him, he would have built a bloody theater out there. Because he had aspirations. I think he really wanted to be an impresario. I mean that's kind of the image of Vic that I have in my mind, because anytime anybody would come in that had talent, he would automatically just grab ahold of them, and he wanted to use them. He wanted to provide venues for people – musicians, actors, it didn't make any difference who they were. He had a good eye for people that were talented, and he wanted to support them. And that was it, but, he was a little bit laughable

I have to say in some of the things that he did, like his English, the imaginary gentleman, this *bourgeois gentilhomme* alone was a little outside of his league, but really funny, he said it's always with a little bit of lubricant so it always had a little edge to it! The folksingers made a great impression on me. Lainey Holland and there was this gal, she was a beautiful woman, I think maybe Latino, with a twelve-string guitar that used to play there sometimes too and she was really great. I really liked her. She did a lot of Odetta songs and, she had that kind of big voice and she was a good guitarist and her guitar had a big sound.

EP: What got you interested in actually heading up to San Francisco and started your interest in macrobiotics?

BT: Yep, yep. Yeah, I went to work at the Ashland Shakespeare Festival in '64, and I did the summer season with them, and when I finished, I decided not to come back to Santa Cruz. I went to San Francisco. And I enrolled in college there, but my college career at San Francisco State was about four weeks long. It was right in the middle of the Free Speech movement, and so I left, and then I did my own theater there in an old firehouse in San Francisco I had converted for a small theater. In order to make a living at it, you've got to do dances there, with groups like Big Brother and the Holding Company, and Jefferson Airplane was not there but one of the pre groups of the Jefferson Airplane, the Great Society and the Amazing Charlatans, and there was a whole bunch of local musicians there. I worked a little bit in a coffeehouse called The Matrix which was down in the Marina, and they were the first place where a lot of the San Francisco folk-rock bands got their start. In fact, they were partially owned by some of the Jefferson Airplane people. And I started getting interested in light shows, so I did light shows there. And then we used to do these events. We did about five of them, I think, in all, at the Firehouse, and we were very successful. I guess now they would be called raves, we had music and projections and all of that. And we lost the lease because they tore it down to build a parking lot. So we started renting out all through San Francisco, and we were the third wave. There was the Family Dog, and there was Bill Graham, and then there was our company, which was the Calliope Company.

EP: Paul Hawkins?

BT: Yeah. He and I worked together at the Firehouse, and then he and I started the Calliope Company. And that's where we produced dances, we also had an old warehouse in San Francisco that we used for checking out light show stuff or having parties and eventually that's where Ken Kesey and the Pranksters hid out when Kesey was on the lam so to speak because they could drive their bus in and we had a big roll up door they could drive their bus inside the warehouse and then you lowered the thing down and the bus disappeared! And we could see the jail from where we were. And when we were doing all that, Paul had asthma, and he came home one day and he said, Look, I'm going to start doing this diet, which is going to cure my asthma, and I thought that was an amusing concept, and he said, it's all based on Taoism. And I'd been reading a lot of Taoism, and I said, Oh, well that's interesting. Well, I'll do it with you. And so we started eating that way, and his asthma went away and I had a serious case of duodenal ulcers. And so I was in pain a lot. If I hadn't been smoking it would have been unbearable and I would have been on painkillers all the time. Which is a good excuse for me to keep smoking!

EP: Yes, of course, that horrible stuff from Mexico.

BT: So when we started this diet, it was very effective, and I was doing a play I directed in San Francisco at the Ashbury Theater, and when I finished with it, I thought, I can either continue on with this, or I can find out what I'm doing with this diet. I don't know what I'm doing with it. I don't understand it. And so I decided to go on a study in Boston, Massachusetts. Paul had already gone out and checked it out, and we ended up starting a little natural food company. It was already started when we got there, it was a little store like 10x10, and we developed it into Erewhon Natural Foods.

We started in San Francisco, but then we both went to Boston. Lisa, kind of the guru of macrobiotics, was teaching there. So we went there, we got involved . Nobody had this food. You're trying to eat this diet, and the food wasn't available. So we backed into doing the business, because nobody was doing it.

EP: So there was no source and so you decided to source it yourself.

BT: Source it myself, and then we opened a few stores. I opened a store in Los Angeles, and then I opened a store in Chicago, and eventually ended up going on a trip the better part of the year kind of looking at the world, looking to Europe and into the Middle East and ended up in India, looking, trying to study a little bit of natural medicine, and looking at what people were eating and what traditional diets were like. I was just getting a little bit of depth in my own understanding, and when I came back to the States, the company said, well look, we're thinking about moving to Europe, we're thinking about opening up in Europe, and you're the guy, because you're the only one that's been there, so I moved to the U.K., and after I'd been there for a while, I thought, this isn't going to work. We're going to be the ugly Americans if we come in here, because there's already a kind of a young food scene happening. And so I decided to stay in Europe, and I opened my own company, and then I decided to get out of the food business and get into education, and so

I started a nonprofit in London called the Community Health Foundation, and it's been a success.

EP: When you were in Santa Cruz, I'm not sure when the Staff of Life bakery opened?

BT: Much later. That was a guy that Jimmer and I hung out with, Gary Bascou.

EP: Right, yeah, Gary Bascou. The business is still going, Bill. It's still there, after all these years.

BT: Yeah, he started that. That was quite a bit later. I didn't go back to Santa Cruz very often. I came back when the Pranksters came down to open up the bookstore that opened on Pacific Avenue.

EP: Oh, the Hip Pocket Bookstore?

BT: Yeah, yeah.

EP: Right, and then the Ron Boise sculpture was too outrageous with this nude couple.

BT: I was there on the unveiling.

EP: It is so vivid. Both days are so vivid to me, because it was just like a jaw dropper for this little community. Who are these people and what are they thinking? Well they were thinking, that was the problem!

BT: Am I making this up? The mayor actually unveiled it.

EP: You know, the unveiling and pulling up that shroud was like opening the curtains on a whole new era, wasn't it?

BT: Yeah.

EP: Oh, that's lovely. Do you have anything else that you wanted to add, particularly any thoughts about the Wicket, because that's really kind of the focus of the chapter I'm writing.

BT: I think the Sticky Wicket was like an oasis. It was really a place that was inspiring, and I thought that Vic and Sidney were inspiring people. They were supporting people. Obviously they weren't into it for the money. They really wanted to breathe culture in, just bring it in. It didn't make any difference whether it was classical or jazz, it didn't make any difference if it was an abstract painting or figurism, it didn't make any difference. They just wanted to get the whole mix happening and I thought they did a really great job of it. I was really saddened when I heard that the highway access was blocked to that road to the Wicket.

EP: Maybe it had something to do with Vic's demise as well – it must have been heartbreaking for him.

BT: It would have been. I just can't ever remember him not being there. Even during the day, because I was going to school at Cabrillo, I used to go down there and read in the afternoon, and I was cleaning the place in the morning. I was virtually living there a lot of the time.

EP: Tell me a wonderful story about Vic. Something kind of dramatic that you would think that might really typify his character. Remember you said something about him thinking of himself as an impresario, and so on, but you know he had some demons. He had some issues he was trying to work out. Jimmer had some interesting comments about Vic. And you'll see those in the book. I'll mail you a copy and you can enjoy and see what Jimmer says about Vic.

BT: Jim was born to be depressed. He was a cynic since he was 10 years old.

EP: You went to Branciforte Junior High School didn't you?

BT: Yeah.

EP: All right, so you remember out there in the field during gym class when Jim Hunt did a thousand sit-ups? Do you remember that?

BT: No.

EP: Oh, he started doing sit-ups and he wouldn't stop. And he stopped after a thousand. And now he's got terrible arthritis, poor guy, but those were the days when you just do what you want to do. I took metal shop class with Mr. Buckner. I rolled in my 1931 Ford, and I was going to chop and cannel it and make it into a hotrod, and I had a cutting torch, and I was about ready to cut the gas tank! Anyway, those are pretty wild days as kids. Jimmer's always been an interesting character, for sure. Bill Helm lived in the original Branciforte adobe on the corner of Goss and North Branciforte street, and he had a sister. What was her name?

BT: His sister was Peewee. That's what she was known as.

EP: Peewee Helm.

BT: Peewee Helm. I don't know what her actual real name was, but she was a cheerleader.

EP: Oh, no kidding.

BT: And years ahead of us in school. And she taught Bill and I to dance in their kitchen.

EP: Then Bill's and Peewee's mom was head of the draft board in Santa Cruz. Do you remember that?

BT: No, because my draft board was in Oakland.

EP: Anything else you want to toss in here?

BT: I have to think, I remember you asking about Vic. Vic did a funny thing one night. He said – he would really get pissed, just really out there – I was washing dishes, and he said to me – he used to cook, and then he would go out and take money from the till. And when he would cook, I don't know if you remember, they had these, one of their big things was these steaks, they were huge steaks and they did them on a metal platter. He had a platter he would heat up and then he would cook them with mushrooms on them, mushrooms and onions or something like that. When the steaks were done, he wouldn't put those plates right, and they would slip down, and there would be like this double grill, and they'd slip down the grill and they would hit the edge and that steak would come off. And he did this tremendous trick he used to do where he would catch them on the top of his boot.

EP: I love it! I love it!

BT: He would turn around to look at me he would say, stabbing it with a fork, There's another one trying to escape!

EP: That's a good one. That gives you a sense of his character and sense of humor and so on. Well it's been a delight talking to you.

BT: Nice to talk to you.

Bill Helm

To me, singing at the Sticky Wicket was not just another gig. Coming out of high school I was a lost soul in many ways, just trying to make sense out of this new adult world. The opportunity to work there for Vic and Sidney was a life changing experience for me. Being there, I began to feel like I was where I should be at the time, and I feel that way today. I wish they were still alive to tell them how much that whole association meant to me.

My time at the Wicket began just after high school when I would go there on weekend evenings with Gary Bascou and other friends to hear Dick Bailey sing. I was a novice musician at that time and enjoyed Dick's rich voice and his varied repertoire of folk songs. Dick moved on to bigger venues at some point, and his successor was Jack Traylor, who equally impressed me with a totally different style. Jack lives near Sacramento and we are friends on Facebook, although we really never communicate. Al Johnsen told me once that he would travel anywhere in California to hear Jack sing. Finally, the entertainment moved to Carol Bruhn, a beautiful woman with a rich contralto voice who was accompanied by her husband on guitar. I never tired of these musicians and I wish they were still around. I believe that Dick died some years ago, I don't see Jack, and I haven't a clue about Carol.

Jimmer Hunt and I were renting a flat in Capitola in 1962 while we attended Cabrillo College. A mutual friend, Steve Tortorici, came over one night to announce that he had spoken to Vic Jowers and had set up an audition for me at the Sticky Wicket. I about fell off my chair from both excitement and fear, chiefly because I only knew about 5 songs that were worthy of performing in a professional setting. I went to the audition that was, thankfully, just me being the evening's entertainment, totally without introduction. Vic and Sidney were there, but working along with all the help and seemingly were not paying a lot of attention to me. After a few hours, when the business calmed down, Vic took me aside and said that both he and Sid liked me and that he would pay me $25 per weekend along with all the food and beer I could drink. I thought I had hit the big time. Minimum wage was $1.00/hr., my half of the rent was $25 per month and all I had to do was sing on Friday and Saturday nights from 9:00 pm to 1:00 am. It was more like going to a party than to a job. Well, I did that happily for two years or so, until the place closed in late 1964. Often, musicians would sit in with me and I enjoyed that immensely. You have to do that to stay fresh and to continue to learn the craft. Now and then Vic would come over to the mike and we'd sing "Knees up Mother Brown" and "I Don't Want to Join the Army", two English pub songs that he taught me.

Sidney rarely worked in the restaurant. She occupied herself with the business end, payroll, bill payment, etc., and worked hard with Lou Harrison and members of the Oakland Symphony to create the first Cabrillo Music Festival. That was a huge undertaking that was a marvelous success and is still going strong after many years.

Victor was something else. He worked in the restaurant tending bar and cooking, delicately insulting boorish customers, and hitting on women, sort of an early version of Basil Fawlty of Fawlty Towers. Vic's sense of humor was classic British cutting humor. I loved it. It was just like his mother's humor --"mumsie"-- as he called her. After closing time was the most fun. Vic would be counting the cash and the waiters would be cleaning up, and we would all be laughing for another hour with Vic. Times like that are fleeting. I remember when Jimmer had to go into the Army Reserve basic training at Ford Ord. Jimmer got really drunk and slouched in a corner saying that he didn't want to go. All the time Vic was shouting drill sergeant, marching orders at him. All Jimmer could say was "I don't want to be a soldier." Vic didn't like phonies, so I think that's why he liked me. I wasn't flashy, but I wasn't phony either. Vic admitted that he did not like any stranger until they proved that they were worthy of his respect.

The people who worked there and those who were friends of the restaurant were very interesting. The place was Lou Harrison's second home. He lived in a beautiful, smallish house in the Aptos hills about a mile away. He often came in during the afternoon. He always ordered his "usual" that was some vegetarian concoction we would fix for him, and he'd sit in the reading room speed-reading 2 or 3 books. Sometimes we would get into conversations with Lou about anything and everything. Never once did he say that he did not know anything about the subject. Seemingly, he knew everything about any subject and would love to tell you about it. Lou was the smartest man I have ever met. But more importantly, with all his musical talent he was always kind to everyone who worked there. That was in stark contrast to the orchestra musicians who came in after concerts at the Cabrillo festival. Generally, all those folks were arrogant. But Lou had more talent than all of them put together, yet always found time to show genuine interest in his "family" of workers at the Wicket.

Another guest was one of my favorite singers, Salli Terri. She came in one night after a concert at Cabrillo. It was a night when I was singing and I couldn't believe my eyes when she walked in. I got right up and took a break to talk to her. She, like Lou, was so kind and was thrilled that we had her record that I had put on the phonograph.

Then there was David Johnson, a guy with two front teeth missing, dirty work clothes, messed up hair, etc. He looked like a homeless man. It turns out that he was a piano mover by day and a composer by night. He came in one afternoon with a record of some of his compositions and played it for us on a quiet afternoon. When he moved pianos, often he would sit down at someone's Steinway grand and blow away the owner because his appearance did not match his talent. However, he cleaned up well when he wanted to, and even had false teeth to show off his smile. Dressed in a suit he was really a handsome guy.

The Sticky Wicket was rich with culture, art, music, good food, humor and talent. When we grew up as kids in Santa Cruz, the town was a retirement community. My grandparents retired to the Seabright area in 1940, paying $1,800 cash for their house. The politics was conservative Republican. Everyone liked Ike, mom and apple pie. Looking back, it was a paradise to grow up in. The cops used to give us a ride home after a movie at the Del Mar. It was really a safe Midwest-type of town, but right on the ocean. It was clear, however, that if you wanted to move on in life past high school, you had to go away to San Jose or San Francisco to go to college. There was little economic opportunity in our little town.

Then Cabrillo College, and later UCSC came to town with all their wonderful education and leftist politics. And along with that, a coffee house started down on Cathcart Street and later moved out to Aptos on Highway 1. It was owned by a bearded 30 something guy and his wife. They had folksingers, house concerts, art shows, and a little live theater called the "New Vic Theater". They got a lot of good press in the Sentinel with their monthly art shows and a lot of bad press from conservative elders who just thought the world was going to hell.

Bill Tara acted in various plays. Vic really liked and respected Bill's talent, but said that he (Vic) had to learn to let him do it his way. Once he did, everything worked out fine. I saw Bill at our 40th high school reunion and had a good time talking for quite awhile. That was the only thing good about that strange get-together.

Arlene Freitas was a talented artist and a friend of Vic and Sidney. She and my sister were close friends and both were talented artists. She painted the mural on the wall by the bar with life-size figures of 19th century men and women drinking in an English pub. She also did a similar treatment on the menu margins. That place really had a pub-like atmosphere, especially at night.

The Wicket was the first of its kind, a true catalyst of art and music, and good times. I met my first wife there. I learned to appreciate witty humor, and in so many ways, in just a few years, I grew up there. Vic died at age 39 of aplastic anemia. Sid took their two children to England to live. At Vic's memorial service Lou Harrison wrote a beautiful tribute to Vic and played it on the piano. The Wicket had closed in 1964 as a result of being fenced off from the freeway for public safety due to so many accidents there. It all was over so quickly.

Five months after closure, Manuel and Alice Santana opened a small Mexican Restaurant in Seacliff. Many of the Wicket crowd simply moved a mile down the road to Manuel's and a lot of what Vic and Sid started was carried on there.

Bill Helm: When the Wicket closed in late 1964, Bob Levy of the Watsonville Register-Pajaronian wrote an article with a good history. I'm sure it's available in their archives. Bob was the brother of Cabrillo teacher, Fred Levy. After graduating from Cornell University, Bob came west to live with his brother and sister-in-law, Robley Levy. He got a job at the Pajaronian as a reporter and knew no one in Aptos. So he hung out at the Wicket and befriended everyone. He was devastated when it closed and he wrote a heartfelt article about his home away from home. Then he drifted over to Manuel's, fell in love with the waitress there and got married.

Jim "Jimmer" Hunt

Jimmer: My Dad was from Los Angeles, he said he just wanted to get the hell out of the whole fuckin' mess – When he was in the Navy, he stopped by Santa Cruz at one point, and liked it.

Ed: A lot of soldiers from Fort Ord did that too.

Jimmer: He said, I like Santa Cruz, you know, it had the Casa Del Rey Hotel, and of course the Boardwalk was there. And he probably had fun and got off and had a beer and bullshitted with his buddies. He came up here right after the war. He was in the navy for about 13 years. He was in the navy before the war started. Anyway, he wanted to get a new start, I don't blame him. So he came up here in 1943, and he bought that house on Grant Street for $15,000 I think he paid for it. So that gives us an idea of comparison to your parents' place, and there were places like that all over Santa Cruz. Sometimes I think we would have stayed in LA, what a mess that is. Santa Cruz has been pretty good, up til now.

Ed: So it was just you and brother Bill, you and your brother?

Jimmer: : No, I had a sister, an older sister who died. Anne was her name, and she was six years older than I am, and then my parents had a surprise child. She was thirteen years younger, and so they had four kids.

Ed: Oh boy, I didn't know that. I always thought it was just you and your brother. Our family had a surprise child as well, Mark, and ten year my junior. I turned 76 in May. And I had a horrible thought the other day, I'm only four years away from being 80! You're laughing. I'm cringing! I know, I know.

Jimmer: You always think I kind of want to make it, I want to have some control, to plan it or configure it, I want to be in control over the escape.

Ed: Well, I wanted to ask you about the years of the Sticky Wicket. There's this project that's going on, and we are trying to document a lot of the activity that was going on back in the late '50s, early to mid '60s, and somewhat into the '70s. And so I remember playing music at the Sticky Wicket with a group, because I play the guitar, but that was on Cathcart Street.

Jimmer: Oh, that's the ancient place.

Ed: Did you work there?

Jimmer: No.

Ed: Where did you first hear about the Wicket?

Jimmer: When it was out on the freeway, and I don't know how – oh, Bill Tara. Bill Tara got a job there. I think he had a job there. Or he knew Jowers or something. I think it was through Bill, initially. And of course we still liked to go hang out there. And I thought Vic was a rather arrogant smart-assed opinionated son of a bitch. But then I ended up working for him for a couple years. And God I really liked the guy. He just came from a different personality.

Ed: Yeah, a different culture. He was British, wasn't he?

Jimmer: Yeah. He was English. And he was a newspaper man.

Ed: What else do you know about him?

Jimmer: When he first came and he had that place down there where you played, on Cathcart Street, he had a newspaper, a small independent newspaper. I don't know if that's true or he wrote articles and submitted them, because he was real opinionated, sarcastic and had his own take on things. And it seems like he was writing things,

Ed: Like kind of a left-leaning –

Jimmer: Not the Sentinel. It was not the Sentinel, it was like a different political don't know the name. Then he was out to Aptos and I think he got involved in the Wicket quite a bit. And... I don't know why he ever – I really didn't ask him, Why the hell are you in this stupid business anyway? Because when you have a business like that, it's a pain in the ass. I'll tell you why. It's 24 hours a day. It has to be cleaned every day, you have to order food, bread and junk, hire people and yeah, toilet paper, all this dumb shit. Then you gotta clean it once in a while, or all the time, and – fuck that! Who needs that, you know?

Ed: So he must have liked the people that came there and that must have been why he did it.

Jimmer: It was stimulating. And then he had that old homosexual composer who would come out there all the time.

Ed: Maybe Lou? Lou Harrison.

Jimmer: Lou Harrison. Who was just bizarre, but he was a nice man. When I say bizarre I don't mean any negative thing about him. He was genuinely a great human being. The fact that he was flagrantly homosexual gay whacko, that's his problem, but I think he was a good human being.

Ed: Well, when you were there, what timespan – can you remember the years you were there?

Jimmer: Ah, sixty-two, three I think.

Ed: Sixty-one and sixty-two, yeah. I was going to Cabrillo then.

Jimmer: We all went to Cabrillo then.

Ed: Was Manny Santana ever, anything to do with the

Wicket? Did he ever go there?

Jimmer: Absolutely, all the time. They were buddies.

Ed: All right, so Vic Jowers and Manny Santana were friends.

Jimmer: As a matter of fact, I think that's why Manny got in the restaurant business.

Ed: Oh, no kidding, I think it was '65 when they started Manuel's, if I'm not mistaken.

Jimmer: Did you know Manny?

Ed: Yeah, he was an artist.

Jimmer: I know.

Ed: He's a great colorist, Mexican expressionist

Jimmer: I like Manny.

Ed: Yeah, me too, I liked him a lot. And Alice. Alice was really beautiful, I remember her. Do you have any memories of Vic's wife Sidney Jowers?

Jimmer: Absolutely.

Ed: What was she like?

Jimmer: Now, the first thing you have to know is that Sidney was Vic's teacher, and he met and married his school teacher. I think this was college, okay? And that was bizarre right there. And I don't know, some college and/or regional college like situation, or I don't know, so anyway, he married this gal who teaches the class, and Sidney. Sidney was a person who didn't particularly approve of Vic's character to a sense. But on the other hand, she loved it, okay? And Vic just was outrageous, with a wonderful sense of humor and laughs like a son of a bitch, and could be real sharp and heavy sometime. But then if you didn't like your ass or something, he could be that way. But I ended up really liking the guy. He's a wonderful, wonderful man. But you had to get over these barriers first. He's the guy that, you gotta pass his tests before he would approve of your ass. And somehow over the years I passed all the tests, so I was okay. Vic liked people after he actually got to know them a long time, after a year or so, it didn't mean anything to him.

Ed: Well, what were his politics like? Did you ever get any sense of what his politics was?

Jimmer: No I didn't. I don't think he was interested that much in politics. I think he was more interested in people, and having a decent business that was viable and reasonable, where interesting people would come. Like Manny. Like Lou Harrison.

Ed: And what about Roy Rydell, I understand, he had something to do with it, or at least he had a collection of photographs that he had collected over the years. However, Roy was older than us. He was like, maybe fifteen years older than us. Yeah, but, he's dead.

Jimmer: Well, you got to remember what Jowers had. He always had a folksinger. He always had an art show going on. He had special concerts for Lou Harrison and anybody else that was interesting. He promoted the arts. Now Lou was interesting. Because Vic in many ways I think he thought the arts was a bunch of bullshit. He never said, for example, I'll be putting up a show by X, you know, and that he really got inspired putting on these shows. Or, Lou's got a new composition he wants to present, he could give a shit. Vic talked about art and music and I think it was people that he was interested in. And he liked people. I think he tested it, or tested himself. He seemed rather arrogant in certain respects. If somebody was an asshole, he'd tell them.

Ed: Well, how did you happen to get the job there? How

did that happen, that you started working there?

Jimmer: Bill Tara knew Vic and knew the place and I used to go there with him a little bit. And then I got comfortable with the Wicket, and there were jobs available. So I got a job there as a dishwasher.

Ed: Did Bill Helm ever work there?

Bill Helm? He played guitar and sang folk music out there for a couple of years.

Ed: No kidding.

Jimmer: And he was terrific!

Ed: Yeah, he was.

Jimmer: And – it's so funny about Bill. I think Bill was drinking every day and all that business.

Ed: You know, it's interesting. He and his family lived in the original Branciforte Adobe right there on the corner of Goss and Branciforte.

Jimmer: That's right. God, if I lived in that fuckin' place, I'd have torn down all this stuff and support it somehow and put plastic sheets over it so you could live there.

Ed: Yeah. He was an interesting guy, he was an intelligent guy, though. I liked Bill. It was restored by Joe and Edna Kimbro.

Jimmer: Very, very nice person. And when he got to singing, and he married one of the gals who was a waitress out there.

Ed: Was Diane a Santa Cruz High School graduate?

Jimmer: No. She was from out of town somewhere. Anyway, she became an attorney, and so did Bill.

Ed: So you worked out there a couple years. So when you first went there, what was your feeling about it, like the vibe? What did it feel like? Because there hadn't been anything like it before. If we had coffee, it was at the Delmarette or the Bubble Bakery,.

Jimmer: Well, I'll tell you what Ed, and it's a good question you ask. And there is an answer. But, I will say this. Never any place I've ever been to, ever, in Santa Cruz or anywhere else that's ever had the same kind of feel that the Sticky Wicket had.

Ed: I would agree.

Jimmer: I think everybody would agree who was actually in there. There was a little bit of folk music, there was a little bit of drinking beer, and coffee.

Ed: I mean the whole thing was set up like a living room, as I recall. It was a lot like a living room.

Jimmer: Yeah.

Ed: In a certain way, there were books everywhere if you wanted to read there were a couple tables.

Jimmer: That was another aspect of it, old books and all that stuff. So he tried to make it into his own personal little club, yeah. It was also a place for him to generate enough money to live reasonably. Vic was a wonderful, wonderful man. But he had, for his own reasons, his own personality that he displayed to the general public, but when you'd get to know him, he was this wonderful, wonderful guy. And it'd take a long time to get to know him.

Ed: Oh really.

Jimmer: Oh, hell yeah. You know, I remember, eventually, we played tennis a couple times, and, the employer-employee situation no longer existed, you were just a couple of assholes out there on the tennis court.And he was a really loyal kind of guy. And, I don't know. I think he was fair. For me now it's even funny to think about all this stuff. He was a really good guy and I think his wife wanted him to be X, and he couldn't be X. But he loved his wife, and they never had problems, and then they bought the old adobe out almost to Watsonville. I forget the name of who he sold the adobe to. He's working on it today.

Ed: He and Sydney and family lived at the Castro Adobe on Old Adobe Road in Watsonville. I think that's where he tried to put in a little theater or something, didn't he?

Jimmer: No, not that I know of. Anyway, he moved out there with her, and I felt so sorry for him. You know, it's hard for me to talk about him sometimes.

Ed: Really? You really liked him, huh?

Jimmer: Yeah. Because I knew him. I knew him after the work stopped. And he – well, what happened in the end was, last time I saw him he told me, he says, Jim, he says to me – this is when he had a terminal disease, he had some sort of blood problem, so he had to have these fuckin' transfusions, like seven or eight, getting new blood. He told me the last time he saw me, he told me, he said, Jesus, Jimmy, I was so worried my drinking would get to my wife and she bitched about it but it wasn't that at all, it's the god-damned blood stuff. He felt he was dying, but he felt better knowing that it wasn't drinking and that he hadn't and he didn't want to fulfill her concerns, about his drinking.

Ed: Do you remember anybody who was kind of regular that used to hang out there? We're going way back there. This is kind of fun to kind of explore.

Jimmer: Well, Bill Helm, Bill Tara, aw Jesus – everybody used to go out there. What the hell you gonna do? Because one of the good things about it, Ed, was, if you were of age you could drink, but if you weren't of age, you ordered a cup of coffee or a coke or something, and you could still be there with the people that were singing. So that was a quality. It was an in-between place. It was for adults and entertainment and all that stuff, but if you didn't fulfill that requirement, you could still be accepted. And I think that's never been achieved in Santa Cruz. I think it's the only restaurant in Santa Cruz that's ever achieved that.

Ed: I think you're right, because even the Catalyst has areas for minors and for people of age.

Jimmer: The Catalyst doesn't even come close to the concept of what Jowers had. All his contact with the artists was always kind of interesting. I don't think he had any interest in particular about these guys. Most of them, I don't even – I never talked to him about how he acquired these art shows, but I think guys came down, maybe, from San Francisco and asked Vic if he could show their stuff.

Ed: I think it was much more of a happening place than we realized at the time. We knew it was where we would go, you were really involved in it. I would go occasionally, like Santa Cruz guys would go there, it's kind of like where Santa Cruz people first started to what we called "hang out." We used to hang out at the beach at Cowell's, and we'd hang out there.

Jimmer: Well another unusual thing is, listening and talking about it, is, it was a concept, an idea, that was never tried before, and he came over, tried it, made a success out of it.

Ed: I wonder who knows more more about the original place, more about the Cathcart location. I played jazz guitar there with pianist Bill Davis and drummer, Ted Templeman.

Jimmer: I went there once or twice.

Ed: It wasn't there for long, I don't think.

Jimmer: It wasn't. I think just a year or so. And then – course in that place out there on the freeway, you know, the State or County closed the freeway off ramp.

Ed: Yeah, that was a big deal. You couldn't even get into the restaurant. People had to go way the hell around. I don't know if the Wicket being there and the body politic seeing it as counter culture rather than the emerging culture of a new generation drove the highway exit closure. It was kind of a transition time too, of, when you think of how we would call people Beatniks. It seems like the Beat generation of New York and all that stuff, and kind of San Francisco, that kind of Beat generation – some of those poets and stuff like that. And I think Bill Tara, because he was interested in poetry and theater, and he would have been paying attention, he was a real smart kid, if you remember. So you know, I think he knew what was going on there.

Jimmer: Something happened to him, which is interesting to me, because I used to be a really good friend of his, and – I don't even know why we were good friends. Not that I disliked Bill, even though he got to be pretty arrogant. And then he left town. And he was into acting and all that. He went to New York, and upstate New York, and was into summer stock and what the hell did he get involved in? And then I heard he went to Europe or someplace.

Ed: Well, do you remember anybody of any note, like musicians, that ever came to the Wicket? Because I either heard a rumor or maybe dreamed it, that Joan Baez played there one time before she was famous.

Jimmer:I heard that. But I never had it verified. The Limelighters were there a couple of times. Not when I was working there. I wasn't there at the time. And I think that sort of thing happened a couple of times. Maybe Joan Baez stopped over, I don't know.

Ed: Do you remember anything about any theatrical productions or anything like that when you were there? Any plays or any kind of productions?

Jimmer: I know Bill Tara used to be in the plays occasionally in the summer, and they would have I think one, maybe two plays a summer.

Ed: Where'd they have them?

Jimmer: They had them out in the bottom of the Wicket. Downstairs – against the building there was a platform – this is actually part of the end of the parking lot, and they would have the shows out there. And that's another one that Bill Tara was in, because I remember he was in *Waiting for Godot* out there. But that's another thing that Vic did. He had these arts, music, and shows.

Ed:Yeah! So you were like a fly on the wall, I mean you're a young guy, you're working there, and you're observing the whole scene, and I'm sure you had ideas about what it was like for you being there and seeing these characters coming in and out.

Ed: Do you remember George Dymesich being there?

Jimmer: No, I don't remember George.

Ed: He told me that Sidney used to fix him a free steak every once in a while.

Jimmer: Oh, god!

Ed: And Vic came back after some pints and jumped on George, said, "Ya bloody bastard, you're eating me out of house and home" and he went over and he grabbed the steak and threw it against the wall and told him to get out. Then he passed out, and Sidney fixed him another steak after they put him down for the night. Does that sound like Vic? I mean would he do something like that?

Jimmer: Vic did? Yeah. But I don't remember seeing him that angry!

Ed: No, that's just again hearsay, it's what I've heard. But evidently he was a real strong character. It was a phase, and it was an effective transitional one.

Jimmer: Absolutely effective.

Ed: You'd wear a certain kind of clothing. You'd wear a black turtleneck, you'd let your hair grow a little bit, or –You'd find out what the coolest new words are and you'd use those, and you were, in a way we were all kind of experimenting with our identity at that time. But there were these different, distinct groups, like the surfing group, remember the surfers?

Jimmer: Oh God yeah.

Ed: Then there were three guys down at Steamer Lane on a good day. I think you did for a while, was it Gene Williams, Dennis Conquest, Hal Schlotzhauer...

Jimmer: Yeah

Ed: ...and – who were some of those guys you were surfing with?

Jimmer: Gene Williams, Richy Novak.

Ed: Novak, yeah.

Jimmer: Gene Williams, what a horse's ass he was, a complete asshole. Ach!

Ed: He died young.

Jimmer: He went off on drugs. I mean you don't want to work and want to take drugs and if you want to get married and have fun and have money, you can't take drugs.

Ed: No.

Jimmer: He's lucky he didn't end up in jail. And of course Novak ended up with a big skateboard business, NHS.

Ed: Richie was always serious I remember those days. But he played just as hard as he worked, which was interesting about him.

Jimmer: And Gene, I remember Gene from junior high school, and he was always kind of a con artist. But you'd put it aside, because who the hell wasn't, a little bit.

Ed: Well, he and his brother. He had an older brother.

Jimmer: Oh, the brother was a horse's ass.

Ed: I think it was his older brother Vince that got him into drugs. But Gene and his brother, they used to go abalone diving, deep sea diving, and they were into the ocean. We all were in some way.

Jimmer: Right.

Ed: Way before wetsuits and all that.

Jimmer: Yeah, right. That's correct. I knew Gene and his brother and family quite well for a while, there was something wrong with all of them. The days we lived in our Santa Cruz, they will never come again. There was some nonsense. But everybody had a lot of fun and there weren't so fucking many people.

Ed: Thanks Jimmer, I appreciate the time you spent with me.

Jimmer, Yeah that was interesting to remember all that stuff.

George Dymesich

Ed Penniman: I'm sitting here with George Dymesich, master potter, in his Santa Cruz Mountains studio above Cabrillo College this sunny, clear, and somewhat chilly day. Hi George.

George Dymesich: Hey, Ed, good to see you man!

EP: You too. I made friends with Ralph Abraham, who wrote a book on Santa Cruz called *Hip Santa Cruz*. I don't know if you've heard of that.

GD: No, I haven't

EP: It traces the history of Santa Cruz from the inception of the Hip Pocket Bookstore and Ron Boise and his sculpture, and then The Barn up in Scotts Valley and Big Daddy Norse and the Merry Pranksters and dawning of the hip culture in Santa Cruz. I was having a conversation with him, and the subject of the Sticky Wicket came up, and so I told him that I had some experience with the Wicket, but at that time I was involved with the band, The Dukes, and a lot of other things. I told Ralph I would talk to a few people that may have some memories and between all of us we can piece something together about the Wicket and give him a good flavor of what it was like, who was there and what was going on. I thought I would call you, Bill Tara and another Santa Cruz native Jim "Jimmer" Hunt. Jimmer worked there for a couple of years at the new location in Aptos.

GD: I remember him.

EP: I'm going to give Jimmer a call.

GD: Did he perform music there?

EP: No, he worked in the kitchen and doing the work that made the place operate as well as cleaning and organizing the place.

GD: Busboy, probably.

EP: Whatever, yeah. For Vic Jowers.

GD: Vic Jowers, right. Scottsman, I believe. Also, if I remember correctly, Alice Santana worked there for a while, and if my memory serves me right. She's a little bit older than I am, and she's so beautiful. When I got near her I couldn't talk. And she kind of knew it, you know what I mean? But she was very kind to me. I was on the skids pretty much, so I was part-time job there, waiting tables and bussing and so on. I was working there one stormy night, I mean it was coming down, and Vic was gone.

Well, Vic was quite a drinker, so he was gone that night, and Alice said, How's it going George? And I said, It's going okay, and I really appreciate the little tidbits you're putting in my jacket when I leave. And she says, It's been really slow tonight, why don't I cook you up a nice steak and some nice things for you here. I said, Gee, that's great. I started cleaning up, putting the chairs on the tables and so on, and so she brings it out and I sit down and I'm just getting ready to eat it when Vic comes in. And he looks at me and says, Ya bloody bastard, you're eating me out of house and home! And throws it against the wall, and then he passes out. So he's laying on the floor, and we go downstairs and get Sydney, his wife, we carry him down and tuck him in, and Alice goes back upstairs and by the time I get back up there she's cooked another one for me. And then that's when I met Al Johnsen, who was a painter at that time. He wasn't a potter yet, he was folk singing. I had been folk singing around and about for probably since about 1958, '59, thereabout, '60.

EP: You know, I recall it was a two-story location.

GD: And the house was underneath it. So that's where they lived. There was a driveway that went outside and around.

EP: How would you describe what that place looked like inside. Do you recall?

GD: Yeah, I do. Where you came in, in the backdoor, which most people did, because they parked in the back, there was a small room with a floor-to-ceiling bookshelf. And there were all kinds of books on all kinds of subjects, a lot of it pretty esoteric. And then there was what they called a plotter's table there, and it was a six-sided table with a glass in it, and under the glass were marine maps and that's why they called it the plotter's table. And then you went into the main dining room, and then to the left of the dining room there was a smaller room on the side with an open doorway, and then this open area where maybe a window was at one time, pretty good sized, it was about, oh, three foot off the floor, so the folksingers could sit there and play and everybody could hear them, and that kind of thing.

EP: I recall, it was the first place I'd ever gone to where the chairs were comfortable when you wanted to sit down. Also, there were candles and flowers on the table, and it was completely unusual to have candles –

GD: Yeah, lights were down low.

EP: And it had a nice mood to it.

GD: Right. And they served some alcohol there, it was pretty minimal, and another thing I remember that this was the first real coffeehouse in the Santa Cruz area, maybe in the county at that time. And we were just moving into the end of the Beatnik era. So those of us that were there were mostly holdovers from the Beatnik period, the turtleneck sweaters, the berets and that kind of thing. We were too young to have gone through the war, right? So Al Johnsen and some of these other guys that were there often talked about, you know, the Wobblies, and Sacco and Vanzetti, and Joe Hill – all these people that were in the unions, in the 30s, see, some of them were born in the 30s and got this information from their parents who talked about the unions, the unrest that was going on at that time, and then the war came and snuffed a lot of that out.

EP: I wonder if Tom Scribner ever was there. I don't ever remember him at that time when I was a kid.

GD: He came later.

EP: Because he was a Wobbly.

GD: Yeah, he was a Wobbly too. He carried a card and was proud to show it, and he played at a place that was right where Soquel crosses the freeway. I think it's where that blues place is now, on Commercial Lane?

EP: Mo's Alley?

GD: Yeah. There was a woman who ran that, and I can't remember her name, and that's where he played a lot, and we used to go there and listen to him in the evenings. But the Sticky Wicket was far enough out of town, it felt like you were in another part of the county. There were no buildings around us, there were no houses.

EP: Well that was when 41st Avenue was essentially undeveloped.

GD: Right.

EP: I'm sure you have childhood recollections, like I do, of it simply being a large field,

GD: Yeah.

EP: And the first development that went in I think was Bank of America on the corner.

GD: Right, right.

EP: And I guess that was when George Ow Sr. bought a good sized piece of land. Also a lot of that area was the Brown's Bulb Ranch, Shaffer's Tropical gardens, Antonelli, and Vetterly and Reanult. Brothers, begonia growers, plant and bulb sellers.

GD: On Soquel near 41st was Daffy Don's, that was a furniture business there, and Garbini's was around the corner.

EP: Do you know who Daffy Don's daughter was? Linda Epperson. She married Fred McPherson IV.

GD: Yeah, I dated her way back when I was in high school.

EP: Oh, no kidding.

GD: Yeah, because her father ran the Miss America pageant.

EP: Oh that's right, yeah, Don Epperson. I met the family when they lived in La Selva, she was a knock out.

GD: And so Don Epperson and my dad were good friends, and there was a whole group of them. Brad McDonald -

EP: Brad McDonald, yeah, he was the one that first owned The Shadowbrook.

GD: Yeah, and Dave Yakabovich, you know, had a Babe's Bandstand down there.

EP: But let's get back onto the Wicket.

GD: Wicket, yeah.

EP: And some of the people that played music there, if you recall. Did you ever play music there?

GD: Oh yeah, yeah I did.

EP: Did Phil Reader and Dick Yount play?

GD: No, they never –

EP: They weren't with you?

GD: No, that was a little bit before that the three of us got together. Al Johnsen was playing there. There was a couple that did beautiful harmony, Carol and Dick Bruhn. And I think his brother (Karl T. Bruhn) or cousin played at the bandstand over at the Boardwalk in – what is that room where they did all the dancing?

EP: Coconut Grove?

GD: Coconut Grove, Harry Bruhn or something like that. And let's see, who else? Bill Helm?

EP: Bill Helm, I liked him.

GD: He became an attorney or something.

EP: Bill Helm is still around. He's another person I want to talk to.

GD: Yeah, I remember he was an attorney, and he's working for a legal mediation group up on Mission Street.

EP: Oh super, I'll give him a call.

GD: I haven't run across him or run into him over the years. And then there was some people that just kind of came through town and would stop there and play. But those people were steady. You could almost count they'd be there almost every weekend or during the weeknights, especially during the winter months when Capitola buttoned up during the winter, right? They pretty much closed all the buildings, all the business was down. Then there was the Greek restaurant was the only one that –

EP: Spiro's?

GD: Yeah, Spiro's.

EP: Let me ask you, did you ever hear that Joan Baez played at the Wicket? I had heard that, but I didn't remember –

GD: No, I never heard that.

EP: Yeah, it may be false memory, or –

GD: She could've, because different folksingers were wandering up and down the coast.

EP: It was probably the end of the Kingston Trio days, Glen Yarborough, those guys were all being phased out, but yeah, we were at that point between the Beatniks and the hip culture, and I think the difference was that the hippies were smoking weed and taking acid, and we were still drinking beer and smoking cigarettes.

GD: The hippies – at least the hippies, or the Beatniks I hung around with in San Francisco were more into jazz, and it was all North Beach where we hung out. So I spent some time up there too. And the only guys drinking hard stuff were the guys in the band. Everybody else was drinking wine.

EP: Yeah, it was before weed. In those days, weed was like a really serious, serious offense. But, I remember the Sticky Wicket –It was just someplace I went. It was relaxed, cool and my friends were there. And I have more vivid recollections of the cigar store on Pacific Avenue.

GD: Oh yeah, Joslin Brothers. The United Cigar Store.

EP: Yeah, like the heart of Santa Cruz, with the little eternal flame.

GD: That's the only place you could get the magazines, right?

EP: Well of course, Playboy. Yeah, but anyway, but I remember Vic Jowers and, yeah, it was a dynamic time.

GD: And Vic was a very dynamic guy, and he wrote for the Sentinel periodically.

EP: I didn't know that. Was he was a political writer?

GD: Op-ed, I don't remember. I was reading books more than newspapers, but yeah, he contributed to the Sentinel periodically. It was a good period of time, what was going on, not only in Santa Cruz. It was getting, moving toward

'65, university negotiations started and everything started to change.

EP: I remember I completely missed that time between '62 and '66 because I was in art school in Los Angeles. I'd experienced the Watts riots and the Police Riots in Century City with the demonstrations against Johnson and all that anti-Vietnam war stuff. So I was really extracted from Santa Cruz, so when I came – I remember-

GD: You were protected though.

EP: [Laughs] I remember coming back to Santa Cruz, driving down Ocean Street, and I couldn't remember all the franchise – Dunkin' Donuts, Jack in the Box and all this kind of stuff, and it was like the beginning of "Generica" happening to Santa Cruz, where you have all these franchises moving in. Used to be the Spivey's Five Spot, the Drive-n-Eat, and the one that was down by the beach and train depot, the Crossroads.

GD: I remember the Five Spot was at the end of the pier, that was over by the tracks, and we would drive in.

EP: Was that the Five Spot? No, Five Spot was on the corner of Water and Ocean Streets that's what I remember. See, there was the Drive-n-Eat, that was on the corner of Soquel and Ocean, and the Five Spot was on the corner of Water and Ocean, and then at the end of Pacific Avenue was the Crossroads. It was like the third tier of the places we would go to.

GD: Right, right, right. Depending on how work was going, yeah.

EP: So back to the Wicket, yeah, it had a different kind of vibe. It was different than anything I'd ever experienced before. However, it was not like The Barn. When I went up to the Barn, the Barn was real different. That, you know, was almost a little bit intimidating to me, because I think those guys knew something I didn't know.

GD: Really?

EP: Yeah. For me, I mean they were already on acid, and I had no knowledge of anything like that.

GD: Well the Wicket was more intellectual, I think.

EP: I think so.

GD: Well you know who else was there, was – oh man, the Gamelan guy (Lou Harrison), uh, shoot, he died just a few years ago. He did his first concert there, and then he taught at Cabrillo, but he's the one that created the Gamelan band, I mean the ensemble. Oh, hell's bells.

GD: And the first time I heard it, it was so bizarre, because there would be a bing bong over here, and then there would be silence, and then something would happen over there. It wasn't like any music I had ever heard before. It was just so different. But then he went on to make some hell of a career and became I think world famous, basically.

EP: Yeah, he did. It was really an incubator kind of a time, that gap between kind of where things disintegrated and began to solidify this different kind of consciousness.

GD: It was almost like progressive jazz was positive, but with pauses. Jazz never got down to Santa Cruz, basically. It was all in San Francisco. Because that's where all innovative and hardcore jazz players were coming, and a lot of them would come out from back east just to play with guys on the West Coast, because the West Coast was doing what they called progressive jazz, but it wasn't happening on the East Coast. It was all happening here. It was all in San Francisco, and it was all down at North Beach.

EP: Do you remember Lambert, Hendrick and Ross that was some really early jazz, it was spoken word jazz.

GD: Yeah. And Miles Davis kind of started that way, with Sketches of Spain.

EP: Oh man, what a great album it was to get stoned to.

GD: Yeah, he was just really early. But the Wicket introduced some interesting artists, I don't know to the community or not, but to the people that were interested in that culture.

EP: Well did Manny (Manuel Santana) go there at all?

GD: You know, he did.

EP: I never met him there, however I knew him after that.

GD: And years later, when he used to hang out with Al Johnsen and a few guys – what was the place, before the earthquake there was that place where you could get coffee, not where Kelly's was, but it was right behind.

EP: Oh, Cafe Pergolesi? Frank Foreman's place.

GD: Yeah, Pergolesi. University was starting, there were a few professors that would comedown there, called the Penny University.

EP: That was Paul Lee. I attended that.

GD: So Al took me there, invited me to come.

EP: Page Smith was another one.

GD: Page Smith, yeah. And I remember talking to Manny about art, you know, I was just not really getting into jazz, and he said, I think art's for the people. I says, really! I think that's wonderful. I was really impressed. Then about six or eight months later, they've having a thing on the mall, where I guess Chuck Abbott had already done their thing, changed the mall. So all these artists are down there on the mall, I'm walking down the street and I see Manny's got these pictures all over, and I'm looking at them, saying, Damn, to myself, Geez they are expensive. Funny, he's doing art for the people. So I said to Manny, I said, Hey Manny, I thought you were doing art for the people. People can't afford this! He says, Oh, fuck the people! I couldn't believe it! Six months ago he's making art for the people, but the people can't afford his art. I've kept in touch with Manny on and off over the years, when he was out on the Westside there, you know, in those buildings. Well, but the Wicket was a short time. It didn't last long.

EP: I think the city fathers, they knew something was percolating out there, and they closed off the freeway, Highway 1 to him, and that was kind of the end of it. So that fell apart, and then I remember his cricket paddles showed up at Zachary's on the mall.

GD: No kiddin'!

EP: Yeah, Zachary's Restaurant had his cricket paddle for years. So there's a linkage between Zachary's and the Wicket.

GD: That's interesting. Are the paddles still there?

EP: I haven't been there for years. I think they were gone the last time, and I don't know if somebody bagged them or – I imagine Zachary's has changed hands since then, and maybe whoever sold the place kept the paddles. It was owned by Mike and Diane Williams I think, brother and sister, not sure of the connection.

GD: Well, did you ever know Dick Yount?

EP: Yeah, yeah, I went to Santa Cruz High School with him.

GD: You know, he and his Dad were making surfboards.

EP: Yeah, way back when.

GD: And they are a collector's item now. If you can find a Yount surfboard that is in good shape, it will command a good price. Because him and his Dad were about the first ones in Santa Cruz that were making and shaping.

EP: But they were doing balsa wood boards, if I recall. It was before foam and fiber glass.

GD: Because I surfed in the '50s, and it was a plank. It was a plank of redwood about two inches and a half thick and about twelve feet long that took two guys to carry it.

EP: Yeah.

GD: And if it hit you, it'd kill you. And we didn't wear wet suits.

EP: My surfboard was balsa wood, and it had a coat of fiberglass over it, and if you got a ding in that, then it would soak up water, and it would never dry out. It would always get a little bit heavier, it would get heavy and kind of lead to one side, you know. I finally quit surfing and got into a band. Well, that's interesting, your recollections of the Wicket, and I just remember the vibe. The vibe was different. It was new.

GD: Yeah, I worked there for about half – almost a winter, like from October til maybe April, when things started picking up, and then I went back and worked on the wharf.

EP: Well, thanks George.

GD: Sure. I can't give you a whole bunch more on it. I loved the hamburgers there. They were good.

EP: The Wicket Burger, yeah. I was talking to Michael Riley, who's nickname is Seal. Cheryl (George's wife), Seal was saying the Wicket was not your cup of tea as a young girl in Santa Cruz.

Cheryl: Yeah, yeah I never went in there.

EP: What was the Wicket's reputation as far as you remember? What was it about, that place?

Cheryl: Gosh. I was ultra, ultra, what would you call, prudish. Oh my gosh. So anything that was dark and drinking was not anything near where I wanted to be. I've always been that way. Or any kind of drugs, that was the last thing in the world that's I'd ever – now I have a little bit of beer with George when we have Mexican food, and that's a huge thing in my life. I don't know what made that happen, other than seeing my uncle drunk one time, at a very impressionable age, and that's all I can think of that would have shaped me – my parents didn't drink either.

EP: The Wicket was dark, and there was drinking there.

Cheryl: It was kind of like, when the hippie, or the – the Beatniks, they felt very uncomfortable for me, so no, that wouldn't be someplace, but I think I walked in one time. Walked in and walked out!

EP: It was the end of the Beats and beginning of the Hippies, it was kind of in that transition period.

Cheryl: And being a woman, I think a man is much, you just have different –

GD: One of the neat places was around after that was the Coffee Cabaret in Capitola. It was the first gay-operated place in the county, I believe. It was out there in Mr. Toot's. It didn't last very long. Probably a year, year and a half. It was a very short-lived. But it was kind of a gathering place for gays.

EP: That's great, man, I had no idea. Yeah, in those days Capitola was "Crapatola," or "Capatoilet," remember those days? We local kids had slang for that place, because it was so funky. That little crappy merry-go-round that they had there, a sad effort of an amusement park area.

Cheryl: There was The Capitola Theater, though, that was a cool theater.

EP: Yeah, I recall the sisters that ran the place.

GD: I used to fall asleep in there, and they would come by and she'd wake me up and say, George, you gotta go home. I'd go there after work. We'd start at 5 in the morning, get off at 5 at night, go get something to eat, and then I'd go watch a movie, and I would fall asleep. So I'd go to see the same movie two or three nights in a row, and finally, you'd get to see the whole thing.

Part 3
MUSIC

Chapter 3
Kenneth L. Koenig:
Jazz in Santa Cruz, 1950s to 1980s

Jazz history in Santa Cruz reflects the cultural trends that helped shape jazz in general. Before the Beat and Hip generations of the 40s through 60s, swing bands dominated popular music. The tunes these bands played and those sung by their "crooners" became standards and filled the airwaves. Jazz music which had been steadily evolving since its inception around the turn of the century in New Orleans, had for the first time become part of the mainstream.

In the mid-30s swing bands, such as the band of Gil Evans, who eventually became famous for his beautifully arranged recordings with Miles Davis such as Sketches of Spain, brought his big band from Stockton for the summer to play at the newly renovated Capitola Ballroom. At the same time, other name big bands, such as Duke Ellington, Count Basie, Lionel Hampton, Artie Shaw, Glenn Miller and Harry James were playing to packed houses at the Cocoanut Grove Ballroom and Casa Del Rey Hotel on Beach Street in Santa Cruz near the amusement park and boardwalk. This continued until the mid-60s.

The 1950s

Coming on the heels of World War II, bebop as developed in the mid-40s by Charlie Parker and Dizzy Gillespie represented a new and more progressive form of jazz. Big band music was primarily music for dancing and these big bands played in the many large ballrooms all over the United States and throughout the world. On the other hand, bebop with its sometimes frenetic, angular and complex sounds and its young, innovative, masterful improvising musicians such as Parker and Gillespie as well as Bud Powell, Max Roach, Thelonious Monk, and Miles Davis set the trend of playing a form of music primarily oriented for listening rather than dancing. They often played in smaller clubs with no dance floors.

Bebop was embraced by the Beat Generation of the 1940s and 50s. Bebop emphasized spontaneous self-expression rather than the more structured big band music that it evolved from. The Beats, with their anti-conformist, free-flowing style easily related to this new form of jazz. In "On The Road," Jack Kerouac, while visiting San Francisco's "Little Harlem," gushingly describes hearing a "wild tenorman with a bawling horn across the way, going "EE-YAH! EE-YAH! EE-YAH! and hands clapping to the beat and folks yelling, "Go, go, go!" He goes on to describe entering a "sawdust saloon" and the proceedings of the evening's encounter with this jazz man in exquisite, loving detail for the next few pages. John Clellon Holmes wrote a jazz novel called "The Horn," which was published a year later (1958) in which he takes us into the life of a black jazz musician as well as into the life of the music.

During the 1940s up until the mid-1960s, as many as nine music clubs were open along Beach Street featuring a wide variety of performers including jazz musicians. Beach Street, for a time, became the musical heartland of Santa Cruz, especially from Memorial Day to Labor Day. The activity on the street back then was compared with Broadway or New Orleans French Quarter. There were blues singers like Big Mama Thornton at The Beachcomber. (See photo #1) Other clubs, such as the

Mamboo Gardens, the High Hat, and the Casbah provided opportunities for jazz musicians to "sit in" and play bebop with the house band. In fact, during the years of World War II and the Korean War in the early 1950s, musicians assigned to Fort Ord would make the drive up to Santa Cruz on a regular basis to have an opportunity to play in clubs along Beach Street. Many of these musicians later became famous in the jazz world. Lennie Niehaus for example, who was a long-time musical director for Clint Eastwood's movies, was a regular in the clubs.

Walking down Beach Street these days, it is hard to believe that the area was so rich with music venues. Parking lots, pizza parlors, beachwear stores and seedy motels line the street instead. One club, the Saint Francis became the Opus de Jazz which finally became Monk's (named after owner Monk De 'Anna). It stood where the Beach Street Cafe is today. In those days you could even hear Dixieland jazz regularly played at the Dream Inn and on the Boardwalk. This was a part of the West Coast Dixieland Revival of the 40s and 50s spearheaded by Lu Watters and Turk Murphy up in San Francisco. The joint was jumpin'.

Many of the finest black jazz groups came down on weekends from Oakland because of the opportunities to play on Beach Street. Ralston Brown, a popular jazz drummer and vocalist who lived in Santa Cruz and worked for a number of years on Beach street, reported that patrons would come in off the beach dressed in bathing suits to listen to the music and dance during the day, then go home or to their motel, get dressed in their finest and head back down to Beach Street for an evening of fine music and more dancing and revelry. At one time, one of the clubs even hosted Kenneth Patchen (the well-known poet) reading poetry to jazz.

Another place to hear and play jazz during this time was in Capitola Village. The Coffee Cabaret, opened in 1958, was the place to go after the clubs closed on Beach Street. It was said to be the only jazz coffeehouse with live entertainment between San Francisco and Los Angeles. The bands would start late and the jam sessions often ended in the early morning the next day. This establishment lasted into the early 60s before it was closed because a noise ordinance was enacted allegedly promoted by "squares."

In addition, in 1954 the Saba Club and the Caribbean Ballroom were opened side by side in Capitola replacing the old Capitola Ballroom. The Saba featured small groups and the Caribbean had the big bands. They were decorated in the faux West Indies style, popular at the time, complete with many carved wooden Tikis. The Saba burned down in 1957 and was not replaced.

The 1960s

By the mid-1960s the scene began to change. This change parallels the shift from the Beat Culture to the Hip Culture. Growing up in the generation of the Beatles, Bob Dylan, Joan Baez and the Rolling Stones, the hip generation was prone to listen to rock n' roll rather than jazz. Their taste in music was earthier and less intellectual. Once again, dancing rather than listening to music became favored and rock n' roll provided that dance music. In the latter part of the 60s and early 70s some jazz musicians with decreasing audiences and places to play developed "fusion" jazz, thereby attempting to capitalize on the popular appeal of rock. As rock and fusion bands began to take over the clubs on Beach Street, reportedly a "rougher" crowd moved in and the old club owners, jazz fans themselves, closed up and moved elsewhere. The number of venues in Santa Cruz featuring jazz decreased.

Fusion added the sophistication and complexity of jazz, with its spontaneous improvisation and the interplay between musicians. From rock, fusion got its power, rhythm and simplicity. Groups primarily used electronic, not acoustic instruments, rock rhythms and simple harmony. Rock fans were more likely to support fusion than the jazz fans. Many jazz musicians did not consider fusion "real" jazz and wouldn't play it. Others, like Chick Corea, Herbie Hancock and even Miles Davis took a different approach and figured out ways to make the music "artistic" and expand on its emotional and commercial appeal. Groups like the Miles Davis groups in the 70s, Weather Report ,The Yellowjackets, Blood, Sweat and Tears and Chicago transcended the jazz - rock cultural divide and became quite popular even opening for rock bands at concerts.

The big band scene at the Cocoanut Grove also started to fade in the mid-1960s and finally gave way to artists like Sonny and Cher, the Four Freshmen and other more commercial, pop music groups. And for a time, as jazz became superseded by rock music, many jazz musicians found themselves even playing in rock bands to keep active.

However, jazz music remained alive in the Santa Cruz area schools. In the late 60s and into the 70s, teachers Don Keller at Aptos High School and Dave Leets at Soquel High School continued to train students to play jazz. This foreshadowed a resurgence of jazz in Santa Cruz in the 1970s.

The 1970s

In 1970, Lile O. Cruze was hired as head of the music program at Cabrillo College, a community college in Aptos. Cruze found himself in charge of a stodgy "pep" band that played standard big band arrangements from the past. Instead, befitting the times, Cruze was determined to morph the band into playing more fashionable progressive jazz. He recalled though, that at the beginning he wasn't allowed to use the term "jazz" in describing the music.

Cruze searched for appropriate but unusual charts for the band to play as well as for the best young musicians to play them. He blended Vietnam War veterans and hippies who had developed their skills on the rock music of the 60s. The band developed in 1973. Cruze was demanding at rehearsals and very exacting in promoting music reading skills as well as playing skills. And, he had to be firm with this very free-wheeling group. What he accomplished was to turn out excellent jazz bands and a number of world class musicians some of whom went on to productive careers in music locally and internationally.

In 1975, Cruze was joined by Ray Brown who took over a part of the jazz program while Cruze developed the Cabrillo Theater program. Brown had been a member of the Stan Kenton band in the early 70s. He grew up in a musical family and taught at the jazz camp that his father started, one of the first programs of its kind. Under Brown, the Cabrillo program became renowned for training musicians with classes in arranging, music theory and even music copying. Three big bands of different levels were formed. Feeding into the program were already skilled students from bands at Aptos and Soquel high schools. This continued until California

Proposition 13 was passed in 1978 limiting property taxes. Funding for arts and music dried up in the schools and the programs at the high school level suffered greatly limiting the number of available skilled student musicians. Musicians were drawn from other areas to live and study in Santa Cruz because of the reputation of Ray Brown as an outstanding educator and the dimensions of his jazz program. The Cabrillo jazz program continues to the present day with Brown still a part-time participant.

In 1973, Rich Wills, a DJ at KUSP-FM had the idea of forming a non-profit jazz center to provide audiences a chance to hear good jazz without being in more expensive, commercial clubs. He joined with Tim Jackson as the two co-directors of the project. Soon, a group called the Friends of Jazz was formed. Rich and Tim were joined by Sheba Burney, a grant expert, and Peter Davenport, who kept books and handled publicity, and many other volunteers. Tim booked the bands. Developing a series of benefit concerts over the next two years, the group was able to afford to rent a 2000 square foot space in a building at 320 Cedar Street that formerly was a bakery. With some outside volunteer help and donations, as well as selling some of their personal possessions at the flea market, the group was able to fashion a workable jazz club after extensively remodeling the space.

The club opened its doors on May 25, 1977. It was named the Kuumbwa Jazz Center (pronounced Ku-umb-a, a Swahili word suggested by another volunteer, James Coleman, meaning "the act of creativity." Over the years many world renowned jazz musicians have played at the club. At the end of 1987 the interior was remodeled, the stage shifted, the kitchen upgraded, and more seats added. The sound system has also periodically been upgraded over the years to provide a more professional presentation. The club, under the guidance of

Tim Jackson and Bobbi Todero, the executive director, has developed a reputation among musicians as one of the world's finest jazz clubs to play in. Audiences and management are respectful of the musicians and the music is legitimized as a unique art form. Tim Jackson became the general manager and artistic director of the Monterey Jazz Festival from 1992 to 2010. Since then he has remained the artistic director of the festival as well as remaining the artistic director at the Kuumbwa. This connection has served to enhance the reputation of Santa Cruz and the Kuumbwa Jazz Center as friendly to jazz and has brought many artists of the highest quality here to play.

Also contributing to the promotion of jazz in Santa Cruz at this time was Frank Leal. He was a top flight saxophonist that had moved to Santa Cruz from Los Angeles in the 50s. Leal had played in big bands at the Cocoanut Grove. Upon coming to Santa Cruz he continued playing music but also became a restauranteur opening a number of music-friendly venues in town including one on Beach Street. After that scene ended, he operated the 2525 Main Street Restaurant and music venue in Soquel. His groups played on the wharf and other places in the area.

The Dobson family, Smith and Gail along with their children Sasha and Smith Jr., were at the forefront of jazz in Santa Cruz beginning in the 70s. Smith was a world-class pianist who chose to remain in Santa Cruz to be close to and raise his family. Gail, a vocalist, and Smith gave private lessons and encouraged many of the area's budding jazz musicians for many years. Tragically, Smith died in a car accident returning from a late night gig in 2001. But the dominance of Smith and Gail, and later Sasha who is a vocalist, and Smith Jr. who is a multi-instrumentalist, earned them the reputation as the "first family of jazz" in Santa Cruz particularly during the 70s through the 90s.

By far, one of the biggest promoters of the Santa Cruz jazz scene in the 70s and beyond was the presence of the jazz group Warmth playing on Pacific Avenue nearly every day from noon for three hours or so and sometimes at night right in the heart of downtown. The Cooper House, originally the county courthouse, had been converted into restaurants and shops and had an outdoor patio for dining. The band played right next to this patio and the music could be heard all over downtown much to the delight of locals and tourists who flocked there for some mid-day fun.

In 1972 Max Walden, owner of the Cooper House hired Don McCaslin to put a band together to play jazz during the afternoon lunch hour. Don hired the best musicians he could find. Many graduates of the Cabrillo jazz program played with Warmth at some point. Some of the other musicians included Harry Woodward, Dave O'Conner, Jim Brown, Phil Yost and Jim Lewis. Musicians, some quite well known, came from in and out of the area to "sit in." Don's son, Donny was a bright and talented young sax player who studied at Aptos High School, performed with the Warmth when he was twelve years old. He later studied back East and went on to international stardom. Besides the music, there were a bevy of street performers who frequented the Cooper House area. These included, Ardis The Spoonman, Tom Noddy, the bubble man, and the Flying Karamazov Brothers. The atmosphere remained loose and tinged with hip culture. (See pages 113-114, 139 in *Hip Santa Cruz 2*)

Warmth continued as a central downtown institution until the Loma Prieta earthquake in 1989 when the Cooper House was red tagged and demolished. Even prior to that, new owners had carted away and demolished a large mural built behind the band that honored many of the musicians that played there over the years. (See photo #2)

Besides the Cooper House, other jazz venues of note in the area during this time period were Gatsby's, which became Hillary's, Holy Donuts, the Riverside, and the Bayview Hotel in Aptos. Mr. Toots coffee house in Capitola Village featured jazz part-time.

The 1980s

Early in the 1980s the music scene in Capitola Village along the Esplanade thrived in a number of clubs including the Edgewater and Zelda's. In the summer of 1980, Paul Jackson who wrote the tune Chameleon, came to town and started a funk, fusion band. That band included vocalist Ruby Rudman who also performed regularly with Warmth. Along with Ruby, a number of other jazz oriented vocalists performed in the area such as John Lawrence, Windy Day, Charmaine Scott, and Darlene Alexa. Darlene sang with a band organized by pianist Bobby Payne who had come to Santa Cruz from Chicago. In the early 80s, Santa Cruz was a relatively inexpensive place to live. The natural beauty of the area and great climate as well as the low cost of living appealed to many artists and musicians who made Santa Cruz their home. The band included Max Hartstein on bass (see pages 53-73 in Hip Santa Cruz). Max Hartstein was an artist, writer, musician, and philosopher who continued to be very much a part of the hip Santa Cruz scene for many years.

Many of the institutions that developed in the 1970s continued to flourish into the 1980s. The music at the Cooper House with Don McCaslin and Warmth remained a core part of the jazz scene every day of the year unless it rained. The jazz program at Cabrillo College continued to be a source of excellent training for those inclined to follow the jazz improviser path training both those who intended to become full time musicians and adult amateurs from the community. The words, "I studied with Ray at Cabrillo" offered easier entry into the local jazz fraternity.

The Kuumbwa Jazz Center continued from the 80s to the present to feature all-star jazz musicians regularly. In addition, they expanded their reach into the community by starting jazz education programs. Since the music funding in the schools remained decreased, the Kuumbwa filled a much needed gap by developing a Kuumbwa Jazz Honor band made up of the best high school music students from Santa Cruz and neighboring counties. The band was (and still is) chosen on an annual basis and prepares for a performance at the Kuumbwa Jazz Center as well as other venues. A summer jazz day camp for 8th through 12 graders held on the Cabrillo campus introduces students to jazz improvisation and jazz appreciation. Another program sponsors musicians going to local schools to play and teach.

The number of privately owned venues available for playing jazz decreased as the commercial viability of jazz continued to decrease during the 1980s. Audiences at clubs preferred blues, rock, folk, and country music which seemed more easily accessible and provided more opportunities for patrons to dance than jazz did. Nevertheless, drummer Red Malone led many small groups and a big band weekly at the Mount Madonna Inn for many years after coming to Santa Cruz in 1981.

As the cost of living rose in Santa Cruz under the influence of commuters from Silicon Valley and others who moved into the area, the feasibility of a full-time artist living in Santa Cruz diminished and there was a steady migration to other cities with a lower cost of living. A smaller but active jazz community existed during the 80s providing those interested in playing and preserving this art form the opportunity to do so. Still, very few musicians were able to play jazz on a full time basis. Youngsters with the talent and ambition to be full-time jazz musicians left to study and live in New York and other big cities.

Mamboo Gardens, Beach Street, 1950s

Photo courtesy of Ken Koenig

Chapter 4
Ed Penniman: Santa Cruz R&R History

Some background and interviews on the arrival of R&R in Santa Cruz.

Sound track of a Blues documentary video by Ed Penniman.

1953. This is a story about a thirteen-year old guitar player getting hooked on the Blues when he heard Willie Mae Thornton for the first time. She wrote and played blues songs, played the harmonica and taught herself to play the drums. A string of small Blues clubs along Beach Street was where it happened. In 1953 she had a hit with "Hound Dog," the song was poached and made even more famous by Elvis Presley. Ed remembers her wearing white cowboy boots sitting behind her drums singing, she was around 30 then with a strong career. Ball and Chain, was a Willie Mae piece made popular by Janis Joplin, with Thornton yet again being stiffed of any royalties. Big Mama was an underappreciated artist who had a huge influence on Rhythm and Blues and early Rock and Roll.

[Music intro – guitar backed blues singer Willie Mae "Big Mama" Thornton, singing "Sassy, sassy Mama."]

2008. Ed Penniman: I'll tell you a little history about the blues in Santa Cruz in the 50's. That's like the songs I was listening to in the fifties. When I was 13 years old in the Santa Cruz summertime we used to have a train called Suntan Special that was coming down from Oakland. Mostly Black people, they'd come down to Santa Cruz, and fool around on the Boardwalk, sun and frolic at the beach.

That was when there were a number of blues clubs along Beach Street. One was called Mamboo Garden and the Beachcomber and I can't remember the names of the other ones (Casbah and the Top hats) but these were the two that were the best ones. And so I'd be walking back from the beach and I'd walk past these places, and I loved that music. They were playing blues music. I loved the relaxed shuffle beat. I loved the sound. I loved the feeling. I remember listening to AM radio at night, and there was this radio station called KDIA from Oakland that always played blues at night. So I'd be listening to these blues players on the radio at night, and damn if it wasn't the same music that was playing in these clubs on Beach Street. I became a fan of Jimmy Reed and others.

Yeah, same music. And I remember I started paying attention to who was playing and I remember this one lady, her name was Big Mama Thornton. She used to play at the club there on the corner of Ocean Street and Beach Street, right there on the corner kitty corner from the Merry-go-round, where there is a big parking lot now. But I think I was probably 14-15, and I'd already started playing the guitar when I was 12-1/2, 13. And so I'd hang out in front. Of the Mamboo Garden. Mamboo Garden. Not Bamboo Garden, but Mamboo Garden. They presented many blues acts in there. So I would just hang out in front, peek in and listen to them live. I loved it, it was free. I'd peek through the crack in the door listening to this music. I did that for about five years. And then they got to know me and I sat in only one time with Willie, and a kid who I thought was her son. Another time I got to get up on the stage in this little crappy blues club. It was another blues club about four doors down from the Beachcomber. I remember I was getting more and more confident with my guitar playing. So, I snuck into this place, underage, and I wanted to play with these guys in the worst way because they were good. The players were natural and, again, so relaxed. The guitar player had a shitty little Gibson amp with a blown speaker. It actually was a precursor to the "Fuzz" amp that became popular in the 60's. They knew that I was a musician and that I wanted to play. You know your peers, musicians, you can tell with musicians. They're watching your hands, they like to watch you, and they are so in to it you know. And so I finally came out and broke the ice with these guys, and the bar is full of mature people. Now I remember them being these sun burned brothers and sisters. And now I'm sitting on stage, so I'm sitting there with his Dane Electro guitar. You could buy them new for less than $150. Now a vintage one is about $4,500. It had a unique funky sound. I'm up there on the stage and he says, so what do you want to play? And I said, I don't know, why don't you just start playing something and then I'll play with you. And all the people started laughing. But then he said to the audience, yeah, okay, we're going to start playing, and he's going to play with us. He's a Black guy and he's got this sexual bar humor? I finally figured out what the hell they were laughing at, I laughed, we played for a while. I held my own, I knew the changes, and had my own way of interpreting the stuff I heard on the radio and on Beach Street live. That scene of blues bands coming down from Oakland, and entertaining the Oakland people down here planted a seed in me. You know, that spawned one of the first rock-n-roll bands in Santa Cruz. Yeah, Dukes of Rock-n-Roll, and I was the lead guitar player. The Dukes.

Charlie Tweedle: You were the guitar player in the Dukes? Was there – did you have an electric guitar?

Ed: Yeah, very first Fender electric guitar was a Duo Sonic, a little smaller than a regular Stratocaster. My first Strat I got used in 1957 for like $80. Again, those old pre-CBS Fenders are priceless now.

Other Party interviewing Richard "Blinkin" Meynell: Did you ever make a recording or tape or anything?

Blinkin: Yeah, I had tapes made from one of the practices. Ted the drummer had a good sense of humor. Some times he would just go into the kitchen and pull out a few pots and pans rather than setting up the whole trap. I had a reel to reel tape transferred to cassette then to CD, it's a sucky old recording. The music is solid. I made five or six copies for all the original band members.

Do you realize how many hundreds of bands followed in the wake in this town?

Ed: You know, it's interesting Phil Wagner, We called him "Twang or PJ," he was a rhythm guitar player. He was classically trained, could read guitar music and knew more chords than any other guitar player in the region. He and I made a conscious decision to rather than taking the band to San Francisco and going full on into the music in the 60's, we would go and get a formal education. So he went to the University of Santa Clara and graduated with a degree in Economics and Philosophy. I left Santa Cruz and went down to L.A. to Chouinard Art Institute and got my degree in marketing and advertising design. It's just real interesting that I made a conscious shift to go from music with the band to my own thing. But there was one guy in The Dukes, Ted Templeman, he was the business manager and local musicians union rep for the band. He decided to stick with the music business. He reformed the band and called it the Tiki's and they got really popular in the area, and later they morphed and were called Harper's Bizarre. They made a couple of hit recordings back in the sixties. One was a version of Simon and Garfunkel's 59th Street Bridge Song (Feelin' Groovy). And then Ted stayed with it. The band broke up and he continued on with Warner Brothers as their A&R guy, then he also started producing Doobie Brothers, Van Halen and some other artists. And he made a career out of it. He, like us, was on the ground floor of the music scene then but Phil and I at that time had a little more traditional thinking about what we should do with our lives. I've often thought, that I don't know what would have happened to me, being a musician in the sixties, those were dangerous times in the music business. I recall we were playing as an opening act at the Cocoanut Grove for Conway Twitty's (Harold Jenkins) band. I spoke to the Gretch guitar player (probably Jimmy Ray "Luke" Paulman), he showed me his fingertips, his callouses had callouses. He had played shows nearly every day for years and he was exhausted. That and the thought of packing my amp and guitar at three in the morning helped to cool me off. It was a great time in my life, but I've had a lot of them.

The History behind The Santa Cruz "Dukes of Rock and Roll"

Philip Wagner is a native of Santa Cruz, California. Former musician then poet turned Painter. Peace Corps in Peru. Paris 67-68 befriended Jean Paul Sartre. Made political documentaries, ran an underground anti-war press, had a Poetry TV Show, wrote a couple poetry chap books, taught college level poetry and psychology.

This introduction has been adapted from Philip's writings by Ed Penniman.

The phenomena of this band known as "The Dukes " has to be taken in a large historical context. We were an all-white band of middle class teenagers "crossing-over" into "black music". At that time, the "rock beat" was said by the Churches to (quote) "create a subtle confusion in the minds, wills, and emotions of the listeners, which leads them to question the absolute moral standards of God." We were teenagers, kids who were part of the first middle class that had ever existed in the world, forming a group. We had some economic freedom and knew a small amount of world history: we could get jobs not on a farm; we went to school, had factory-made clothes, and bought cars. Cars enabled us to have privacy, "mobility", be away from our parents, be alone with our girlfriends and listen to whatever music we wanted, not church music!. The black "Do-whop" sound and straight-up Blues music had a huge impact on us. It was our lens on the world, our emotional lexicon. Our cars had AM radios which were forever turned on to our favorite music station KDON. Music was a way of learning: we loved this kind of direct learning from experience. For example, a sax player friend,

Joe Serrano, would cut school in order to sit in his car playing along with the radio. We could be exposed to new ideas outside the class room and add our own forms of artistic expression, essentially "make history", not be "victims of history". Call it "freedom". We could get "on stage" where we had "permission" to shine.

Up until that time, about 1955, the members of the Dukes were lock-step products of history and our parents : Our parents were born roughly in 1910. They were 5-8 years old when they were forced to suffer through WWI. Then the devastating Spanish Flu hit the U.S. about 1917. War, disease and unemployment: They grew up in constant mortal fear: for "safety", they clung to their "group", Catholic, Protestant, Jewish, White, Black, Italian, & etc., as a "source of identity". With rock and roll, teenagers could expand, get out of the trap, away from established, abstract, static "group identities" and base their identities on dynamic, immediate "direct experience", which included free-thinking, sex, dance and rock and roll!

From 1955 on, the fabric of the social structure was profoundly assaulted . WWI, the Great Depression, WWII, Korea, racism, the violence of poverty, etc., all of which are the by-product of fear-driven set of rigid rules for thought and action. Overall religions do not serve humanity, and we knew it. With WWI and the Great Depression, the idea of "civilization" was imploding. Freud showed the world it's repressed material had "gone septic", become poison and was irrupting in wars, racism, misogyny; this repressed mindset projected its "dark side" onto the "out groups" like the blacks, women (labeled "the handmaidens of the devil") or socialists.

Rock and roll allowed for this release of repressed material in a healthy evolutionary process, not war and racism.

Our information and experience contradicted the "official story" of reality. My grandfather's family were all-Catholic for generations, but. the World Wars destroyed the assumptions of their Puritan, Edwardian family-political-social "Christian" structure. "Moral civilization" was irrational: After WWI , none of the waring nations could figure out why they had fought the war! "Morals" and "obedience" were so highly regarded and tightly interwoven, the wars just kept happening, and no one could say "no" or offer an alternative! Youth did not want whatever the old social structures had to offer. The anti-human horrors of the war shook the foundation of any "cultural justification" and of "civilization" itself and its purported "values". The known, accepted social structure was destroying the world. One trauma after another, families were being torn up. For example, in 1915 my grandfather, P.J. Freiermuth, had 9 siblings, but in 1919, he had 4; they suffered the loss of 5 children to the Spanish Flu, an unforeseen by-product of WWI, but for years the news of the flu was suppressed by the U.S. government "for the good of the country" and the future war efforts! Arts tried to release people from this non-serving, false authoritarianism. Post WWI saw people trying desperately to get out of the Edwardian Era with the flappers, "speakeasies", jazz, and some "wildness". But then that generation was reeled back in with the Great Depression 1929-1940. Then WWII started and more repression. Post WWII, the Cold War began, with the perpetual threat of nuclear annihilation. "Moral values" were producing a world that nobody, except those authoritarian rich and powerful, wanted. But in the midst of this Cold War, a middle class America had been born, and we teenagers benefitted. We could purchase Fender electric guitars, drive cars, enjoy a world outside the admonishing eyes of the church, state, or parents, and we did. We endured the continual condemnation by fundamentalist religions. As evidence in 1956, I recall an all-black band lead by a screaming sax player named Chuck Higgins which came to the Civic Auditorium. The teenagers went wild, "dancing indecently". Higgins had a hit "Pachuko Hop" which galled authorities. The Santa Cruz Police Chief shut the dance down and the very next day rock-and-roll was banned from Santa Cruz. That cultural ban "for indecency" did not hold for long, but it reflected the basic thinking of the time: "People had to be trained, to be controllable and controlled at all times; they could not be free!" In 1958 the Dukes were playing a dance at Holy Cross Church Hall and the nuns made us to stop playing and get off the stage. People out-of-control of the "authorities" were seen to be sinners, rock and roll was seen to break the laws of "common decency". Bill Kelly, a guitar-playing friend while singing some suggestive song, was punched in the head on stage by an offended member of the audience. As further evidence, about 1957 a sexy woman was a vocalist in a club called The Beachcomber on Beach St. That bar was frequented by black bands and audiences which would come down on the "Sunliner" train from San Francisco. As it turned out, this sexy woman singing in the Beachcomber was discovered to be a transvestite. He was ordered to leave town or be arrested, essentially for violating codes of common decency, which was a criminal offense. Ed Penniman and I (Phil Wagner) used to go down and hang out in front of the Beachcomber Bar and listen through the door. We heard some mind-blowing great stuff. One time, a black bandmember saw Ed and I listening in and invited us up on stage to play a few chops with the band. I was too shy, but Ed got up there and performed. The bandmembers loved us: two young whiteys digging the blues! 1958-60, Channel 11 TV organized dances, some at the TV studio and some at the same Santa Cruz Civic Auditorium. The TV host liked the Dukes and tried to promote us. Our band, with two tenor saxes, actually sounded somewhat similar to the "indecent" Chuck Higgins Band, the band which was shut down at the Civic by the chief of police 1956.. We played "sock-hops" in S.J at a kind of West Coast version of Philadelphia's "American Bandstand". Teenagers were coming out, expressing themselves; suddenly they were not willing to be tied down to a counter-productive race-driven cultural form which was personally repressive, destroyed potentials, and started endless wars essentially to dominate people, wars to exploit weaker smaller childlike nations, wars to keep the citizens of their own country in line and "going to church", ironically justified in the name of "morals". But, rock and roll was here to stay!

I discovered the guitar when I was 12 years old and began lessons with Mr. Harder who owned the Music Box Music Store on Soquel Avenue, and talked me into buying a 1954 Les Paul guitar and then a couple years later, a 1955 Fender Stratocaster. (Both guitars were first editions and are now worth $20-40,000.) Later when I learned all I could from Mr. Harder, I studied with Jack Springer on Laurel St. He played guitar for his entire life in Los Angeles. The first band I played with 1955 was The Velvetones. Then I was invited to join the Dukes who were more professional and with two saxophones, two guitars, trap set, base and piano, had a bigger sound. Ed Penniman was Stage Manager and Ted Templeman was the Business Manager. We were members of the Musicians' Union. The Dukes were something I could identify with: We were part of this larger social movement: a psychological revolution away from "group-identity" like church, state, and family, and toward a "personal identity" based on "connection", circumspection, non-violent non-racist tolerance, direct experience, a broad cultural explosion wherein "pleasure" and "feeling good" were not sins. We created a "family of adventurous friends", all learning from interactive, immediate, and direct experience. We worshipped emotion, passion, sensuality, intuition, and dream; all the stuff of do-whop, the blues, and rock and roll. We were cross-over whites, although occasionally, Corny Bumpus, a black sax player who later played with The Doobie Brothers and Steely Dan, sat in with us. The Dukes were basically a white band playing black music. Chuck Berry was "the father" of rock and roll and a kind of "father" to us. We loved Chuck's music, his energy, and other black bands, especially harmonica players. We dug the visiting bands, like Big Mama Thornton's, which performed at the Beachcomber Bar on Beach St.

Some of the local venues we played were: the Capitola Bowl, Holy Cross High School, Santa Cruz High School, the Coconut Grove (where once we led on for Conway Twitty), Santa Cruz Civic Auditorium, Channel 11-TV, Ben Lomond Riverside Park, Lompico Swimming Pool, and the Hollister Veterans Hall leading on for a band we all looked up to called the Downbeats.

In about two years, The Downbeats, became very successful and so packed up and headed to Los Angeles. They fell apart because of drugs. The lead singer, Johnny Armilo, became an evangelical minister in Salinas. The base player, Petey Rose, died of an overdose. The Dukes also resolved to follow suit and go to where the music was happening: Los Angeles. I didn't go. Why? Because my father, in 1927-8, had travelled around the world in a dance band on a pleasure liner owned by Dollar Lines, and he knew firsthand the dangers of always being on the road, around alcohol, women and drugs. My dad told me flat out, "You are going to college, not Los Angeles!". The re-populated Dukes of Rock and Roll left Santa Cruz for L.A., changed their name to the Tikis who had a sissy white, beachboy sound which I hated: It wasn't black; it wasn't rhythm and blues; it had no soul. The Tikis morphed into a stage band named Harper's Bizarre, which had a couple hits: Feelin' Groovy, Chattataooga Choo Choo. Harper's Bizarre was headed by our drummer, Ted Templeman, who later joined Warner Brothers Studios and produced the Doobie Brothers and Van Halen. Our piano player, Bill Davis, was super talented; he joined the navy and played in navy bands. Later, Bill was successful; he went big time jazz, won many jazz awards, played with some wonderful bands and headed his own group, The Bill Davis Trio, which once opened for Ray Charles and an audience of 90,000 people. The Dukes of Rock and Roll is definitely part of the history of Santa Cruz and of a changing society which momentarily opened up and refused to be forever victims ruled by fear.

Dukes, rough time line.

1956

A group with no name is put together to play for the girls at the Santa Cruz High School as part of a boys performance program including several acts. Bob recognizes Bill from SLV. Girls go nuts.

1957-58

The group adds several people who worked at Opal Cliffs market. Add Don Stewart .The band plays at dances and local venues.
1956
Second semester, 9th grade, SLVHS. Bob Cecil hears Bill Davis play piano at a school assembly in the gym. Bob and Bill have not met at this time, however, Bob recalls thinking that Bill was a great pianist.

Bill Davis, Original founding member of the Dukes

Bill D.: When I was 15, I began playing 2 nights a week at the Moose Lodge. My mom got me the gig based upon a deal that she would let me join the Musicians Union if they found me a gig. She was tough!

The leader of the band was Hal Leath who owned a very successful music store. He was the drummer. It was he who made me aware of the The Dukes of Dixieland, a very good, nationally known dixieland band. I told him we were trying to come up for a name of our band. He said, you guys (my band) should be "The Dukes of Rock n' Roll". Hence..........The Dukes.

Early on, the band was myself, Bob Cecil vocal, (I'm still in touch with him)" Mel Stanley (Sax) and another horn player, alto sax, Bill (can't remember his last name) and, of course, Ted (according to Bob Cecil the original drummer and founding member who's idea it was to have a band was Bob McPherson). We never had a bass player, at least that I can remember. I've lost contact with everyone out there except Bobby Cecil (Robert Brooks) who lives in Alabama). Bobby hasn't changed much from high school. He's a very nice, quiet dude and looks great!

Bill D.: Thank you for undertaking the project and for being part of The Dukes history.

Ed P.: Happy to do it. Good times!!

Bill D.: Bobby will tell you how he and I got together and the interesting story of how we found Don Stewart. I have a humorous story of Bobby as well: We were to play a major talent event at the Civic Auditorium, in front of several hundred people. Bobby wanted to play guitar but...............he didn't know how to play guitar. So,.... I suggested, "I have a guitar. just strap it on before we go on. I told him to just dance around with it while he was singing (he had great moves) and use it as a prop, you won't have to play a note". I told him the girls would go wild. He did what I suggested and the house came down, girls screaming, couldn't hear ourselves think. He never played a note. I remember I was laughing so hard during the performance that I almost couldn't play! He tells the story better than I do but it is definitely one of those things that you don't forget. From that point on, we used the guitar.

We were actually called back for an encore after the audience started chanting, "we want the Dukes". When we did come back out, the applause and screaming was so loud we were overwhelmed. Bobby and I gave each other a look like "what in the hell have we got going here"?

EdP.: I had no idea that essentially you and Bob founded the band. I knew you were an original but Bobby was presented to me as just a fellow who wanted to sing with us once in a while. I'm embarrassed now that I wasn't more inclusive and encouraging.

So Ted was added after you learned his uncle had a music store with rehearsal rooms you could use. Seems like Ted's uncles played a pivotal role!!! All interesting to me.

Don Stewart taught me a lot about the guitar, he was talented and I think came from more of a country music background like Sammy Carson who was around at the time. I became a big Chet Atkins fan because of Don teaching me how to finger pick melody and bass at the same time. Not sure when I replaced Don, I have a photo of him on stage with us and I don't remember that gig but there it is in the photo in the Civic. It would be interesting for us to work out a timeline of personnel.

Bill D.: Yes, for a short period we called ourselves "The Dukes of Rock and Roll" but the more I heard that name the more I thought it would be more "hip" to shorten it to "The Dukes". By "dance band" I meant music the kids could dance to not ballroom style dance music of the 40's. Traditional swing dance music is what I had to play with Hal Leath's band at the Moose Lodge (I was so embarrassed) but there were no kids there, thank God. Ask me about Sal Basile when we Skype. He also played a role in directing my music career path in a much different way. He may still live in S.C. Not sure. (Sal passed away of ALS in 2016).

Ed P.: Little Richard and I have the same last name, a story in itself. After you went into the service, I took over the duties of the leader of the band and Ted continued managing booking and union contracts. My intent was to model the band after Little Richard's band. Piano, bass, drums, two tenors saxes and a baritone sax, two guitars lead and rhythm. When I hear "Lucille" I still get goose bumps as it reminds me of our sound! I abandoned searching for a piano player, as you were irreplaceable. I wanted Corny Bumpus on lead tenor and shifting Allen to baritone sax but that never happened.

Bill D.: And, you remember correctly. Little Richard changed the musical course of my life. Up until that point I was going down the classical music path and more focused on playing with "traditional" dance bands. I heard Little Richard and thought, "yeah, that's what I want to do". My mom supported it too. Thought it was great. I began to listen to more black artists. Their sounds, instrumental and vocal, just hit my ears right. That led me to listen more and to try and mimic them. In the process, though I wasn't aware of it then, I was taking the first steps from classical to jazz via R&B and Gospel and wound up at the door to jazz. Little did I know that I was building the perfect foundation to be a jazz musician. I remember hearing Red Prysock's record (R&B more akin to jazz) and was fascinated with the sound and feeling. Having perfect pitch was a huge asset. When I listened to those artists I knew pretty much what they were playing and I would go to the piano and mimic what they played. Got the notes but not the feeling. That took years! Doing that allowed me to "see" what they were playing and to learn different "licks", how they improvised, etc. Most of my "basic" jazz education occurred at the Navy School of Music in DC. I was 17 when I went there from boot camp and all of that listening I did when I was younger paid off.

Eventually, after many, many years I was playing very "black", hence the Ramsey Lewis stuff. I played so much like Ramsey, in my late twenties, an attorney for Chess Records (Chicago) heard me and I was signed to them. Their "stable" was mostly very popular black artists (Etta James, T-Bone Walker et. al.). Being a young white dude I was an anomaly. BTW, Charles Stepney (one of the original founders of Earth, Wind and Fire) produced my record. Unfortunately, it did not go anywhere but that's another whole story way too involved to go into for this project.

Ted and I went to San Francisco one time to try to market the band. Can't remember how that turned out (obviously not so good) but it certainly was an adventure driving up there and in the "big city". We had no idea what we were doing.

Ed: Few know of Ted's lighter side of his personality and how he used to "spaz out" playing the drums and knock over his set and end up on the floor. Of course today it's not politically correct, but we had a lot of fun and it was innocent. I think Ted knew he had a gem with you and realized that you were a unique talent. I'm surprised he never produced an album with you on piano. I do remember you could out Ramsey Lewis Ramsey Lewis!

Do you have any memories of the Sticky Wicket, the various band members, what kind of group was the early iteration; a dance band, a jazz band, a rock or jazz band? Really anything you can add about those to subjects will add to the mix. Ted has not responded to my outreach and that is his prerogative, no foul.

Bill D.: Original band members: Me, Bob Cecil and Mel Stanley (Tenor Sax)

Ed P.: Played where?

Bill D.: Hard to remember. Civic Auditorium, a couple of times. Boardwalk stage. Sticky Wicket a few times. SCHS, several times. I'm sure there were other places, just don't recall.

Ed P.: Always union band?

Bill D.: No. We were not union. Because we were kids they left us alone but if we had gone on to achieve something everyone besides me and Bobby (he was not a musician) would have had to join.

Ed P.: What year did Dukes start.

Bill D.: Probably '57. That's when I was a Sophomore and met Bobby. He heard me play at an assembly and was really impressed so he initialized the friendship and it went from there.

Ed P.: Were you on TV with us? Don't recall.

Bill D.: No. In the Navy. I was in boot camp as of June 28, 1959.

Ed P.: I had no idea that essentially you and Bob Cecil founded the band. I knew you were an original but Bobby was presented to me as just a fellow who wanted to sing with once in a while. I'm embarrassed now that I didn't be more inclusive, respectful and encouraging. So Ted was added after you learned his aunt had a music store with rehearsal rooms you could use. Seems like Ted's aunt and uncle played a pivotal role for his career!!! All interesting to me.

Ed P.: Wow, that explains a LOT, the uncle working for WB. I'd like to use some of the info you have shared with me. I do remember playing with you in the band then later taking Don's place.

Bill D.: He had a sister.

Ed P.: It was his sister Bonny, does that sound familiar, I thought she was alluring and pretty. Zip response from her for most guys I ever talked to.

Bill D.: Yeah, I think you should contact Bobby and pick his brain. In the past, he has reminded me of things that I had totally forgotten. Keep in mind it was 3 yrs of my life a long, long time ago.

It was Ted's mom that owned the music store. His uncle came into the picture long after I was gone. It was he who was with Warner Brothers.

Bill D.: Don was a talented guy for his age and obviously had a bunch more experience than we did. He was a man (18-19 yrs old) and we were boys. The last thing I heard about him was that he may have had some legal trouble and just "disappeared" from Santa Cruz.

Interview with Bob Cecil
Original member of Dukes, singer.

Ed P.: No one gave me an orientation when I got into the band. Nobody said that you were one of the founding members. And so it was interesting for me to think of. The underpinnings of the Dukes and how you Bill Davis played with a dance band sort of thing and then from there it sort of evolved.

You really started fresh with Bill Davis and then as it grew you added Mel Stanley playing the sax, then Bob McPherson on drums and I understand Sal Basile played bass occasionally. I think that's what Bill said. But then adding Don Stewart who was really an excellent guitarist and then myself as rhythm. I came across this photograph of Donny and myself and Ted and Allen Ross and Mike Huntington on stage and I don't know if it was a San Jose Channel 11 or if it was at the Coconut Grove or at the Civic Auditorium.

Bob C.: It was after I left.

Ed P.: But I remember you clearly singing with the band.

Bob C.: I remember talking with you about the Dukes a time or two..

Ed P.: I just wish that you would have sung more often; we didn't have any vocal component to the band and you would have added so much. We all were not in agreement on what you had to offer.

Bob C.: Well let me tell you how it got started. And this goes back to Bill and I when we were 14 years old. The year would have been probably 1956. He and I were both living up in the Felton area. The first time I ever heard Bill

Davis was in the ninth grade. I was just a kid. I wasn't doing anything in music. However I had sung since the fourth grade. Coming from Roswell New Mexico where I was born. I had always been around music always had a voice, always singing and I just loved it but I was not in a band. And Bill Davis being a piano protege he was playing since two or three years old. His mom taught him how to play probably as long as he has been talking.

Ed P.: He's a great talent, a terrific musician and he's done some recording but I always thought that he was not really recognized as well as he should have been. He was so gifted with a perfect pitch.

Bob C.: Exactly Ed, I always felt the same thing. Bill could have done anything. He was 14 years old just coincidentally we happened to be at the same school in our freshman year. Living in the Felton area, he and his Mom and Dad.

Ed P.: So you met in the assembly.

Bob C.: I think we had an assembly in the gymnasium and the entertainment was Bill Davis. They introduce him and so this kid comes on the gymnasium floor and they had a big piano and he played several songs. And I sat there listening and thought, Wow. This kid is really good but I didn't go meet him. We never met at school. So you might say that I was a fan of his but didn't know him. So then my family moved down to the Twin Lakes area. That was just the Twin Lakes State Park and we lived in a State house right on the lagoon.

There was another fellow by the name of Bob McPherson. It was a year ahead of Bill and he was a senior now. He worked at a food market (Opal Cliffs Market) and was a drummer and was a senior one year older than Bill. He was in the Musicians Union. That's how good he was. We learned the school was going to do an assembly and the boys were going to put on a program for the girls in the gymnasium. Bob McPherson says to me why don't we get together and put a little group together and play for the girls. He said I'm a drummer. And he said I understand Bob that you're a singer and Mel Stanly who was working at the market played sax. And so we said Yeah that would be fun just a one time thing. The football team does fashion show in drag and you make everybody happy. So Bob said I know a piano player, his name is Bill Davis and he really can play piano. He says why don't I give him a call if he wants to do this. At that point I did remember that the Bill Davis he was telling me about was the young man I saw earlier in my freshman year at San Lorenzo. I connected the dots.

Ed P.: I remember his Mom.

Bob C.: Ma was an extrovert talking and friendly and Dad, pretty much you wouln't see him. There was a little bedroom in the back where we met for the first time. So we had two sax players, Bob McPherson drums, Bill Davis piano. And me vocalist. That was the first meeting and we were not the Dukes, we were just five guys that were going to do an assembly for the girls. It is the beginning of the year so it may be early September 1958. Right after school started. So we figured out that we could do two instrumental songs.

Bill was so good, and Bob was a union professional at a very young age, and now Mel Stanley who would really make his sax wail.

We came up with two songs I could do. The first one was Chuck Berry's "School Days" and Elvis Presley's "Don't be cruel." So we practice those pieces for days. We would just start playing and making it up as we went along till it took form. I would start making up lyrics and making something and we would go for 10 or 15 minutes or longer.

He said, "Bobby if you played guitar..." I'd never played anything! "Elvis hardly ever strums a note when you hear him sing. What if we use the guitar as a prop. You wouldn't have to hit the strings, it would just be the look. Do you know anybody has a guitar?" Yes there's an older guy at church who has one.

So I take my older friend's guitar and we go get ready for the show. We were at the gymnasium. 500 girls packed into it.

The shows start and then our group started to play the instrumental numbers. And I was in the back myself. I started getting really nervous like what are we doing this for? How do I get out of this? So I did the classic cop out. I left the guitar prop behind.

The place was applauding for the band as they had already heard the first two tunes. I was introduced and went out to the microphone really nervous. And Bill sees me come out without the guitar. It's exciting and basically I didn't know what was happening to me. And I don't even know what Bill's doing. He goes back to get the guitar and gives it to me. And the next thing you know as I'm standing at the mic singing my first number, Bill looks over my shoulder at me and announces Bobby will be playing his guitar and the place went crazy. So I just turned around and the guys and we were all laughing and then I said, as I did most of the time, "Okay guys let's kick it around."

Ed P.: OK so now you're on stage with a guitar around your neck.

Bob C.: So Bill looked at me and he's got that big Bill Davis grin like "I gotcha!" So we started in playing. "School Day" by Chuck Berry.

"Up in the morning and off to school
the teachers teachin' the golden rule,
American History and practical man,
studying hard and hopin' to pass,
working your fingers right down to the bone.
The guy behind you won't leave you alone."

So what I want to get I just had it. What I did with the guitar is I simply adlib and I went for it 100 percent I was playing that thing but my right hand never hit the string. I moved, the guitar moved, we went crazy, wild, and evidently we went over. After that we went right into "Don't be cruel" and the place went crazy.

Ed P.: I love it, that's what Bill said it was absolutely amazing. He said it was magical. You guys were so uplifted by that and you were so shocked at the same time.

Bob C.: Yeah exactly.

Ed P.: Bill said, "Oh my God what have we got here?"

Bob C.: Afterwards at that point we're saying, "You know I think we're a band."

Ed P.: You, just like the group, decided that.

Bob C.: Then later Bill was telling me he spoke to an older gentleman who owned a music store, and he's talking to the guy, and said we were trying to come up with a name for the band. So this guy told Bill that there is a group called the Dukes of Dixieland. Why don't you call yourselves the Dukes of Rock and Roll?

Ed P.: Yeah!

Bob C.: We all loved it. So that's where we actually became the Dukes of Rock and Roll.

Ed P.: What year was that then. Would it be fifty nine?

Bob C.: It would have been September 1958. So officially at that point there was a "Dukes of Rock and Roll" Because I was the singer and the lead person who usually gets a lot of attention. So some people would refer to the band as Bob Cecil and the Dukes. But you know that was never our title. I was just a member of the band. It was Bill that basically moved everything forward. Bill was the musical component and I was the front doing the singing and the talking, a year with the musical background. At no time did I ever want to claim that this was my band. I understand you know that.

Ed P.: Yes I do.

Bob C.: We started playing every thing every place we could go and one night at Civic Auditorium with Bill Race at Record Hop. The place was absolutely packed, I don't know how many thousands of people. It was a lot of folks, and we were just one of the acts on the show. And some of these people were in show business.

Ed P.: So you said it was called "Record Hop" because I know there was a show with Frank Darian who did that on TV. But I think that was a little bit later like it might have been 1959.

Bob C.: Yeah. And Bill had been in touch with them so we were booked on the show and I believe it was 1959. Now that was I guess backing up into my high school junior year, it was Bob McPherson, our drummer. Since he was a senior and upon his graduation he went into the Navy. At that point we were needing a drummer and there was a fellow named Ted Templeman who we were aware of and knew. And he was in a little three-piece cha cha band. And we had seen them at various places around.

But you know Ted was fantastic on drums. He was a better drummer than the band was a band. So when we were looking there was a little bit of rivalry but Bill and I approached Ted and asked him if he would consider being a drummer in the Dukes. Ted was a little cool and said you know I'll think about it. And he said Yeah I'll do it. And so that's how Ted became the drummer it would have been in our senior year in the summer 1958. It was a very smooth transition.

Ed P.: I know it was happening and then you added I believe Don Stewart (guitar).

Bob C.: Well here's the story on Don. By this time I get Bill Davis a job at Opal Cliffs Food Center. OK. So now I'm working there. Mel Stanley (sax) is working there. Bob McPherson (drums) is working there and then Bill (piano) too. I was checking groceries. Bill was bagging and the people were coming, a neighborhood supermarket. We were friendly so we were having fun. You know we always liked the people. A grandmotherly type lady came up in the check out line and there was a young fellow with her, kind of reddish hair as I recall, and not too friendly, not talkative.

Ed P.: He was quiet

Bob C.: So I was talking to the lady, checking, Bill bagging. And I tried to make some conversation with the young man. But he was not receptive and I think it turned out to be his grandmother apologize for him. You'll have to excuse my grandson. He is tired. He's been practicing all day. Oh and for some reason I said do you play tennis? Maybe he is practicing playing tennis. Why I said that I'll never know. She said he plays electric guitar. He's really good. We found out that his father was a guitarist in a country band traveling around the country.

Ed P.: Oh no kidding.

Bob C.: I said we have a band. Would you be interested in being a part of the band and without any expression he said No. He had no interest in being part of a band. I got their address and said we would like to come by.

So that evening Bill and I went by to visit him. They had a piano in the home and Bill started playing saying here's what we do and I sang a little bit. Don became interested and he got his guitar out. One thing led to another and he joined our band. Yeah that's how we got Don.

Ed P.: I know he was an excellent guitarist and he had a little more of a country thing to what he did. I guess that's because of his dad. He knew about Doc Watson and he knew about the other guitar player Chet Atkins and so he taught me how to do the finger picking style where you pick out the bass with your thumb and then you pick the melody line out of the chord structure with your other fingers. He really was a good guitar player and so I sat and practiced with him a lot of times. This would be after my audition and joining as a regular member.

Bob C.: Well let me tell you of this whole incident from 1959. The place was packed, all kinds of acts. they were out at night so we called the guy that did the TV show the Record Hop thing, it was kind of like the Dick Clark show. And we did our stuff. We had a blast. And after our performance we went into the crowd. Bill and me and my girlfriend Darlene. And he was with somebody. You know he never had a steady girlfriend. So we were just hanging out, it was bumper to bumper people. And we listened to the show and it was just a great evening. Then for some reason a chant started in the crowd. "We want the Dukes, we want the Dukes, we want the Dukes". We looked at each other and it got louder. We looked at each other and shrugged our shoulders saying how did this happen? It took us by complete surprise. It was so loud. We wondered what we wanted to do. The MC came back out on stage and quieted everyone down and said, I don't even know if the Dukes are still in the building. He said if they are, we invite them to come back up on stage and then the crowd went crazy. We look at each other and we wonder if any of the other guys still are here. So we went backstage and fortunately everybody was still there.

We went back out on stage. And everybody that was in the auditorium came out of their seats close to the stage not dancing but standing there. It was wall to wall people and they were loving everything we did onstage. It drove them wild. Yes, that was the first time I ever experienced something that was incredible like that. Well we had five hundred girls in a gymnasium but nothing even close to this. To be on the big lighted stage and all these people packed up there was exciting. So we said we are going to do this song "Juge" we played it and the place went nuts.

Ed P.: Can you tell me about that particular song, where it came from? It was kind of the Dukes signature song.

Bob C.: It was a song that was a lot of people's favorite. And when we would be performing people would say do "Juge". And people would say hey I really like that but we would get requests for it because when we started playing it, it was such a rocking song the place would just rock.

Ed P.: The song was like an incarnation of the Little Richard sound.

Bob C.: That is exactly what happened. And here is the story behind that as far as the Dukes are concerned. You know I'm not sure exactly where I was at the time but I heard this song or a reasonable facsimile of Juge and it was being performed by a Mexican group out of Salinas California.

Ed P.: That would be the Downbeats. Johnny Amelio on the Downbeats.

Bob C.: And Bill and I incorported our version of it into the Dukes repertoire.

Ed P.: It was rock and they had also recorded a song called

"Red X". I remember their lead guitar player named Grover York big tall guy with a pompadou hair do. You know just he and I. We came up with what we could do with it. We started doing it and then we had to play it every place we went. It was a crazy kind of nothing song but it had a feeling we all needed. Absolutely kind of nothing.

But you know, look when you sang it on stage at the Civic with the band when I was in it, it was the same thing. But I think at the time that we played it at the Civic Auditorium I think Bill had left for the Navy and I think it was 1959. When we would play that song and I'd sing there was always a great reaction. The band was restructured at that time.

Bob C.: I went to college, I started school. I never planned to go. But. In the fall of '59 Cabrillo College was starting up. I got serious about going to college. In the middle of the senior year. Because certainly you're facing graduation. And I had this girl friend. Truthfully. We will probably get married I gotta get a job I'd better get going to college. I went over to Watsonville High School and registered for Cabrillo.

Ed P.: That's right. That's when they had the junior college there at the old Watsonville High School building. Did Bill send you those scrapbook photographs that he sent me? Wonderful Yeah. I was shocked to see my picture there auditioning for the band. Yeah, I guess that was my audition photo. I couldn't believe it. Oh yeah we had charcoal suits with baggy pants, skinny black ties and white bucks. That was the Dukes trademark.

Bob C.: When the Dukes walked in to the place it's almost like the Beatles. We weren't arrogant or snotty we were just kids but we really were confident. We had fun doing the shows.

Ed P.: We were much better musicians than we gave ourself credit for. Yes certainly. You know Bill was talented and Don was talented and we were all talented but I think probably the one thing that we lacked is this. You look at things in retrospect but we didn't have a mature person to give us any kind of a guidance, to suggest you really do need a bass amp for that bass. So you could do an equipment lease. There were just practical things we needed perspective on because we were so busy and involved in the band itself. There was some mentorship that really could have really helped us out a lot.

Bob C.: We didn't have a manager who knew what to do with us. We were going like gangbusters having a lot of success. Each one of us knew what we could do and were having a lot of fun too.

Ed P.: We made a conscious decision to further our formal education which we did. And when Phil and I left the Dukes that was kind of the end of the Dukes. That was when Ted restructured the band as kind of a Beach Boys knockoff, more of a vocal group than an instrumental group and so it shifted to the "Tikis."

Chapter 5
Rick Alan: R&R in Santa Cruz

More history of early Hip Santa Cruz music
.

Ed Penniman interview

Rick: Hi, this is Rick Alan, I am here for the Hip History project, talking with Ed Penniman, local rock-n-roll pioneer in Santa Cruz. How you doing, Ed?

Ed: Doing good.

HH: Good. You mentioned something just before we sat down here, and that was my first question for you. You are a native?

E: Yeah, I was born in Santa Cruz and came up through the local school system and left Santa Cruz in the mid-sixties to go to Los Angeles to college, but I went to local schools.

HH: What was Santa Cruz like in the fifties? Those were the years that you were in high school, right?

E: Well, I graduated in 1960 so I was in junior and senior high school in the late fifties. But Santa Cruz was essentially a beach town. The Boardwalk was the main draw. Everything was really focused around tourism and the beach boardwalk. Those were the days when, you know, small businesses were all up and down Pacific Avenue and they were catering essentially to a combination of locals and tourists. But mostly the tourists didn't range out beyond the beach boardwalk area and all the little hotels. They had hotels from the sleaziest, crappiest little ones before the Dream Inn, so there were little hotels running along Beach Street up along the hillside there on the other side of the beach boardwalk, where people stayed. But yeah, it was a beach town.

HH: People who came after may not remember or know that Pacific Avenue was just a Main Street, USA. It wasn't the Mall.

E: Yeah, it wasn't until the seventies that Chuck Abbott's wife, I can't remember her name, and they built the lighthouse out there on Lighthouse Point as a memorial to their son Mark who perished in a surfing accident. But you had Chuck Abbott and some of the movers and shakers decide they were going to try to kind of mix up Santa Cruz and gentrify it and, you know, make it more interesting. Those were the days that Chuck Abbott changed the main street to the Mall and Max Walden a developer of the old county building, the Cooperhouse. There's a whole bunch of stories that go along with that - myself and Max - but that's not what we're talking about today, but yeah.

HH: As you say, we're talking about the music of Santa Cruz, and you were a rock-n-roll pioneer. How did you get started in music?

E: Well, my dad was very musical, so we always had musical instruments lying around the house, in the living room. And he played about, oh maybe six, seven instruments really well, and he played with the Santa Cruz Symphony and Watsonville Band and kind of swapped off instruments. So as a kid I started playing the drums. That was in junior high school. And then from drums I shifted over to the bass horn, so I played the bass horn, it was like a b-flat bass. But that was too heavy for me to schlepp around, so then I started playing the trombone, played the trombone until my thirties or forties. I picked up a guitar that was lying in our living room. Carl Jorgenson, who was a pitcher for the Red Sox, left the guitar there and he had retired and moved to Santa Cruz with his wife and they were friends with my parents. They called him Pinky, that was his nickname. So Pinky left his old hollow-body Gibson, I think it was a Gibson. I'm not even sure what it was. So I picked it up because I kind of thought it was cool. I had written some guitar works. I think those were the days of Les Paul, maybe. I'm not even sure if Les Paul was before that?

HH: Probably before.

E: But anyway, I liked the sound of the guitar, so I picked up the guitar, and I remember playing guitar and making sounds. It was before I learned how to make chords, but I would just put the guitar hollow body up to my ear and hit the string and it would just resonate and make sound and it was just really cool. And then a couple of strings at the same time, and my dad said, "Oh, you want to learn how to play the guitar?" I said, 'Yeah, that would be pretty neat (neat was before cool). Dad taught me three or four chords and I started playing like 'Coming Round the Mountain' and folky type stuff, the traditional Americana type of music. And then we'd get together as a family and Dad would pick up something and I'd play the guitar, and we'd all kind of sing, have a family thing. That was, I think when I was about twelve and-a-half, or thirteen when I started playing guitar, and I really liked it. It was portable, it was fun, and you could get a lot of music out of it. Those were the days of going to Cowell's Beach, hanging out at the Boardwalk, riding the roller coaster, enjoying the river in pedal-boats, having a great summer fun time. We would lay around the beach, and

then after the beach scene was kind of over -those were
the days before cell phones and you just knew you had
to be home before dark, otherwise there was a problem.
We had long summer days, and the bar scene was on
Beach Street, and there were several clubs along the street.
One was called The Beachcomber, and the other was
the Mamboo Lounge. And there was another one, but I
don't remember the name of it. But those two clubs were
catering to black folks coming down from Oakland on the
Suntan Special. We had a pretty strong contingent of black
people coming down and the clubs catered to them with
blues music. I had discovered some of the blues music on
KWBR (KDIA), which was an AM radio station. This is
well before FM Radio and I had a bit of wire hanging out
the window and a crappy little radio playing blues music.
And I liked it. Plus, for me it was easy because it was just
three chords, and once I figured out the keys that they
were playing in, I could just change keys and play those
three basic chords in a different key and play along. So,
listening to that music on radio and I don't know what
inspired listening to that, whether it was an accident that
I heard it and I said, oh, that's what they're playing down
at the beach, or it was the other way around, I'm not sure.
But the combination of those clubs and the radio station
got me interested in playing blues. So I started playing
blues, and continued playing that kind of music kind of
solo. I had some experience in the different clubs down
on Beach Street. There's a videotape that I'm going to give
you and you can transcribe that and plug that in, because
that talks about the beach scene in Santa Cruz at that time.
Willie Mae Thorton, you know, Big Mama Thorton, and
other artists whose names I don't remember anymore.

Some were A class acts, some were B class, but the music was all A class. It was all really good, good stuff. There was that kind of a sloppy shuffle beat that was just infectious, and, it set the tone for a very mellow Santa Cruz beach scene with the doors open and this music coming out, and people walking around. In those days there was some fighting. Usually people had been drinking on the beach all day long, but it was a pretty mellow scene down on the beach boardwalk. So that was kind of the beginnings of my interest in blues, and for me, rock music was just blues speeded up. I mean that was always my take on it. So for me it was, again, it was easy to play. It was uncomplicated.

Music didn't get that complicated until like in the mid-sixties. White guys were playing it and competing with each other to see who could play the most complicated leads. But the soul was still there for sure. So I started playing guitar and I guess I was good enough that somebody heard about me. There was this group called The Dukes. And this would be 1958 probably. And it was comprised of Bill Davis, Alan Ross, Ted Templeman, Don Stewart and myself. Actually, Don Stewart was the original guitar player in The Dukes. And they played essentially dance music and jazz. Bill Davis was a pianist that played like Ramsey Lewis. He was really, really good. And so, I guess the original Sticky Wicket had a piano in it and that was one of the places we played. It was one of the first places I played, in the band, and I had been practicing with Don on my finger-picking style, so that I could do the bass note with my thumb, and then I could pick out the melody with my other three or four fingers, and 'it's like Doc Watson's style. That came in real handy, what Don taught me, in terms of the finger-picking style. I had become a big fan of Chet Atkins, and the more Chet Atkins I listened to, the more I appreciated the musical instrument I was playing, because it had such amazing versatility. So Don quit the band and I started playing on a regular basis. Just chording kind of, rhythm playing. And it was kind of like progressive jazz, so I could understand chord changes and that sort of thing. When we played, Bill Davis started playing more rock music, I think, when I got into it. He understood how to play the changes and all that sort of stuff.

I always was a big fan of Little Richard, and so Bill picked up that style very easily and we played a lot of Little Richard's music. We were union members, and Ted did all the contract work. Well we're still kids, we're still minors, but we belong to the local musicians union.

HH: Was it Local 342? I used to belong to that Local.

E: Might have been. I don't even remember the number, but that sounds vaguely familiar. So we had a split in responsibilities where Ted would do the business part and we all had opportunity to chime in on anything. But I acted as the "band leader" and Ted the "band manager". So I wanted to fill out the band with more instruments, and again, I liked Little Richard's sound, and of course we had the same last name – Penniman - so I thought that was cool, yeah, Richard Penniman. We did meet at one point, but that's another story. So, I started with adding a tenor sax player, and his name was Mike Huntington. He was from the same town up in the Santa Cruz Mountains as Ted Templeman, which was Ben Lomond. So it was Ted and Mike Huntington and myself, then Bill, and then we kept adding. I added a second sax player, and then I added a rhythm guitar player, Phil Wagner. The second sax player was Alan Roth. He lived in Santa Cruz. He was a good-looking guy. All the women loved him when we were on stage, so he was always like the cat. Anyways, he was super shy and that was probably part of the appeal, you know what I mean? I mean you're safe with Alan. I had a girlfriend named Karen who I unfortunately was nuts about, too nuts. Thank God she broke up with me or we would have had nine children! We practiced often and played gigs, and the band got tighter. Often we would practice without Ted. Or if we did practice with Ted, he would bring a pair of drumsticks and then go into the kitchen, bring out some pots and pans, and [laughing] he made a good jury-rigged drum set out of pots and pans, which was always kind of fun, but we he kept re-arranging pieces to make them ours. So, those were fun days.

HH: I noticed you didn't mention a bass guitar.

E: Yeah, bass guitar didn't come until much later. That was near the end of the band, actually, and I added Mike Gray to the band, and he was so passionate about learning the bass guitar and passionate about being in the band. I guess I - god rest his soul, Mike - but I think I used poor judgment in not doing auditions, yeah, I really should have had auditions for a bass player. But I liked Mike, he was, so sincere and passionate about it, but it didn't work out like I wanted.

But we had a lot of really good gigs, actually, with and without a bass. And again it was solid, kind of like the difference between playing music with a Zildjian cymbal with those little grommets in it so it rattles and is always making this constant sound. It was like that versus, playing without the bass, like I always found that has more of a jazz sound. Anyway, so the band was really solid and we played a lot of local parties and school functions. We were on TV a few times. We played at the Civic Auditorium many weekends in a row, dance parties and things like that. And then we played at the Cocoanut Grove again, those were more like performances that featured major recording artists. We played as warm up for Conway Twitty, for Connie Francis. I don't remember some of the other artists. It's funny how you don't pay attention to that stuff. You just ended up doing it.

HH: So, this is Santa Cruz in the fifties, and up here in the North County there was one high school, right? Soquel wasn't built yet. San Lorenzo Valley High probably, but…

E: Yeah, SLV was real small.

HH: And Santa Cruz High.

E: And Santa Cruz High and Watsonville High and Holy Cross.

HH: Did Watsonville have a Catholic school in the sixties called Mora? Don't know if they existed in the fifties.

E: I remember Mora. And St. Francis was another one.

HH: St. Francis was where guys were studying to be priests, but it's where the catholic high school students go now. They rebuilt it. So there were just a couple of high schools. You guys were it.

E: Well, there was nobody else powerful. You know how that goes, we were kind of like the default band. But I have to give credit to other musicians that had little dance combos and so on.

HH: From Santa Cruz High?

E: Well yeah, from Santa Cruz High. There were bands, they had drums, accordion and saxophone, and there was Corny and the Corvettes (Cornelius Bumpus). And one of the things I should have done and didn't do was invite Corny to jam with us and play with us. And it didn't happen. He had his own band by that time. For short time as kids we had this older fellow, he was old by our standards. He was like in his early 40s. His name was Tony Hill and his son was a local drummer. So Mr. Hill would give us direction. But we really didn't have like a mentor. Our mentor is more of an audio mentor, trying to sound like certain people, and then also, almost by default, having our own sound. The more you play, draw, write or whatever you will develop your own style and signature. I keep using the word solid because that is the only way I can describe a band, it's something I hear, it's a clarity, confidence, sensitivity to the group sound, being in synch with the unit and letting individual members be expressive without ever stepping on them.

HH: Now didn't Ted Templeman end up as a music producer - he played in Harper's Bizarre later, but didn't he end up producing music?

E: Yeah, Ted's trajectory, and when you talk to Ted he can give you more in-depth information. Wikipedia doesn't even talk about The Dukes. And whether he put that Wikipedia page together or somebody else did it, I don't know, but it picks up, I think, right after The Dukes broke up, and he starts this band called the Tikis, which is kind of like a surf thing, like with Jan and Dean and who were the other guys before…?

HH: I don't know. I know Duane Eddy had his band and the surf guitar sound back in the late fifties.

E: Dwayne Eddie was a crossover. He was a country boy.

HH: He was, but again, he had that sound. Forty Miles of Bad Road. Cannonball. Wasn't Corny Bumpus playing with the Doobie Brothers when Templeman was producing them?

E: That's later, yeah.

HH: And so that's kind of interesting.

E: Yes. So Ted and Corny, we're all contemporaries. Ted started this Tikis band, and it was like a surf thing, and then that chorus, and then I think he realized that he wasn't interested in making that happen, or again, you'll have to talk to Ted about why that change happened. Personnel changes maybe. And then from there to, yeah, Harper's Bizarre, which was essentially a vocal group. And so the musical, instrumental aspect was more secondary to the vocals. Again that was Ted's call, I wasn't around, and they did fine. They did great. They did that cover of the 59th Street Bridge Song, and that became popular. They were able to continue. I don't know how Warner Brothers picked up the group. I really don't know how that happened. Again, Ted can tell you. But then he was working at A&R for Warner Brothers and he went from A&R to producing. And that was when he started working with the Doobie Brothers. I don't know the personnel in the Doobie Brothers. I know a few of them.

HH: You mentioned Little Richard and the blues influence when you started, and you mentioned that surf sound. Who were some of the other rock-n-roll musicians from the national scene that might have influenced you?

E: Elvis, when he did Hound Dog, I knew it was Willie Mae's song. And that woman was working hard. You could tell she was working awfully hard. And I'm sure it broke her heart when Elvis played that song and it was, it was wonderful in a way. It was a different take on the song. Ball and Chain by Janis Joplin was Willie's song too. The beat was different. Her beat was a shuffle beat, and his was more of the driving kind of a rock beat. But it resonated. But I liked Elvis' guitar player. I don't remember his name…

HH: Scotty Moore, wasn't it?

E: Is that who it was?

HH: Yeah, he was his guitar player in the '50s, I think.

E: I don't know. But I remember playing that song, playing those chord changes and so on. But mainly, as lead guitar player, I was listening to leads. I was listening to different lead players. Bobby Darrin "Splish Splash", I think, did it first class, again good instrumental, good sax section. But again, I just kind of kept going back to Little Richard and that music had the energy, "Lucille" and…

HH: "Long Tall Sally"?

E: Long Tall Sally, yeah.

HH: How about folks like Lloyd Price and Bobby "Blue" Bland?

E: Bobby "Blue" Bland for sure! But again, on the radio, on KDIA, I listened to these guys, and probably at that time knew all the people who were playing on the radio.

HH: Fats Domino?

E: Yeah, yeah, yeah, you know, New Orleans. But I don't remember now. It's just like it was massive. But I mean I still listen to 50's blues music, I love the music still. And I regret being paralyzed and not being able to play the guitar anymore, because it brought me a lot of joy and it's been replaced by my artistry now, as a painter I can paint and spend time by myself painting, just like I used to do when I was playing. It's very introspective and meditative.

HH: So as it transitioned into the sixties and that period of Santa Cruz when it turned into a kind of a hip mecca and the Pranksters moved here, and the Hip Pocket Bookstore, etc - what were you doing in that period between, let's say when you got out of high school and the early sixties?

E: Okay, so I graduated in 1960, I was still going in '60, then continued, I think, in '61, maybe '62, and then I left town and went to Los Angeles to go to art school. But I remember going to The Barn, which was where all these guys were doing acid then, and I didn't feel comfortable there. It wasn't my scene. I didn't smoke weed until I was down in L.A. I was a pretty straight guy.

HH: You're talking about going to The Barn in…

E: In Scotts Valley.

HH: In what year?

E: Gotta be '63?

HH: So that's when Big Daddy Nord owned it? Before Leon Tabory?

E: When I was there it wasn't all decorated psychedelic.

HH: Right. That's before Leon Tabory got it in the middle sixties.

E: I was gone. I was in L.A. I auditioned for a couple bands down in L.A., but the practice time was cutting into my studies and I thought, I already made my decision. I'd made my commitment and I wanted to honor my commitment to my chosen career, and so I can't say that they were on fire, that they wanted me, but auditions are tough, because, first of all, there's a lot of self-doubt. You know, trying some music that you maybe don't know, and you're scrambling to find chord changes and stuff, and heck, I remember playing, oh it was a Paul Butterfield tune, something about Chicago…

HH: Born in Chicago?

E: I can't remember what the band was playing, but god they were a good band, it might have been. I don't remember again, it didn't mean much to me, because the more time I spent in L.A., the more I started getting interested in jazz. So I started frequenting the jazz clubs, and I particularly loved the Hammond organ, because, again, it was based on blues and kind of had a rock beat to it. I was a regular at the Interlude on Sunset, and I would be going to listen to Jimmy Smith, and that was some seriously good music. Damn, man, it was just like I got my soul filled up with that stuff. And so, yeah, saw Lou Rawls when he was just like 23. Those were the days. I remember I was working at night in this photo lab. It was this little international clique of guys that were working at night. There was a Chinese guy, a couple of black guys, Japanese guy, me, a Puerto Rican guy. And so the Puerto Rican guy and I were buddies. There was an Australian guy too. Couple bit-part actors.

So anyway, guy named John (who had to change his name) and I, we buddied up and I was interested in jazz, and he said, "you know, if you really want to appreciate jazz, you gotta smoke some of this stuff". So we're on the 405 San Diego freeway, and we lit up a joint, a little skinny cigarette, and I said well, that's kind of weird. It was nice. But that's when I started smoking weed on a pretty regular basis, and continued with my studies and was able to focus on my studies and continue. But it changed my sensibility in terms of music and art positively for sure.

I just continued following jazz, and still enjoyed blues, but the beat is like a real thing for me. I'd go and see Jack McDuff, and Jimmy Smith at the Interlude on Sunset and others who were playing in those days. Really, the pioneers like Groove Holmes, the pioneers of Hammond B3 organ. Who was that guy that played oh jeez, it doesn't matter. He did Green Onions.

HH: Green Onions, that would be [mimicking the beat] those guys from up in Northern California.

E: Yeah. But, anyway, that was…

HH: Booker T?

E: Yeah, exactly, Booker T. and the MG's! He was 19 when he recorded that record, maybe even younger. He's a wonderful guy. He is really a good person. Very, very mellow guy. So I left Santa Cruz during the what they're calling now the 'Hip Santa Cruz' era. I equate Hip Santa Cruz with LSD Santa Cruz. Like, when I went to The Barn, I didn't feel comfortable there. And the whole acid scene, I wasn't comfortable with it. Maybe I doubted my sanity or was afraid I'd have some kind of negative bad trip or something, so I've never done acid, and I never felt like doing acid. But I'm a real big fan of mushrooms, and that changed my color palette. Talk about a painter doing mushrooms, boy you find out which colors love each other and which colors hate each other. It really makes a difference in your work. So maybe that's a candid recommendation for artists to do mushrooms, but it made a change in my opinion. It was natural and the Indians had been doing it forever, and so I felt well that's fine. But yeah, the Hip Santa Cruz thing, I wasn't any part of that. But definitely just the early pioneering of rock music in Santa Cruz, I was definitely part of that.

HH: I was asking you about some of the venues and clubs around the valley and Monterey Bay. You mentioned the Interlude in L.A. There used to be The Interlude on Pacific Avenue, right at the Del Mar Theatre.

E: At one time it was owned by a former schoolmate of mine, Carol Curtis. And she always had good bands in there, but this is like in the seventies now, mid-seventies. I'm not sure who played there. But there was a whole lot of music. Did you play there? You may have played there when I was getting a free beer from Carol. I was enjoying the music at the bar. I'd come in and see the drums set up, amps, and PA and get a yearning!

HH: We played there one night when Wilt Chamberlain walked in.

E: Oh my god.

HH: He used to come and play in these pro beach volleyball tournaments when his basketball career was over.

E: I had no idea.

HH: He was in Santa Cruz one summer night when Jango was playing there and he walked in, and I swear to god he walked past the stage, which was a couple of feet high. You remember the stage? And he walked past and looked us right in the eye.

E: That was actually a nice little club, and Carol was always a perfect hostess, a perfect lady, she was a lovely lady. She out classed the place. You remember her?

HH: Yes.

E: Yeah, real beautiful, beautiful lady to me. That was a

good thing.

HH: And the Sticky Wicket. This was when the Sticky Wicket was downtown in central Santa Cruz, is that right?

E: Yeah, it was on Cathcart. It was right there by the Catalyst, it was around the corner from the Catalyst on that side. Because Johnny's Bike and Sports was on the corner, and then there was a little shoe repair shop called Sam's Shoe Repair, and then there was something else next to that, but between the shoe repair place and Johnny's Bike and Sport was the Sticky Wicket. It was when Vic Jowers was just starting the place. He liked to sing, and it was always interesting. I just played there a few times. The band started morphing into more of a rock thing, that was not what the Wicket was about. That was more about being cool, and I was cool, but I was never hip.

HH: Did you ever play at the Sticky Wicket after it moved out to Aptos, before you went to Los Angeles?

E: I used to go there, but I don't remember ever playing, no. It was a coffeehouse scene. There was definitely, separation, music was starting to separate at that point. So where before, my interest in playing at the Wicket was blues, jazz, folk kind of stuff. And then later, as the band started to morph, so did my interest. And so even though I was going to the Wicket and hanging out with my friends, I didn't play there. But if I did, it wasn't with the band. I may have played individually or something, but there was a guy named Bill Helm who was a regular player there, and I'm not sure who else played at the Wicket. It may have been maybe Dick Yount and George Dymesich, Phil Reader and some of those guys.

HH: I know George. So he played there?

E: Played guitar. Decent player, too. I did a whole interview with him about the Wicket, and so on, and also Jim Hunt. Do you remember Jim Hunt? He worked at the Wicket out there for like two years, so I got a really good interview with him, like an hour and a half, just really irreverent, funny, good Vic Jowers stuff. He has a really good memory, which was funny. He was really animated when I was talking to him. The more he remembered, the more he remembered, so it was really rich.

Anyway, that was the Wicket. And they cut him off, they closed the road to Highway 1 and that was the end of the Wicket. And there was some connection between Zachary's Restaurant and the Wicket, and I'm not sure what it was. Was it family connection or what?

HH: Diane and her husband?

E: Williams. Diane and Michael Williams. Brother and sister, right?

HH: Right, I thought he was her husband.

E: He worked days at IBM in a "think tank", I recall.

HH: I met Diane in '65, at Cabrillo College. For a short while she ended up working on a newspaper I started in the late sixties, and after that, she said, 'Well I'm going to start a business, and that's when she opened Zachary's.

E: Still there. Just a brief thing about Zachary's is that, I think the Barn Brothers carved that sign, if I'm not mistaken. It's still there. And I don't know if I designed it or if Terry designed it, but that was one of my accounts.

HH: Terry King.

E: I had my graphic design business in Santa Cruz, just started in the seventies. Ed Penniman Associates Design. And we used to do trade-outs. So I would do their ads for the papers and things like that, and then I would get a credit for food, and actually, one of the guys that is still around town, Andrew Miller, Drew Miller worked there. He was like an assistant manager or something like that.

HH: You might have designed the ad that they used, that

they still use…

E: I may have.

HH: Do you remember much about Corny who grew up here, and do you know much about the African-American community in Santa Cruz, as opposed to the clientele that would come down from Oakland. Was there much of a music scene in the local black community?

E: I can't speak to that, but I know that historically, Santa Cruz was a real racist community.

HH: Yep. There was a lot of racism here.

E: And there was a small contingent, a small group of black families. In my junior high school there was one black girl. In Santa Cruz High School there was three black guys. That was it, like out of hundreds and hundreds. So it was a real small group. Now, musically, I'm not sure what was going on, but Corny, you know, he was a natural. He was so good.

HH: Did you know Prince Lashay? A jazz musician, drummer.

E: No.

HH: I think his son was a manager for Max Roach, and also played sax, I think. I met him years ago.

E: The local black community was very small and lived mostly around The Circles. There was…like military unit here back in the - I don't even remember when it was, but there was like a contingent of black military guys that were bivouacked, I guess. I don't know how many of those guys stuck around.

But no, I don't really know much about the African-American music scene. Just a few guys I went to school with, and it wasn't easy for them, I can tell you that. There were a couple brothers named Dab. There was Bobby Dab, who was a super baseball player. And I have a picture of him and me on the Tijuana Pirates team, and I think I was like thirteen.

(Shows Picture) And yeah, here he is, he's in the front row and he's a really good baseball player. But I don't know whatever happened to Bobby. He was a good football player, a good basketball player.

HH: Did you know Bob Lowery, the local blues singer/guitarist? He was from Arkansas and located here in the late '50s. Delta Blues man who played around town, down on the mall, Blues festivals. He passed away a couple of years ago. Or his cousin Ron – Shaker Ron – a percussionist, who's still around, I think.

E: I don't know Ron, but I know Virgil Thrasher who played harp with him. He's a blues guy, been around the Santa Cruz music scene since 1970. You probably know him. Played traditional blues harp. Nice guy. Good traditional musician and artist.

HH: Heard him play but never met him. What about the school music scene?

E: Oh, interesting question.

HH: Did you play in a school band?

E: Yeah, in junior high school, playing the drums, I switched as I said earlier over to the trombone. I played trombone in Mrs. Mueller's orchestra.

I remember we played some kind of American folk music thing, so they needed a harmonica player. I got a little Marine Band harmonica and I started playing harmonica and learned how to play a few ditties on that. So now I was playing the harmonica and listening to these blues players play harmonica on KWBR/KDIA.

I thought, "oh yeah, this is pretty cool". So then, from Mrs. Mueller's class to Branciforte Junior High School playing the trombone in the marching band. We had the junior high school band with uniforms and all that stuff. I played the trombone and then I became like… I guess I had leadership qualities, but I became like the drum major. So I was the drum major marching this band around the field in the eighth grade and from that into high school, playing the trombone and the guitar, the high school band. Merle Good was such a good-natured guy and for some reason I decided to drive him crazy. He was the band teacher. And with a trombone, anybody that has a musical ear, you can drive them crazy with a trombone, because you can play it just a little bit flat, every note, just a little bit flat or a little bit sharp. I used to torture him. And one time he went nuts on me, and he took me outside and veins are bulging out of his neck and out of his forehead, and his teeth were clenched, and he was asking me, "'Why are you doing this? What's wrong with you? Why are you doing this to me?" I acted out badly but I thought it was really funny at the time, twisted humor my specialty. But I stopped doing it. I think I was just juvenile. [laughing] But I enjoyed touring with the high school band, that was fun. After that, I played for a couple years in the Watsonville Band. So I was always talented. I had music in me. I played for the Watsonville Band for about 16, 17 years and went to various events. The Seattle World's Fair and many State Fairs, different parades and all that marching band stuff. It was fun. Camaraderie among musicians is always fun. And then the band parties. You'd break up into different groups and there would be the German Sauerkraut band, Dixieland band, and all these different styles. I would bring my guitar and we had like a little blues thing. So it was always really fun and always musical. That was my experience with music and music ultimately took a second seat after I moved to L.A., as far as my musicianship was concerned. But certainly I always had a real respect, love and admiration for the musicians, because it was a tough life, man. You'd get these guys playing jazz and they'd reach into their pocket for another reed for their saxophone and all these bennies are dropping on the stage, and what an evening. That was at Adams West Theater or the Parrot Cage, not sure.

HH: Understood, understood. This has been a really nice reflection on a part of Santa Cruz history that most people who live here now didn't experience.

E: In 1955, we had the major flood and I was here for that. I was down on Pacific Avenue when it happened. We had had torrential rains and the reason I'm telling this story is because it's in Santa Cruz. You know, the scene on the San Lorenzo River was beautiful. It was bucolic. And the flood came and you know what happened. All the debris and logs and everything got jammed up on the Water Street bridge and diverted the river down Pacific Avenue. And we had a business at the time, at 1537 Pacific Avenue, the Penniman Title Company, and family were down there filling sandbags, and that water was right up to our door. But the county courthouse was under water, all the hall of records, all those records underneath, all the old hand-penned records of property ownership and all that stuff was lost in the flood. The city fathers saw it as a real opportunity, because now Chinatown was wiped out. So now it's like these guys have dollar signs in their eyes, and they're after reparation money from the state and the federal government for disaster relief, and you've got a whole group of guys thinking, oh, all that land, the Chinatown land, we can redevelop all that. So what they did essentially is they just redeveloped Chinatown right off the map. And that's where my friend George Ow grew up. My dad owned an old warehouse across from Bud's Furniture where I worked in order to earn money for my first electric guitar. My job was cleaning refrigerators and stripping furniture and stuff like that. It was nasty work. But across the street from Bud's was my dad's warehouse. And that was the gambling hall for the Chinese. So my brother and I, we didn't know that Dad owned it! So one night we're being mischievous teenagers, and we broke into this place. As kids will do. And it was really mysterious, because there was all these strange little pieces of paper with Chinese writing on it and everything, and blackboards with Chinese writing on it and all this stuff. And we were busted. The police came. They found us in there. So they called the owner. A couple of delinquents have broken into your place, come on down. It was Dad! Oh man! Anyway. Yeah, growing up in Santa Cruz was pretty amazing. It was golden. I have a million stories.

HH: Before we finish up this interview I wanted to ask you - what was available if anything, and how were women and young women participating in any of the cultural things around town…?

E: I like that question. I think that's a really intelligent question, and I need to think about that, because - are you finished asking the question?

HH: Well, I was just going to mention, as an example, that one of my mentors when I first settled down here in Santa Cruz was Dolores Abrams, who was teaching…

E: Drama

HH: Yes, drama out at Cabrillo, and her family owned the Abrams' Department Store downtown. She was involved in theatre, and then went back to New York and worked professionally, then came back here to teach.

E: You know, of course, she was older, but she was a teacher at Santa Cruz High School along with Roberta, god, what was Roberta's last name? She taught theatre. But, well my interest in girls, or young women, at that time was limited to the young ladies that liked to listen to our music and go to the parties, go to dances and stuff like that. But from a cultural standpoint, I know that Ms. Abrams had an influence on a number of people in Santa Cruz, including Bill Tara, who did frequent the Sticky Wicket often. He was a theatrical person, did some acting, but, moved to San Francisco. Did I show you that article about what Bill Tara did up in San Francisco? I mean he's living at the former Russian Embassy with a couple of other people. One guy was a pioneer of the light shows where they'd get an overhead projector and put together some oil and water between sheets of glass and do all kinds of visual stuff. So he was instrumental at adding, with this other guy, more of a theatrical kind of aspect to the rock concerts. But back then, San Francisco was a different scene than Santa Cruz, for sure. But I don't know about the women in Santa Cruz.

HH: Well, you know, Santa Cruz, as you mentioned, had a light side, so to speak. We had somewhat of a hip subculture, drugs and stuff, the Beats, hippies, on the cutting edge perhaps. At the same time, as you also indicated, there was somewhat of a dark side. It's not much of a surprise in a nation with a deep racist heritage. There was a strong racist current. San Francisco, for all its liberal history, has a racist heritage. But there was, and is, a lot of denial. At the same time I asked the question about what it might have been like here for women. We're known for the Miss California Pageant, which became a lightning rod in the '60s and '70s, to do something about that, to change the nature of that. So that's why I was curious about things that you might remember about it.

E: Isn't it interesting how feminist things were kind of germinating in Santa Cruz at the time, you know?

HH: A lot of stuff. That's why it's a special place. Even with baggage.

We've all got baggage. I've got baggage.

E: Let's talk about racism for just a second.

HH: Please.

E: It's a dangerous, dangerous thing, because prejudice

doesn't give a person a chance. Like when people, a white person and a black person come together, the white person is afraid for some reason, because maybe a black guy's different looking, African-American, whatever you want to call him. And the black person doesn't know what to expect. Is this guy going to be friendly? Is it an act? Does he want something from me? And so, in Santa Cruz. I know for a fact, and I'm friends with the two McPherson brothers. I was in Rotary with Fred McPherson II. But the grandfather I understand, was a full-on, full-on bigot. And so you have his daily newspaper "The Santa Cruz Sentinel" as his mouthpiece for a little town. In this way, a little town can become a racist community almost by default. Just ignorance. And just like I said, if there are only three kids that are African-American in your high school, well it really makes them the other. Now Corny was always warm to me, and always nice to me. I can't say that I didn't invite him into the band because he was a black kid. That didn't have anything to do with it. He had his own thing. But I regret not having him in the band. With his talent? But anyway, so to me, yeah, then there are some painful things I heard about I'm not going to go into.

HH: Oh, there are some incredible stories. Do you know Stan Stevens?

E: No.

HH: He co-founded the local ACLU in 1961. Stan told me a story about Eleanor Roosevelt coming to Santa Cruz to speak to the Democratic Club in 1962 at a restaurant down by Aptos. She had some prominent local African-Americans with her including Erva Bowen, president of the NAACP, and the owner refused to let them in, including Roosevelt. He finally relented but they had to come in through the kitchen.

E: Yeah, that's the kind of bullshit that is still going on in some places, believe it or not.

HH: Sure. Well, believe it or not, look at our president.

E: Yeah. We're these days living in the Chinese curse, "May you live in interesting times." And these are interesting times.

HH: That's a Jewish curse too.

E: Is it really?

HH: Yeah. There was a lot of racism here and nationally against the Chinese too. But one thing that music does, is it brings us together.

E: Amen. Absolutely true. Great, yeah. You know, and sports too.

HH: Sports too, maybe a little less so than music, but it's a redeeming cultural thing as well, yeah, absolutely.

E: You can't close your eyes when you're playing sports, but you sure can when you're playing music. Yeah, yeah. Wow! I want to add one thing. As you probably don't know I was an Art Director in an Ad Agency in LA. I worked on the Revlon, Baskin-Robbins, Mattel, and Max factor accounts. I recall seeing a magazine ad for an association to assist the blind. It said it all to me. There were these two little blind boys with their arms around each other's shoulders and the headline on the ad read, "The blind are also color blind."

HH: Well on that note, I'm going to say, Ed Penniman, thank you very much. It's been a pleasure just being able to sit here, laugh with you and listen to you rap. Now people can read all about it in the third edition of the Hip History of Santa Cruz.

E: As an ending note, I just want to say that I do have that video that talks about my personal experience on Beach Street, playing in one of the clubs down there when I was a kid, so I'll get that to you.

HH: Maybe Ralph can put it up on the Hip History website.

Rockin' Santa Cruz into the '60s and early '70s:

On June 3rd, 1956, Santa Cruz California enshrined itself in rock and roll history, though not for reasons you might think.

Santa Cruz had produced its first homegrown band, the "Dukes of Rock and Roll", in 1958 (see Ed Penniman interview). But just two years earlier Santa Cruz went the mid-1950's equivalent of viral by becoming the first town in the U.S., and maybe on the planet, to literally ban Rock and Roll. You can look it up on the web, as it's well documented, but basically, Chuck Higgins and his Orchestra, playing their hit single "Pachuko Hop", had the teeny-boppers, in the racially vigilant and prurient prose of Police Lieutenant Richard Overton, "engaged in suggestive, stimulating and tantalizing motions induced by the provocative rhythms of an all-negro band." And, "Authorities have imposed a ban on 'rock and roll' and other frenzied forms of Terpsichore in Santa Cruz as a result of 'obscene and highly suggestive dancing' by teenagers at an affair held at the Civic Auditorium Saturday night," hectored the Santa Cruz Sentinel on its front page.

An old family friend, a veteran of progressive politics and the labor unions, waded in: "'I attended that dance, and with the exception of one offender, a white girl, I thought it was the tamest affair I ever saw in all my 70 years of life and dancing,' wrote H.C. Bollman in a letter published in the Sentinel." (S.F.Gate, June 3, 2018).

The city elders soon took a second look at the hasty decision as the kids pushed back and the tourism trade began to sport a black eye. But not before San Antonio,

Texas and Asbury Park, New Jersey jumped into the ring as the nation and world looked on with a mix of amusement and, no doubt, high dudgeon.

And, like the Hip Pocket Bookstore/Kama Sutra Statue brouhaha eight years later, this illustrates a feature of our great town that we might bear in mind when recounting the origins and history of the local hip culture: in the words of a S.C. Museum of Art and History blog post…

As it turned out rock is still alive and well. With that said… it's amazing that cities went on to ban rock and roll and in Santa Cruz no less. …Santa Cruz on the surface is to some the leftmost city in the country. As of now, in my opinion, it is, but it took us a while to get there.

Alive and well indeed! For the past nearly sixty years Santa Cruz has incubated, nurtured and showcased an amazing array of musical as well as artistic and literary talent. What I would like to do here is give a shout out to some of the notable rock bands that have emerged from Santa Cruz and the surrounding towns in those "Hip History" days following the "Dukes of Rock and Roll." (And for the record, not being an historian, I apologize up front to anybody I've neglected to include. May you rock and roll forever!)

Gotta start first in the late fifties and tip my hat to another pioneer of Santa Cruz Rock 'n' Roll: the late, Cornelius "Corny" Bumpus. Corny played in the school band at Santa Cruz High and had his own band, Corny and the Corvettes, playing alto and tenor sax at local high school dances, the Coconut Grove and Civic Auditorium. In the mid '60s he played with San Francisco's Bobby Freeman and later in his career he toured with the Doobie Brothers and Steely Dan.

What I've been able to dig up starts with the Cobras, who actually hailed from Pacific Grove. The Cobras evolved in 1963 from two bands, and started with Dave Kibler (The

Vistells) and Bob O'Neill (not sure which band Bob O'Neill hailed from). They added Gary Thomas, a Watsonville kid, on keyboard and made Santa Cruz their home base, playing around Northern California and opening for a variety of prominent groups.

In 1966 Kibler and another band mate got drafted. O'Neill formed Talon Wedge, which eventually evolved into Snail, with Ron Fillmore on drums. When Dave Kibler returned from the service he joined Snail on bass, and sometime in 1968 Ken Kraft joined on guitar. Chris Bishop, on his fine website "Garage Hangover", writes: "Taken together, these groups show the evolution of '60s music from surf to garage, from psychedelia to hard rock." In the late '60s and through the '70s Snail had a great run, gaining wide-spread notice playing clubs, headlining shows, opening for other acts, as they mixed in players such as Jimmy Norris (Fly by Night) on drums, local legend and singer/songwriter, Salinas' own Larry Hosford on bass and Dale Ockerman on keyboards. They produced recordings, which you may be able to get through web sites.

Jeff Blackburn, singer/songwriter and local musical treasure, is one of the talented musicians that migrated up to the Monterey and San Francisco Bay Area from Bakersfield in the '60s. Centered in Berkeley, he teamed up with Sherry Snow and, as Blackburn and Snow, they performed at major venues around San Francisco (Avalon, Fillmore, Matrix) and Northern California. In the mid-'60s he and Snow recorded an album's worth of material for Trident Records, which was finally released as a CD in the late '90s. In the later '70s Jeff was a member of the legendary, short-lived Ducks, along with Neil Young, Bob Mosely (Moby Grape), and the late, local drum great Johnny Craviotto. And, though I can't confirm it, I swear I saw Blackburn performing in the late '60s with some combination of Jerry Best, Bob O'Neill and Ken Kraft in a band named Silver Wings at The High Street Local. I remember the club as having been opened by Tom Louagie, who owned The Local in Capitola, and later, the Club Zayante.

The first band of mostly UCSC students that I can recall playing around town was called Chaw. I first heard them in some local club –probably the Old Catalyst – sometime in the late sixties. Members included Jeff Commons on guitar, Fritz (?) on bass, drummer Michael Knight, lead singer/flutist Jimmy (?), and guitarist Tom Ferrier. They played a smooth, laid-back rock style and did covers and originals.

Jerry Miller, of the charter "San Francisco Sound" rock band Moby Grape, was living up in San Lorenzo Valley in the late '60s and performed in many configurations of the Grape, as well as with many other local musicians in various bands well into the '70s, including The Home Wreckers – with Bob Stern and Tim Ackerman of Oganookie (they're covered elsewhere in this volume), Kenny Stover, and Michael Been of The Call. In '69 Miller formed The Rhythm Dukes along with Don Stevenson, John Barrett, and John "Fuzzy" Oxendine. Organist Bill Champlain from The Sons of Champlain also joined for a year. They recorded an album for Columbia Records.

The '70s produced a lot of great local bands and performers, some who went on to record deals. In no particular order I'd like to shout out to Jill Croston (Lacy J. Dalton); Fly By Night (with amazing singer Annie Hubbard, Pat Hubbard (piano), Gary Roda (guitar), Duane "Beans" Sousa (bass), Jimmy Norris (drums) – this great band recorded with Shelter Records, Larry Hosford and Lacy J. Dalton; Red Ragged Rose; Chameleon, with Tod "Doc" Epstein (guitar), Kenny Stover (piano), "Groove" Groves (bass) and Jim Baum (drums); The hugely talented Jimmy Mahoney on keyboards and lead vocals (can't remember the name of the band he played in locally – maybe Loaded and Rolling?); Jasmine, with Steve Venom on guitar; Women and Children First; Original Haze and Airtight, with Michael Been; The Call, who garnered national attention, with Been, Tom Ferrier (guitar), Scott Musick (drums) and Steve Huddleston and Jim Goodwin (keyboards), Greg Freeman, (bass); the fabulous Chokes with Dave Adams (bass), Eddie Rich and Tom Ferrier (guitar), Michael Johnson (drums), Terry Hardin (lead vocals and percussion); and (full disclosure) a couple of bands with whom I had the good fortune to play: Jango, (we played the Catalyst several dozen times, as well as venues all around Santa Cruz and the S.F. Bay Area), with sizzling "Hot Rod" Annie Steinhardt (electric fiddle, vocals), "Slippery John" Weston (pedal steel, vocals), brothers David (guitar, vocals) and Jonathan Schneider (banjo, vocals), Ron Ogle (guitar, vocals), Zack Bass (drums, vocals) and myself on bass and vocals; and the Ravers, with The Schragg Brothers - Sweeny (guitar, vocals) and WeWa (guitar, vocals), Christine Hawley (keyboard, bass, vocals), Michael Knight (drums) and myself on bass and keyboard.

P.S. Here's a no doubt incomplete list of local clubs and venues from the '60s - '70s. I'll list as many as I can remember.

The Coconut Grove; The Civic Auditorium; The Catalyst – both Old and New; The Interlude; The White Buffalo; The Crow's Nest; The Opal Cliffs Inn; The Sail Inn (owned by the house band – The Allen Brothers – they were Country slick); Margarita's; Mumboo Lounge; Monk's; The Beachcomber; The Back Room; The Edgewater; The Crossroads/Shaggy Fish; Town and Country Lodge; The Chateau Liberte; The High Street Local; The Zayante Club; The Brookdale Lodge; The Burl Theater. There also was a little club (who's name I can't remember) at the corner of Hiway 9 and Mt. Hermon Rd. in Felton, where I first saw Jill Croston; Another club, on the north end of Boulder Creek - whose name I also can't remember but was owned by Kemal, a Turkish fellow – was the first place I ever played locally, with "The Lonesome Strangers", in '69.

Chapter 6
Peter Troxell, Jack Bowers and George Stavis:
The Oganookie Story: More Than Just a Band

Oganookie was a quintessential jam band a couple of decades before that term was coined. Their blend of rock and electrified bluegrass instrumentation and their tendency to play extended versions of bluegrass tunes, notably their trademark pairing of Bill Monroe's "Uncle Pen" and "Orange Blossom Special" made them one of the most popular acts for dances on campus and in town. They also epitomized the people's band ethos, playing many benefits and extolling the virtues of the back-to-the-land lifestyle the group modeled.
  - Michael Parrish

Oganookie was more than just a band. It was a way of life to the musicians in it, their family and friends, and to the Santa Cruz people who listened and danced to their music. Oganookie remains in the memories of many who mark significant moments in their lives by remembering what happened to them "the night we went to see Oganookie." During the spring of 1971, Oganookie's appearances at UCSC and clubs, and the band's growing reputation, attracted an audience of people who looked around at themselves and discovered they were a community. And the community was a reflection of the band, five individuals for whom the importance of community was equal to their music.

George Stavis, Jack Bowers, Tim Ackerman and Bob Stern met each other in the late 60s when they were students at Haverford College near Philadelphia. George and Jack got there first and lived across the hall from one another and soon were picking bluegrass songs together – George on the banjo and Jack then playing guitar. Tim was the school's one and only rock and roll drummer and George traded the banjo for an electric guitar to play in a band with him. When Bob, a serious violinist with credits at Julliard, came to Haverford he roomed with George's younger brother. George taught Bob that a violin could also be a "fiddle" and introduced him to the fine art of folk fiddling. Bob also played bass in a group called Federal Duck. A friend of George's in New York needed a band to record and George rounded up Federal Duck as well as Tim and Jack. The record has disappeared into near oblivion but at least the four friends (all philosophy and/ or religion majors in school) got a chance to play together officially for the first time.

After graduation, George went to Purdue in Indiana for grad work and student protests and Jack went home to Wisconsin to drive a cab, play the piano and write songs. George had an idea for an unusually eclectic instrumental record and went east to make a tape with Tim which Vanguard Records accepted. The album, recorded in New York, was called "Labyrinths, Occult Improvisational Compositions for 5-String Banjo and Percussion." The reviews were great but sales slim. When Tim finished at Haverford he went to New York to play in a rock group and Bob went to Brandeis in Boston for graduate study. After a year at Purdue, George received a fellowship in Philosophy to study at UC San Diego. The money was more than one person needed to live on so he contacted Tim, Jack and Bob to ask if they wanted to join him in California and form a band. Everyone said yes.

In San Diego George, Bob and Tim played together at clubs as the George Stavis Trio, taking advantage of the fact that George had his name on a record. At home they jammed together with Jack, now on piano, and with a singer and guitarist they had met while performing. The singer, Bruce Frye, had been studying and teaching pottery at La Jolla

Museum by day and playing folk clubs at night. He had won top prize as a blues guitarist at the San Diego Folk Festival. He started coming over to the house and sitting in with what was soon to become Oganookie. (The name has ancient roots and is shrouded in obscurity.)

After a year in San Diego, Tim decided to return to college and received a scholarship for the History of Consciousness program at UC Santa Cruz. George, too, signed up for school there. The group, which now included Bruce, took a vote and decided to move north with Tim. They sent an ad to the Sentinel newspaper: "Four Ph.D candidates seek study retreat in mountains." They were offered a hillside farm beyond their wildest back-to-nature dreams (and financial resources). Unable to live solely on Tim and George's study grants, the high rent literally forced them to get it together and play music for pay. Soon to join them was Peter Troxell, a former managing director of the Stanford Repertory Theater and one-time recipient of Ford and Rockefeller grants. His extraordinary vision and organizational abilities were just what the musicians needed to free their time for writing songs and rehearsing.

As a band, Oganookie brought diverse musical experiences to the group. Bruce Frye's music was strongly rooted in the acoustic blues tradition of Mance Lipscomb, Mississippi John Hurt and Muddy Waters; he was also a songwriter with a strong melodic sense and intelligent lyric sensibility. Tim Ackerman had grown up playing and listening to music in the New York area. As a teenager he heard jazz greats on 52nd Street, and played gigs on Long Island with Little Eva. Bob Stern was a classically trained violinist, and performed for a while as part of the Julliard Youth Orchestra. In college he took up electric bass and applied the same highly disciplined practice ethic to that instrument as he had used on the violin.

On electric violin, he was able to meld his formidable classical technique with bluegrass fiddle repertoire. George Stavis continued to evolve a unique style on the banjo by electrifying his instrument, somehow accommodating the styles of Eric Clapton, Ravi Shankar and Earl Scruggs at once. Keyboardist Jack Bowers primary influence in the band was as principal songwriter; his songs drew on the entire American songbag, from Appalachian music to Fats Waller to Broadway show music.

Upon arriving in Brookdale in 1970, the musicians of Oganookie dedicated themselves to developing a sufficient repertoire to fulfill the four set, four-hour gig expected of working bands at that time. The repertoire evolved in several different directions.

First, the Appalachian music tradition provided many of the songs that were to become performance staples. Chief among these were tunes from the Bluegrass songbook such as "Orange Blossom Special," "Uncle Pen," and "Little Maggie." These songs, and other Oganookie tunes from the American folk repertoire, took a psychedelic left turn from their roots, electrified, framed in rock and jazz rhythms with extended solos. Bob would introduce "Orange Blossom Special" by saying "Get ready for 10 minutes of sweat and boogie." "Orange Blossom Special" became an ecstatic celebration of expressive hippie dance that left dancers and musicians elated and exhausted. The improvisational dynamic of Bob and George spurring each other to greater heights of inventiveness was something to behold, even for their fellow band members who heard it every night.

Bruce contributed several blues classics to the repertoire including a beautiful version of "Corinna", and the Muddy Waters' classic "I'm Troubled." Bruce's fine original songs such as "My Way" also became part of the song list.

Jack's songs constituted about half of Oganookie's repertoire. They ranged from reimaginings of traditional Appalachian songs like "Black Jack Davy;" blues influenced love songs, "The Blues Ain't Nothing but a Bad Dream;" Fats Waller style humorous songs, "(That's Not to Say That) Your Woman is Ugly;" jazz tunes a la Lambert Hendricks and Ross, "Play It Cool;" and songs with a Broadway flavor, "Under the Old Apple Tree." Lyrically, many of his songs chronicled the individual and social changes that were rampant in 1970s Santa Cruz. They reflected the complexity of love relationships in this new world and the search for a meaningful life outside of the traditional social structures we had grown up with.

Long listening sessions with local record collector/ musicologist Glenn Allen Howard exposed Oganookie to diverse musical influences, from jazz violinist Stuff Smith to the lyric humor of Fats Waller and the ground breaking big band arrangements of Fletcher Henderson.

It all came together, embellished with the complex vocal and instrumental arrangements that the group layered over Jack's songs as well as reimagined traditional tunes. Bruce's soulful voice, Bob's and George's harmonies and instrumental virtuosity and Tim's incredibly tuneful drumming, together with Jack's tunes and piano playing created a blend of lyric sophistication and powerful instrumentals that reached out to listeners and revelers.

When Oganookie arrived in Santa Cruz in September, 1970, there were a few local bands but no music scene to speak of and hardly any musicians made a living wage. The George Stavis Trio played the Whole Earth Restaurant at UCSC several times. Oganookie's debut as an official, professional band was at a benefit for Cesar Chavez at Merrill College. The next breakthrough came a few months later when Oganookie played a concert at UCSC's athletic field supposedly featuring Crosby, Stills & Nash. When the headliners failed to show, the local musicians averted a near riot by turning the disappointed audience on to their own particular brand of music.

From there the band pressed forward, supported by a growing following who came to see them at clubs and in concerts, often with their children in tow. City people and mountain people and students who came not just to sit and listen, but to dance and be part of the performance. They shared potluck spaghetti dinners with the band at the Town and Country Lodge and buffet dinners at the Plantation, and learned to look upon the musicians not as untouchable celebrities but as friends and neighbors. Oganookie played for the community at street fairs and at benefits for Switchboard, KUSP, Sundaz and other organizations. Oganookie was the house band at the Catalyst as well as the Town and Country and, what's more, they were the Santa Cruz band and the community felt included enough to take pride in their growth and accomplishments.

The "Oganookie Plantation", as the band's communal residence became known, was composed of the band members, a core group of family and close friends, and a rotating cast of visitors, men, women and children. For most of its history the commune had 15 stable members. In addition to the band members mentioned above, the core group was composed of Sherry (Bella) Frye, *Consuelo* Barragan, Jessica Frye, Maria Lucinda "Lucy" Garcia, Acacia Fruitgarden, Diana Troxell, David Bowers, Adriana Troxell, Candis Halverson, Courtney Maguirre, and Janette Walsh. The commune was very accommodating to short term and long term visitors.

Life at the Plantation was an experience. There were hundreds of visitors, friends, family and curious musicians who came away with a full stomach, heads reeling with music, and insights about communal living. In the beginning everyone lived in the main house which had six bedrooms, a huge living room and a full porch overlooking the redwoods. When Peter came he lived in the room next to the garage and the garage was turned into a rehearsal studio. Jack and Acacia built a dome out in the orchard. George and Janette renovated the guest house and moved in. Bruce and Lucy turned the chicken coop into a home.

One of the great joys of our communal life was the children who lived among us. Consuelo Barragan, age nine when she arrived, Jessica Frye just one year, and two infants, Courtney Maguire and Adriana Troxell helped bring an expanded sense of family into our world. Though most of us were not biological parents at the time, we were privileged to observe and participate in their lives as they grew.

When there wasn't music to rehearse there were vegetable seeds to plant, bread to bake, wood to chop, cars to fix, septic tanks to rebuild and meals to cook (not to mention dishes to wash). Though living in harmony with a large group of creative people was a great challenge, we also remember the joy and union we felt as we sat down and held hands for our nightly communal dinner.

Oganookie went north to play in Berkeley, Stockton, Marin County, and south to audition for the men who controlled the music business. But the band away from Santa Cruz was never quite the same. At their highest, Oganookie was an astounding interplay of energy between musicians and audience. Without that audience to play their part in the performance, something was missing.

Why did Oganookie end in 1973? There is no one clear reason. Some thought it was their lack of success in getting a recording contract. Others cited economic reasons – the difficulty in supporting nearly a dozen people by only playing locally. The public's unwillingness to allow their music to evolve had something to do with it. The predominant reason, probably, was that the members of Oganookie grew apart as they realized needs for individual rather than group accomplishment.

Oganookie did finally make a record but it became a parting gift to their community and not a step on the road to stardom. Like the wooden Oganookie plaque that graced the Catalyst wall for 30 years, the record is a testament not to what might have been but to what was: a time of creation and of sharing for both the people of Santa Cruz and for the Oganookie family.

As to the members, Bruce and Jack remain in Santa Cruz. Bruce has become an excellent arborist and photographer. Jack, after working with Jill Croston (Lacy J. Dalton), continues to work as a jazz musician and has had a 38-year career in the Arts in Corrections program in California prisons and jails. Bob became a dentist and continued his musical career; he has retired from dentistry, lives in Montauk, New York and gigs frequently, particularly with the great Mexican guitarist Gil Gutierrez. Tim lives and plays drums in the New York area. George, who built and ran the Louden Nelson Center for a decade, has retired from his law practice. He lives north of New York and performs occasionally, including a recent concert featuring his solo banjo style in a festival near Washington, D.C.

Two Oganookie reunions were held. In 1979, Oganookie performed at the New Catalyst [see Christian Kallen's review below], and in 1991 at the Cocoanut Grove at the Boardwalk.

We remember fondly three who are no longer with us: our beloved manager Peter Troxell, who served his community and the arts with wisdom and dedication his entire life; David

Bowers, who went from Oganookie roadie to work as a sound engineer for musicians as diverse as The Doobie Brothers and Luciano Pavarotti; and Lucy Garcia, whose generous, expanded sense of family touched so many people in Santa Cruz.

My hands are empty
of applause for you
I have no words ringing
Clearly true
Far as I can see
There's one thing
To do when you
Speak to me in music
I will answer you in music
You turn my mind,
My mind to music
Here are my thanks
Here are my praises...
  - Bella Frye

The crucial opening banjo notes and my dad's wrenching vocals in Little Maggie never fail to make me weep, and yet— with my heart in my throat—I harmonize along and stomp my feet with pride. It's at this crossroads of love and loss, elation and fury, where my soul resides. I've got Bill Monroe tattooed on one arm, and Hank Williams Sr. on the other. Holding the precious parts of Americana dear along with a progressive question-authority mindset is not always easy, but I had some danged good models in the Oganookie band.
  - Jessica Frye (age 1 when she came to the Plantation)

I had a band
Five friends and a brother
We lived together in the mountains

Thought we loved one another.

It was peaceful in the mountains
The morning sun awoke us
We lived for the music
Felt it strong and growing
Felt it was a part of ourselves.

The people of the mountains helped us
Held us, fed us.

Flow of the music,
One with the sweat of the dancer's bodies,
Without an owner
Child of the celebration,
Beside which nothing matters,
Returning all that is given.
The stream of all things passing
Time, yet not between us.
- Jack Bowers

We were young searching for aliveness and freedom of
expression. We wanted release and joy. Dancing to Oganookie
was a spiritual experience, ecstatic renewal.
- Diana Wright Troxell

The latest and, just possibly, the last Oganookie reunion is
over. While it may sound corny or even maudlin to say that,
with their demise goes the best that Santa Cruz has to offer.
Yet for a few hours last weekend, that old Santa Cruz
vibration filled the "New" Catalyst and transformed it into a
very warm, familiar place. There was Bruce Frye bending that
Southern California golden voice into the lyrics; Bob Stern,
fiddle bow and smile both flashing; George Stavis, looking clean
cut these days, but community involvement not hampering his
banjo picking one bit; Tim Ackerman, coolly driving the band
from behind his well-broken in drum set; and Jack Bowers,
the seemingly mild-mannered pianist who wrote so many of

the *miraculous songs that made Oganookie a pure local music blend.*
-Christian Kallen, *Good Times*

It is past midnight and Pacific Avenue looks oddly twisted . . . the dense foliage looks like the old Garden Mall . . . there's no place open and I'd like a beer so I stroll over to Front Street to see who's playing at the Catalyst. It must be 1973 or so because Oganookie is into its last set and the dancers crammed in front of the bandstand have worked up a sweat and the cowboys and bikers and hippies and grad students are stomping their boots on the boards of the old carriage-house floor. The music is some kind of Boulder Creek bluegrass, blue as the smoke of cannabis leaves grown and burned in these hills, fiddle-guitar-bass-and-banjo burning as if the musicians fingers are aflame, possessed of some ancient backwoods juju that rocks the big room with primal rhythms that move everyone, even the bouncers and bartenders who rule the place with the force of their studly cool, and the busgirls collecting the dregs of the downed pints.
-Stephen Kessler, Santa Cruz Sentinel

Oganookie group with instruments.
Photo courtesy of Jack Bowers.Bruce

Oganookie group.
Photo courtesy of Jack Bowers.

From left:
Bruce Frye, George Stavis, Tim Ackerman (sitting),
Jack Bowers (sitting), and Bob Stern (top).

Chapter 7:
Jack Bowers, George Stavis and Peter Troxell:
Oganookie in Santa Cruz, 1970-73

Origins

Before there was Oganookie, there was Haverford College, 500 students outside of Philadelphia, where four students, all musicians, met between 1963 and 1965. Jack Bowers and George Stavis lived in tiny dorm rooms across the hall from each other the first day of college. They were armed with banjos. A year later, Tim Ackerman, a jazz and rock 'n' roll drummer, entered the college. And another year later Bob Stern walked in with his violin, rooming with George's brother, after deciding to go to Haverford instead of pursuing a career in classical music. After graduating in different years, these four stayed in touch: in 1968 they recorded, with others, a hip semi-concept record on the Musicor label, Federal Duck, and in early 1969, Tim and George had recorded an unusual banjo and hand drum album, Labyrinths, for Vanguard Records. Later in 1969, the four got together north of San Diego to form an electric band. They met Bruce Frye, a solo singer and guitarist, and the four college mates asked Bruce to join the troop, and he accepted.

Coming to Santa Cruz

In the summer of 1970, the group decided to move north to Santa Cruz, attracted both by the History of Consciousness Program at UCSC for Tim and George, and its spreading reputation as a hip mecca of music and community. They located an incredible home/commune among the redwoods in Brookdale, following an ad placed in the Valley Press. "Four Ph.D. Candidates Seeking Rental." There were eight in all, as Bruce brought his wife Bella and their children Consuela and Jessica.

First things first: setting up the homestead. The home, on six acres with an apple orchard and a broad deck covered with wisteria, was soon dubbed "The Plantation." A commune with music, rather than the other way around. Word of these newcomers traveled quickly to the hip Santa Cruz scene. Somehow, within the first month of arrival, T.Mike Walker visited, and decided that the property was ideal for the hosting of a Moon Festival. All agreed, and shortly thereafter, several hundred joined from all places to play music, smoke dope (perhaps), eat and revel. An astounding introduction to the Santa Cruz of the day.

The band practiced, and Jack was writing songs, building on traditional formats and reimaging them into an electric/bluegrass/country/jazz format. George, Tim and Bob started gigging acoustically, at small venues including the late great Whole Earth Restaurant at UCSC. Word spread of the musicians in Brookdale. Sunday potluck jam sessions commenced at The Plantation, and the newcomers quickly met and were absorbed into the burgeoning music community, which, at that time, was very much a part of the larger community.

And there was a neighbor just up the hill from the Plantation: Peter Troxell, a refugee from the theatrical community in San Francisco, experienced in management, performance and showbiz.

The now electric band, adopting the bizarre name
Oganookie (whose boring origins will not be revealed now,
and maybe never) finally debuted. With Peter as manager,
Oganookie became regulars at the High Street Local, near
the UCSC entry at Bay and Escalona, the Old Catalyst,
Mike's Lounge and the White Buffalo in Santa Cruz, the
Town and County Lodge in Ben Lomond, the Bodega in
Campbell, the Chateau in Los Gatos, the Opal Cliffs Inn in
Live Oak, In Your Ear in Palo Alto, the Cow Palace in San
Francisco, the New Orleans House, Freight & Salvage and
the Longbranch in Berkeley, the Inn of the Beginning in
Cotati, college gigs at UCSC, UC Berkeley, San Jose State,
University of Pacific in Stockton, Fort Ord and Monterey
Fairgrounds in Monterey. Omar's in Salinas and every
other available venue in northern California. Generally,
3-4 performance nights each week, 3 days of rehearsal, and
maybe one day off.

And both the commune and the music grew: Diana
Troxell joined with Peter along with daughter Adriana.
Candis Halverson joined with Bob and brought her
daughter Courtney. Jack joined with Acacia Fruitgarden;
George with Jannette Walsh; and Lucy Garcia joined with
Bruce, after his separation from Bella. And Jack's brother
David, back from Vietnam, joined the family and became
our road manager, with incredible skill and dedication.

The musical and community connections grew as
well. Musically, we connected locally and in the Bay
Area and beyond with, among others, Chaw, Childhood's
End, Swifty Taloose, Fafnir. Jill Croston, Don and Pilar,
Joey Richards and Kai Moore, Asleep at the Wheel,
Commander Cody, Dan Hicks and His Hot Licks, Linda
Burman-Hall, Paul Vorwerk, Joy of Cooking, Tower

of Power, The Crabs, Django, and Fly by Night. In the community, we were neighbors with 1000 Alba Road, a ruralist community and Camp Joy, a biodynamic farming collective which included Terry King, who did many of our graphic designs with Peter and did the wood carving on our album cover (along with Diana's album cover painting of the mountains and the sea). There were USCC connections as well: Paul Lee, Herb Schmidt, Page Smith, the poet Robert Duncan and Norman O. Brown (George became Brown's teaching assistant).

We were larger than our beginnings.

Influences and Influencing

The Music

We are all part of the burgeoning of the folk era, including the old-time music of the New Lost City Ramblers, and then the move from 50's rock 'n roll to the Beatles, the Stones, the Band, and the "art music" movement, represented by such groups as the Incredible String Band. We were into harmony, and so we took from the Bill Monroe bluegrass tradition, the Beatles and the Band's three part, and went to the previous era with gospel and pop jazz harmonies, such as the Andrews Sisters. Our gigs with Dan Hicks and His Hot Licks reflected some of that influence. And there was an Indian music strain, popularized by Ravi Shankar and Ali Akbar Khan, picked up by the Beatles, and incorporated into some of George's banjo playing. We got to know Glenn Howard, a collector of one of the great libraries of recordings from the 20's through the 60's, who provided additional depth on the influences who influenced our influences, and brought us new threads to incorporate in our musical garment.

Each individual brought years of musical background to the collective: Bruce, rooted in the acoustic blues tradition of Mance Lipscomb, Mississippi John Hurt and others, was also a songwriter with both melodic and lyric sensibility. Tim grew up playing and listening to jazz greats on 52nd Street, and modeled Buddy Rich. Bob was a classically trained violinist, and was part of the Julliard Youth Orchestra. In college he took up electric bass, as well. On electric violin, he was able to meld his formidable classical technique with bluegrass fiddle. In Oganookie, George continued to evolve a unique style on the banjo by electrifying his instrument, somehow accommodating the styles of Eric Clapton and Earl Scruggs at once. Jack was as the principal songwriter for the band – to the tune (pun intended) of about 50% of the repertoire; his songs drew on the entire American songbag, from Appalachian music to Fats Waller to Broadway show music.

It all came together, embellished with the complex vocal and instrumental arrangements that the group layered over the bones of Jack's songs, as well as reimagined traditional tunes. Bruce's soulful voice, Bob's and George's harmonies and instrumental virtuosity and Tim's incredibly musical drumming, together with Jack's tunes and piano playing were the glue that reached out to listeners and revelers.

Influencing/Community

Moving from the Sunday potlucks at the Plantation, the Town and County Lodge, in Ben Lomond, started Sunday Spaghetti Diner with Oganookie for $1.00. The place was packed. We became part of the political/communitarian movement that was sweeping Santa Cruz, as well as the country. Every time Oganookie was asked to play a benefit, we did. Many times each month, likely more than 50 over our time. We were reliably part of the broader community: the Santa Cruz Sentinel, the Good Times, the Valley Press and the incredible Santa Cruz alternative weekly Sundâz regularly wrote about us. Progressive political candidates asked for our endorsement, which we provided: Pat Liteky, who became the supervisor in the Valley, and Dale Dawson, who won in Aptos.

What Was It All About?

Oganookie was more than just a band. It was a way of life to the musicians in it, their family and friends, and to the Santa Cruz people who listened and danced to their music. Oganookie remains in the memories of thousands of people who mark significant moments in their lives by remembering what happened to them "the night we went to see Oganookie." During the spring of 1971, Oganookie's appearances at UCSC and clubs, and the band's growing reputation, attracted an audience of people who looked around at themselves and discovered they were a community. And the community was a reflection of the band, five individuals for whom the importance of community was equal to their music.

Life at the Plantation was an experience. There were hundreds of visitors, friends, family and curious musicians, who came away with a full stomach, heads full of music and insights about communal living. In the beginning everyone lived in the main house which had six bedrooms., a huge living room and a full porch overlooking the redwoods . . . Playing music together was never just a job and living together was not always easy. Bu the musicians were always friends first and co-workers second.
  - Peter Troxell, writing in about 1975

The Oganookie "experience" came out of the group's

communal living situation, where we grew vegetables during the day, and went out and played music at night. One of the things Oganookie was, was aspiring to something and everyone around it was aspiring to the same thing. Our audience took us there as much as we to them there. There was really the sense that there was something new . . . at the OLD Catalyst, when after three sets of high energy playing, Oganookie would bring the house down with The Orange Blossom Special . . . a total out of body experience.

--Jack, talking to Rick Chatenever, Santa Cruz Sentinel art/music critic, 1979.

The Santa Cruz sage Bruce Bratton wrote about Oganookie Times as a particular era in Santa Cruz story. Those times were captured quite wonderfully in a 2011 essay in Santa Cruz.com/Good Times by Stephen Kessler, writing Midnight in Santa Cruz, a reference to the dive into the foggy past imagined in movie Field of Dreams (Burt Lancaster as Moonlight Graham):

It is past midnight and Pacific Avenue looks oddly twisted . . . the dense foliage looks like the old Garden Mall . . . there's no place open and I'd like a beer so I stroll over to Front Street to see who's playing at the Catalyst. It must be 1973 or so because Oganookie is into its last set and the dancers crammed in front of the bandstand have worked up a sweat and the cowboys and bikers and hippies and grad students are stomping their boots on the boards of the old carriage-house floor. The music is some kind of Boulder Creek bluegrass, blue as the smoke of cannabis leaves grown and burned in these hills, fiddle.guitar-bass-and-banjo burning as if the musicians fingers are aflame, possessed of some ancient backwoods juju that rocks the big room with primal rhythms that move everyone, even the bouncers and bartenders who rule the place with the force of their studly cool, and the busgirls collecting the dregs of the downed pints.

This is the old Santa Cruz...

It was in fact a simply wonderful, magical time, with a joy and innocence shared throughout the entire Santa Cruz and Northern California area.

Sometime in 2015, George was visiting Jack from New York, and rather than lug his banjo, he rented one from Sylvan Music for a week. On its return, a woman in the store looked at him and exclaimed,

You're the one who played the Black Jack Davey!

Over 30 years has passed, and this was the living memory of one of Jack and the band's great reinvented, rewritten and reimagined folk songs.

The beat goes on.

Epilogue

Oganookie never quite managed the transition from its beginnings as a quasi-fraternity to adults with families. Issues arose as the band was the income (very, very modest) of the commune, and the partners grew tired of being, perhaps, "second fiddles" to the music project of the men. In the spring of 1973, the band announced its final engagements, ending at the Civic Auditorium. A self-produced album, recorded by Tim Dillenbeck and engineered in production by Sandy Stone was announced for subscription, and it quickly sold out.

Perhaps the most touching moment was shortly after the last concert. We got a call from a mother who had tragically lost her daughter in a fire. She told us that one of the joys in her daughter's life was coming to Oganookie gigs, and dancing and laughing the night away. We were asked to play for her at a memorial service on Bear Creek Road, near Los Gatos. We were honored and moved to play a small part in the daughter's life, and the service was a treasured memory.

The band had two reunions, one in 1979 at the new Catalyst, and in about 1991 at the Cocoanut Grove. More treasured memories.

As to the members, Jack and Bruce remain in Santa Cruz, with Jack, after working with Jill Croston (Lacey J. Dalton), continuing as an active musician following a 30-plus year career as the director and creator of the Arts in Corrections programs in the California prisons, and Bruce has become an excellent arborist (his daughter Jessica is the Associate Director of the Cabrillo Music Festival). Bob, becoming a dentist (and continuing at all times as a musician), retired from the practice and lives in Montauk, New York. He gigs frequently, particularly with the great Mexican guitarist Gil Gutierrez. Tim and Bob joined together for several years with the band Juice, along with guitarist Jerry Miller. Tim then went to New York to join his father's children's apparel business, eventually to be joined with George in that endeavor. Tim lives and plays drums in the New York area. George, who built and ran the Louden Nelson Center for a decade, moved first to the Philadelphia area, where he was the Alumni Director at Haverford, then joined Tim, and eventually went to law school at Columbia. He lives north of New York in Dobbs Ferry along the Hudson and performs occasionally, including a recent concert featuring his solo banjo style in a festival near Washington, D.C.

Peter Troxell, our beloved manager, reemerged as a performer in musicals in the area, and founded and ran the Mountain Community Theater, and then became the manager of KUSP for many years. Peter passed away in 2004. And Jack's brother David Bowers, our road manager, had an incredible career, working for Loggins and Messina and then becoming the premier sound man in California, working for, among others, The Three Tenors and the San Francisco Symphony. David passed away in 2011. Lucy Garcia, Bruce's partner for many years, was a fixture of hip Santa Cruz for decades, and passed away several years ago. They were all an intimate part of the entire experience and family, and are greatly missed.

Chapter 8
T. Mike Walker: Don McCaslin Interview --
Warmth: The Cooper House School of Jazz

For nearly two decades—1970- 1989—Don McCaslin's good vibrations radiated from the Cooper House Courtyard in downtown Santa Cruz. Standing in front of James McFarland's amazing Jazz Mural, depicting Don and his ever changing jazz band "Warmth", Don played music outside every afternoon from 1 to 5, seven days a week, to the delight of thousands of residents and visitors who stopped to listen and to dance to the groovy beat of McCaslin's Free School of Jazz: a place musicians could be paid to practice doing what they loved: playing Jazz Music. Saxophonists Paul Cantos, Brad Hecht, and Donny McCaslin were just a few of its grateful graduates.

Born in 1926, Don was raised in the vast flowing apricot and plum orchards of "The Valley of the Heart's Delight" (now known as Silicon Valley). "In the Spring my dad would take us for drives through the orchards so we could see and smell all the blossoms," Don explained. "San Jose was just a little town then. It only had one High School when I started in1941.

"Then—kaboom!-- the US entered world war two. When I graduated in 1944, I joined the Maritime Service because you didn't have to sign up for a specific amount of time like in the other branches of service, and when the war ended the next year, I quit the Maritime and returned to San Jose. I enrolled in San Jose State to play basketball and get my degree teaching English. I was also playing with a band at a Pizza place on the weekends and I continued playing gigs while I was teaching at Washington High in Centerville, CA--soon to be incorporated with Irvington into a new town called Fremont."

After teaching High School for 15 years, Don moved with his wife and three children in 1968 to their family's Summer

Home in Aptos, where it was cheaper. He commuted to Washington High for two more years, but decided to quit teaching and devote his life to music. For Don, the years 1968-70 were years of liberation. He saw Max Hartstein playing bass at the Jazz Cellar in San Francisco, the club that was the center for Jazz and Poetry.Later on Max moved to Boulder Creek and Don got to know him. He played with Max's 25th Century Ensemble, "...a free music group where anything goes as long as it fits—and it always fits because it's 'perfect' music! We just had to stretch our definitions of 'music." Don also met Pat Bisconte at that time and played a few gigs with Pat on his enormous Space Bass.

Although Don did work part-time as a reader for McGraw Hill in Monterey to supplement his now mostly non-existent income, he plunged into music full time. At one of his gigs playing for a political rally downtown, Max Walden, owner of the Cooper House, invited Don and his band to play at the opening of the Cooper House Courtyard. Max liked them so well he hired them to play there as much as they liked. So for the next two decades Don McCaslin and his band *"Warmth"* played out on the Cooper House Patio seven days a week (when it wasn't raining—which it often did back then!). Then in the evenings Don would play from 9-1PM at local clubs with other groups, determined to "...keep up my chops!" He was supporting himself through his music, living his dream.

Warmth recorded four records (vinyl in those days), and introduced a series of BeBop Dramas with Jazz Music, based on the Hip philosophic humor of Lord Buckly. The BeBop Dramas were presented at various locations, utilizing local musicians and actors. The Naz was recipient of a grant from the City of Santa Cruz and was presented by Kuumbwa Jazz Center. Don was also a big Stan Kenton Fan, and he remembered when Kenton brought his full band to the

SC Civic Auditorium in the 70's. When Don got to the Auditorium the place was dark and he joined dozens of people milling around in front. Then the bus pulled up, the band climbed out and Kenton pounded on the front door until someone opened it up. Evidently the promoter had skipped out with the ticket money. So Stan told the band, "Come on in!" and they played the gig anyhow. "I imagine Stan paid them out of his own pocket. It was a nice show, but we never heard from that promoter again," Don laughed.

After his separation, Don would bring his youngest son, Donny, down to the Cooper House on Sundays where Donny would sit in a corner and listen very carefully to the band. One day he announced that he wanted to play music. Don would have suggested piano, but Donny wanted to play tenor sax, so Don got one for him. Brad Hecht and Paul Cantos were Donny's first teachers and Wesley Braxton was his first Inspiration. Donny played with Don Keller's amazing Jazz Band through all four years of Aptos High, winning Statewide competitions, and an appearance with the Monterey High School All Star Jazz Band at the Monterey JazzFestival.

Donny won a full scholarship to Berkeley School of Music in Boston, and while still a student there he toured with Gary Burton's group. After graduation Donny moved to New York where he now lives with his wife and their two small children. During the last few years he has received three Grammy nominations for best jazz solo of the year and won a Grammy for leading his band and writing the musical arrangements for David Bowie's final album, Black Star. Donny and his group perform frequently at the annual Monterey JazzFestival.

For eighteen years Don McCaslin and *Warmth* were the living soundtrack of Santa Cruz, playing the changes of our time. At night they played at Frank Leal's 2525 Club on Main Street in Soquel, or at the Bay View Hotel, or sometimes at word-of-mouth Full-Moon-festivals in the mountains. Two of Don's children, Jenie and Matt, also wove their lives into the fabric of Santa Cruz where they married, raised families, and are still living. Jenie has been a long time waitress working alongside Linda at the Silver Spur Restaurant in Soquel. Mat McCaslin is a retired Santa Cruz Fire Chief and CA Fire Strike Team Leader. He led the first unit downtown after the earthquake. He's also an incredible fisherman, going to Alaska once or twice a year. Don's youngest child, Collette, from a different mother, also plays saxophone, and lives with her husband—also a fantastic saxophonist— in Richmond, California.

As I was interviewing Don for this story, I found myself drawn back to that happy time nearly 30 years ago, like taking a deep cool hit of past. I can still vividly remember drinking beer with friends in the Cooper House Courtyard in late September, 1989, listening to "Warmth" on a sunny summer day with 1,000 tourists crowding the intersection of Pacific and Cooper Streets, all of them grooving to Warmth's Latin beat. Many stopped to listen, while others went inside the Cooper House to taste the crepe's and beer inside the Crepe Place, or to explore the labyrinth of Local Artists and Craftspeople scattered over three floors while everywhere--inside and out, upside and down--the sound of *Warmth* touched our hearts, twitched our feet, lifted our moods and enhanced whatever enchantments we had on board. Outside some of the passing crowd inevitably joined the dance, filling the sidewalk with skipping feet, led on by Ginger Johnson, the twinkling eyed, grey-haired "Rainbow Lady" swirling and dipping through the crowd, waving her colorful scarves, playing her a-rhythmical tambourine as she joyfully led her own parade, dancing in front of the band and astonishing visitors from all over the world, inviting them to join the dance!

What a party it was! A constantly changing crowd of strangers and friends, meeting and parting in a swirl of colors and skins and outrageous costumes, a kind of rolling joy that rippled through the rest of the town and catapulted Santa Cruz's International reputation as a *Wonderful Place to Be.* Between the University and Cabrillo College, creative talent fermented and electricity sizzled in the air. The town was so full of energy it felt like it might explode from pure joy!

Then, on Oct. 17th, the Loma Prieta Earthquake struck with a 7.8 force that ended the era with a bang, and downtown Santa Cruz turned into Tent City, leaving the survivors to clear up the rubble of our dreams.

Fortunately, *Warmth* wasn't playing on the day the earthquake brought the Cooper House down. Don said that McFarland's Mural wasn't damaged, but after Max Walden sold the building the new owner had the mural painted over one night when no one was looking. The Party was over, but the Band played on! That's what bands do.

Shortly after the earthquake a reconfigured *Warmth* started playing weekends on the Capitola Wharf; they also played at 2525 Club and the Bay View Hotel in Aptos, and eventually to Severino's in Aptos, where Don has been playing for the past 20 years. Of course, the clubs reopened soon after the quake and the music scene continued to grow steadily into the monster it is today, with Kuumbwa Jazz Center bringing us the brightest lights in Jazz from all over the world, the Catalyst presenting Rock and Pop artists, Moe's Alley bringing us Blues, Country and Metal; UCSC and Cabrillo's terrific music departments present World and Classical concerts, as do the Santa Cruz Symphony, the Cabrillo Music Festival, the Distinguished Artists Series, The Santa Cruz Ballet and, of course, our terrific theaters (Jewell Theatre, Center Stage,

Shakespeare Santa Cruz, etc) , dozens of nightclubs, even Summer Salsa Dancing on theBoardwalk!

At 91, Don is still playing keyboard on Thursday nights with the help of his family and friends. Every Thursday evening his son Matt picks him up and drives him to Severino's Restaurant in Aptos, and helps him set up the keyboard. From 6:30 – 9:30 PM Don and his musical friends, *The Amazing Jazz Geezers*, play the Great American Songbook—they have memorized over 1,000 of the greatest songs ever written for dancers and lovers, most of them from 1935-45. The group features Stan Soroken, trumpet; Jami Brudnick, bass; Bill McCord, drums, and singers Ron Kaplan, Judy Webb and Rocky Pase. At the end of the evening Jami helps Don store his keyboard at the restaurant and drives Don home.

Don is still a happy man, and he reminded me to enjoy my life as I was leaving his apartment. "I have to practice half an hour or more every day just to remember the old songs—I don't have the energy to learn any new ones. I can talk for a long time but I can't walk around the block. But do you remember that great old standard, *The Autumn Leaves*? I call it the September Song, with its haunting line: '...*Our Lives dwindle down to a precious few...*' That's where I'm at now, at the dwindling down part. Of course, I have a few regrets, but as Hamlet said, '*If we got what we deserved, who would 'scape a whipping?*'"

Santa Cruz Jazz Players mural   James McEwin

Musicians in the Warmth Mural

Top row, left to right: Paul Contos, sax; F#, singer; Jim Lewis, trombone; Ruby Redman, Singer; Harry Woodward, Sax & Vocal; John Lewis, Vocal; Black Lady Singer?; Phil Yost, sax; Guitarist unknown

Center Row Figures: Frank Castellanos, Congos; F#, Trombone; Don McCaslin, Vibes & Keyboard; Thomas Obamswaim, Native American Guitarist; Phil Yost, Clarinet; Glen Rose, Keyboard; Larry Scalla, Guitar

Bottom Row: Dale Mills, Soprano Sax; Gary Griffith, the Bionic Singer; Wayne Goodwin, Violin; Paul Contos, Flute; Dean Davidson, Bass; Don (Hamlet the Dane) McCaslin, Vibes; Wesley Braxton, Sax; John Thompson, Congo Drums; Elliot Kalman, Keyboard; Dean Davidson, bass; Dale Mills, Soprano Sax.

Photo courtesy of T.Mike Walker.

Chapter 9
Bruce Bratton: Tom Sccribner

The Statue, The Musical Saw & Politics.

Tom cared much more about politics than the musical saw. Born in 1899, he was a tree cutter and very active with the Industrial Workers of the World. (I.W.W.). and later he became an avowed member of the Communist Party. He moved here in the mid 60's and from his home in Davenport he published a monthly, occasional, very political publication he called "The Redwood Ripsaw Review" and took on all comers, locally and internationally. Tom lived a long time in the old Saint George Hotel on Pacific Avenue. He'd play on Pacific Avenue just for the fun of it, and would never accept donations. But he did accept brandy old-fashioneds when he started to play at the then Lulu Carpenter's Bar up Pacific Avenue. That's, when Neal Coonerty and Jay Shore (Good Times founder) owned the place. UCSC student Marghe McMahon liked Tom and, as a class project, made the now famous Tom Scribner statue. Santa Cruz was far more to the right back then and Santa Cruz City Council members (Edler, Mahaney & Ghio) back in the late 70's didn't like Tom's left-Socialist-Communist politics and fought hard to stop Marghe's statue from being placed in the then named SCOPE park next to the Town Clock in 1978. The square later became known as Scribner Square. The Square was later tagged for development and Neal Coonerty offered to have the statue moved in front of Bookshop Santa Cruz in July 1993. There's an excellent 11 page bio of Tom written by his granddaughter Laura

Cooper Fenimore at scribnerfamilies.org . This letter (across the page) was actually from Tom to his friend and co-editor John Tuck. He wrote it while he was visiting his relatives. What he didn't know at the time was that Marghe's paying for the bronze in the statue resulted in our creating The Musical Saw Festival as a way to re-pay her.. The Festival continues to draw players from around the world every year during the first weekend in August.

A letter from Tom to John Tuck

La Mesa,Calif, 2 / 22 / 78

Mr. John Tuck, HI!

How is the stem end of your gizzard these fine spring days? Well, I'm packing up to move back to Santa Cruz and will be glad to escape this Megalopolis monstrocity of LA and San Diego with its plastic civilization and its suffocating John Birch atmosphere, and besides they have raised my rent beyond my ability to pay. So--I think I will finish this living bit in the St. George Hotel.

U have given away most of my 40 years gatherings and so just down to a bare minimum, like my musical saw, clothes, etc. like phono, TV, radio and like that. I heard from Margie Mc Mahon and she says that the big benefit to raise money for the bronze in the statue of me, will be held in Vets Hall on Mar. 30th. Of all the Santa Cruzans to be the M.C. of this shindig I would rather have you. Would you do it? I have written Margie suggesting this, and she may have called you already. In case you want to call her, she is "Margie Mc Mahon, 217 laguna St S.C. Calif Phone 427-1901" We will possibly arrive in Santa Cruz on Mar 25, or 26 and will have a room at either St George or Santa Cruz Hotel. My little old $316 bucks a month doesn't give me too much choice of where I live, and I'm quite sure that my next spot will have to be a hollow stump, (goose pen) up in the redwoods, UNLESS I can find a nice young chick about 60 that draws a similar pension and team up again to keep house. If you happen to know of any such let me know. We could at least keep house! Hanky-panky is all in the past!

Enclosing a picture of me on a log down on lower Columbia, Blind Slough, where I was on a rafting job. That's me still on the log. That was in 1927. The mag it was in is long since defunct.

Well John, will close for now and get on with packing.

Sincerely,
Tom Scribner (statuesque blond)

P.S. Will be playing a gig at Cal Poly on Mar 7th at San Luis Obispo.

Chapter 10
Ralph Abraham: The Batish Family

In the 1960s and '70s, Santa Cruz received spiritual influences from the East. Buddhist, Hindu, and Chinese teachers visited and enriched Hip Santa Cruz community. Among those recorded in this book are Ram Dass, Baba Hari Dass, and the Batish family. Here is a brief introduction to the Batish family.

Shiv Dayal (S.D.) Batish was born December 14, 1914, in Patiala, Punjab. Recognizing his musical talent early, his family arranged for his lessons with a well-known composer, Chandan Ram Charan. He learned vocal performance, music theory, and several instruments.

Shanta, his wife, was born in Rawalpindi, Punjab, December 28, 1928. She was also trained as a vocalist. They met while both singing in a radio station in Patiala, and were married there.

In India, S.D. was recognized as an outstanding vocalist, and was signed to a recording contract at age 22. Singing in Punjabi, Urdu, and Hindi, his records went to the top. Invited to Bombay around 1949 to compose and sing in Bollywood films, he served as the musical director for a dozen films.

While living in the Santacruz beach area of Bombay, their children, Surendra, Meena, Tarun, Ashwin, and Ravi were born.

Frustrated by the industry in Bombay, S.D. decided to relocate to the U.K. in 1964. Shanta and the five children joined him in London. There he performed on the radio, and gave instruction to many British musicians, including the wife of George Harrison of the Beatles. He performed on sitar in the Beatles' song, "Help" in 1965.

Following my move from Princeton University to UCSC in 1968, I had a sabbatical in London in 1969. While there I went to the Batish home seeking instruction on the veena. We became friends, and I arranged for S.D. to teach Indian music as a visiting lecturer at UCSC.

He and Shanta stayed with me and my extended family at the large Victorian on California Street, in the heyday of Hip Santa Cruz. After this visit, they decided to stay in Santa Cruz. When the visiting gig at UCSC ended, they opened a restaurant on Mission Street, the Krishna Cafe, in the Fall of 1970. It became a hub for Indian music and food. Shanta was a superb chef, and S.D. helped out in the kitchen. Soon the children joined them in Santa Cruz, and were essential to the success of the restaurant.

When Ashwin arrived, age 23, he continued training with his father, and performed on sitar nightly in the Krishna Cafe.

Over the years, the restaurant migrated to North Pacific Avenue, and finally to Mission Street. Although the restaurant closed, the property remains the main residence of the family. It includes a shop for Indian goods and groceries, and the Batish Institute of Indian Music and Fine Arts created by S.D.

S.D. died July 29, 2006, and Shanta on October 5, 2017. Ashwin is now teaching Indian music at UCSC, and his son Keshav is following the family tradition of classical Indian music, as well as studying the Western musical tradition at UCSC.

Part 4
UCSC

Chapter 11
Paul Lee:
How To Become a Spiritual Millionaire
When Money Is No Object

The story of U.S.A. (University/United Services Agency) and other nonprofit corporations in Santa Cruz, California, their contribution to the local culture as a microcosm of the national contribution of nonprofits and the carryover to the 1970's of the spirit of the 1960's.

Penniless, we own the world.
-- St. Paul, 2nd Corinthians 6:10

After a lifetime of involvement in nonprofit corporations, I am convinced that everyone should have one or get involved in one. The nonprofit corporation represents one of the great institutions between family and government, largely unsung, often unnoticed, as an institution. There are over one and a half million nonprofits, according to the Urban Institute. In a recent editorial in the New York Times, (July 27, 2013) Peter Buffett, yes, that Buffett, who runs his father's foundation, refers to the growth of nonprofits: "According to the Urban Institute, the nonprofit sector has been steadily growing. Between 2001 and 2011, the number of nonprofits increased 25 per cent. Their growth rate now exceeds that of both the business and government sectors. It's a massive business, with approximately $316 billion given away in 2012 in the United States alone and more than 9.4 million employed."

The numbers are astonishing. Anyone with a cause can start a nonprofit, get tax-deductible status, the famous 501c3, and do business. It is one of the great features of American democracy and expresses a deep spiritual strain in American life that is both generous and sacrificial, what we call an economy of gift.

We go into the historical roots of this spirit in the religious movement in Europe of sectarian Protestantism with its beginning in the Anabaptist movement that spawned the principle of voluntary association. I call it the free spontaneous behavior of the redeemed! George Blaurock is its patron saint. He was a Roman Catholic priest who was re-baptised into the new faith on a given evening at a home in Europe (1525). It was a major moment in the new autonomy spawned by the Protestant Reformation, extolled by Kant, in his famous essay: "What Is Enlightenment?" (1784).

I make reference to the Golden Rule as another expression of spiritual substance, following Paul Ricoeur's interpretation that takes the Golden Rule into an economy of gift and an ethic of super-abundance. In doing so, I salute all of those who have eschewed an economy of greed and an ethic of 'what's in it for me', an ethic of self-interest, and instead have followed a life of self-sacrifice, where they have given of themselves for the public good and are exemplary of what I call civic virtue. I have had the pleasure of working with countless people who have exhibited this spirit and I have enjoyed the surplus value of this generosity in behalf of others, this principle of plenitude; it has spilled over in my lap.

I want the reader to learn from my experience as I tell the story of my involvement in a number of nonprofit corporations during the course of my life and to see these examples as a microcosm of a larger institutional structure in American public life. I hope that what I have benefitted from in this work is an inspiration for others who are drawn to a life of public service.

My colleague and dear friend, Herb Schmidt, has contributed his section on U.S.A. We started this nonprofit in 1970 and it was a providential partnership. He was attentive to details as I was not; he worried about the bottom line, when I didn't know where the bottom line was; he kept us in compliance with the I.R.S., always meticulous about reporting and keeping records, which kept us out of trouble. It has been an inspired friendship and one for which I am most grateful. If anyone exemplifies the message of the gift it has been the gift of his friendship that I treasure the most.

Page Smith was another great friend. We left the university in 1972 to start the William James Association, one of the outstanding adventures of my nonprofit experience. I owe him more than I can say, someone who threw in his lot when I was turned out of my teaching career and stood by me when it counted most.

He always expressed gratitude that I had sprung him from the confines of a university career, which always perplexed and astonished me. He was the very exemplar of a public intellectual and knew exactly what the new prospects of nonprofit work meant for us as we launched out into the blue with a shoeshine and a prayer. We made the most of it.

The year was 1966. I had taken up teaching duties at the University of California, Santa Cruz, in a definite move to give my life a new direction. From Cambridge, Mass., to California. From Harvard and M.I.T., to a new campus of the University of California system, begun just a year before. I would own my own home. A swimming pool. The weather. The air. The vegetation. It was paradise. No snow. No freezing temperatures. Sub-tropical. The ocean. We thought we had lucked-out. And we had four more years to go before the tempestuous '60's came to an end. The hip 60's! Oh boy! Was Santa Cruz an epicenter for hip? Let me tell you.

Four years later, I had earned a sabbatical in Wisconsin, at our summer home, at Cisco Point, on North Twin Lake, where I could think about my future now that my present had come to an end. I had had a short shelf life at the university; it was pretty clear that I was going to be denied tenure, partly for starting an organic garden, the first at a university in the country, and pissing off my scientific colleagues at Crown College, because they thought 'organic' meant 'artificial synthesis', as in organic chemistry. They thought nothing of calling a factory a plant.

Our throwback, our practically medieval return, was the garden I started with Alan Chadwick, in 1967, eschewing the use of chemical fertilizers and pesticides; worse yet, it was seen as a hippie plot, devised to embarrass them further. That's what the scientists thought. After all, wasn't "flower power" one of the operative hip slogans of the time, identified with the hippie revolution. Organic schmamick. My career in teaching was on the line. The handwriting was on the wall.

While on sabbatical, I tried to think of what I would do with myself in terms of a new career. I wove muskie weeds I could gather from our lake as a kind of occupational therapy, as I considered the loss of my occupation.

I listened to late night radio and heard the Rev. Ike, a black prosperity preacher, proclaiming his gospel from New York, where he was the ostensible successor to Father Divine, another prosperity preacher, whom I had visited when I was a student at Union Theological Seminary. Ike offered his prayer cloth if you wrote to him. It was free. I thought what do I have to lose. One of his slogans was "you can't lose with the stuff I use," along with "the lack of money is the root of all evil," controverting St. Paul.

So I wrote and days later this little piece of red cloth cut with a serrated scissors arrived in the mail. I put it in my pocket and fingered it in a modestly prayer-like manner and dreamt up a nonprofit corporation. Just like that! I thought of calling it: USA. I was going to reconstitute the country in myself, in a nonprofit corporation, with the initials of my country, what would come to be known as: University Services Agency.

I was going to become a Spiritual Millionaire.

I wrote to an old student from my Harvard teaching days—Bill Russell--who had become a freshman dean at Harvard. Could he send me any material on the Harvard Student Agencies that I might use as a model for what I had in mind. He did. I noticed that their main project was training bartenders. They were in great demand at Harvard. I wasn't interested in that effort but the structure of the agency was what I wanted.

Eventually I would come to understand that my studies at Harvard had prepared me for what I was about to do in terms of the historical background and the institution itself.

I had been a student of two professors at Harvard

Divinity School who had some bearing on what I proposed: James Luther Adams, who taught social ethics and was a proponent of nonprofit corporations as the legal form of voluntary associations; and George Hunston Williams, my church history professor, who taught the origins of the radical or left-wing of the Protestant Reformation, represented by the sectarian churches, in opposition to the orthodox churches, the evangelical protest within Protestantism.

The historical origins fit together with the institutional outcome like hand to glove. This is one of the best applications of what I had learned at Harvard and I marvel that what they had taught me was at hand for me to understand the historical forces that made it possible for us to do what we did. When I reflected on what we had started in our new enterprise, I was reminded of their influence and that we were acting out what they had taught as though they prepared us for our enterprise.

Williams made it clear to me that the principle of voluntary association began on a certain evening in 1525 when a Roman Catholic priest by the name of George Blaurock was rebaptised. It was a matter of starting over. The Anabaptist wing of the Reformation Churches was the outcome. You could gather together at someone's home and exercise the freedom of worship in the context of a voluntary association and it wasn't anybody's business what you did. The most radical expression of autonomy, acting off your own bat, was thus enacted and became an historical event. It is known as taking matters into your own hands free from the domination of others.

Years later, Immanuel Kant would write his essay: *What Is Enlightenment*, celebrating the ability of anyone to throw off foreign authorities in favor of the right to exercise their own personal authority. Autonomy over heteronomy. Self rule over the rule of the other. It was a celebration of venturesome daring and an exercise in courage. "Dare to know" was Kant's assertion. It was revolutionary. When I applied this to the sectarian movement that was the historical background for what we were about to do I called it "the free spontaneous behavior of the redeemed." We were associated with a spiritual movement that was working in the depth of the American psyche, like the old song says: "It ain't anybody's business what I do," implying that it's my business.

This spirit is what I was going to express when I got back to Santa Cruz in January of 1970, when my sabbatical was over. I was going to start a nonprofit corporation in the spirit of the principle of voluntary association established by the Anabaptists in the 16th century and it was going to give me something to do with myself when I was denied advancement and had to find some other means of employment.

I returned to Santa Cruz and got ready for the new quarter with some relief that we were entering a new decade. I was tired of the '60's, as exciting as it had been, and the tyranny of being hip, as I called the pressure to take drugs and act out under the influence of the slogan of Timothy Leary: "turn on, tune in and drop out," his version of Kant's autonomy.

I wanted a fresh start.

A few days into the new year, it was around January 3rd, 1970, I ran into my friend, the Lutheran Chaplain to the university, the Rev. Herb Schmidt, on the border between Merrill and Crown Colleges and he told me he was going to Charles Gilbert's office to sign a lease for the only public restaurant on the campus. I told him we had wanted it for the Chadwick Garden to supply, and that we should collaborate and start a nonprofit corporation I had dreamed up on sabbatical. We would call it U.S.A. He said o.k.; he had been thinking something similar on his own. He got the franchise and we had our first affiliate; we called it The Whole Earth Restaurant.

U.S.A., University Services Agency, would be the nonprofit umbrella for whatever other enterprises came along to add to our affiliates. A child day-care center on the campus was the next addition.

It was that kind of time, a time of hip entrepreneurship. People wanted to start something so they could work together and accomplish something good for the community. Money was not the object. Greed played no part at all—it was the time of an economy of gift wedded to civic virtue. It was called 'right livelihood'. There was a surfeit of good will in the air, a new surge of generosity, an interest in joining with others to celebrate the new consciousness that the '60's had brought about and had given an innovative direction. My metaphor for the students--"oceans of desire"—was meant to characterize the surplus desire of the time, the excess, the longing, the willingness to splurge, to gamble, take risks, and go overboard.

To celebrate the opening of the Whole Earth Restaurant and to get a perspective on what we were doing, I invited Stewart Brand of the Whole Earth Catalogue to come and give a talk about the future of enterprises like ours. I had met him at the time and we had become friends. I had even officiated at his wedding ceremony on the beach at Rio Del Mar, after which we walked the beach and picked up sand dollars as though they were a symbol of good luck. I enjoyed the fact he had his finger on the pulse. After all, we borrowed the name of the restaurant from his publication and we thought of ourselves as part of the new mentality and spirituality that characterized the New Age.

He spoke about the hip sub-economy coming from the 60's to inform the 70's and the new dynamic represented by those who had been initiated accordingly. He spoke of the Briar

Patch Trust, run by Dick Raymond, in the Bay Area, and how we would be another example of the new entrepreneurship, with a strong emphasis on social service and civic virtue, sketching out a pattern of development that turned out to be predictive in an uncanny way. We were to watch things develop just as he said they would when word got out that we would take on any affiliate with a good reason for doing business. Soon various members of the community came to us looking for nonprofit supervision and before long we had a string of affiliates representing the various aspects of community development that emerged from the new spirit of the time. It wasn't long before we hit a million dollars in cash flow.

Alan Chadwick was the great inspiration for me, although it was something I didn't reflect on at the time, even though I registered it. He was generous beyond measure. Everything in the garden was given away on the basis of an economy of gift, as I would come to call it. He had no interest in money. It took some months for us to get the university to pay him a salary and it was around $400 a month. He simply accepted it and put most of it back into the garden. He worked seven days a week, on an average of eighteen hours a day, so what does that come to as an hourly wage? You do the math.

I have written about my experience with Chadwick: *There Is A Garden In the Mind*. I tell the story of the development of the garden at UCSC and the subsequent gardens he developed after he left the university, promoting organic procedures in food and flower production, with his special method and system, the French Intensive and the biodynamic, wherever he went. He is credited with inaugurating the organic movement in California and his influence was remarkable, reaching all the way to the new California cuisine as represented by Alice Waters at Chez Panisse in Berkeley and Deborah Madison and

The Greens Restaurant in San Francisco, developed by the Zen Center. Chadwick did a garden for The Zen Center, at Muir Beach, at their Green Gulch Farm and rural retreat, where he died and is buried, and Alice eventually would orchestrate her student garden at the Martin Luther King, Jr., school in Berkeley, with Chadwick inspired gardeners.

As much as anyone I knew, Chadwick embodied the spirit of the New Age. He gave himself tirelessly to the development of his gardens and to imparting the new understanding of one's relation to nature, although it was a very old tradition, prior to the break from it represented by industrial society as a world above the given world of nature. Students wanted a reverential relation to nature, they wanted to view nature as a sacrament, something given with an abundance that overwhelmed, a veritable principle of plenitude. You got back more than you gave and there was enough for everyone, more than enough. Too much zucchini! What does anyone do with the bounty that nature affords when you know how to work with it? This spirit was what Chadwick transmitted to the countless student apprentices who caught the magic and received the transmission. It was a spiritual substance that was transmitted and the operative term was an economy of gift.

We carried out the economy of gift motif in our nonprofit corporation, partly because we saw it as a spiritual calling. I had been the Protestant Chaplain at Brandeis University and I had studied under the famous theologian, Paul Tillich, at Harvard. I had a divinity degree from Harvard Divinity School. Although my position at UCSC was in philosophy, I was asked by the chancellor to organize a religious studies program, which became one of the most popular electives on the campus. I was ready to apply these influences to a nonprofit corporation.

Two of my fellow incorporators for USA were campus

chaplains: Herb Schmidt, my Lutheran pal, and Jerry Lasko, a Roman Catholic priest. We saw it as a type of secular ministry, although it was more assumed than articulated. I would find a quote somewhat later in an essay by Tillich that defined our situation in his ruminations on the future of Protestantism, which he thought had come to an end as an historical force. He speaks of this new departure from the standard Protestant church as a third way:

The third way requires that Protestantism appear as the prophetic spirit which lists where it will, without ecclesiastical conditions, organization, and traditions. But this imperative would remain a very idealistic demand if there were no living group which could be bearer of this spirit. Such a group could not be described adequately as a sect. It would approximate more closely an order or fellowship and would constitute an active group, aiming to realize, first, in itself that transformation of Protestantism which cannot be realized either by the present churches or by the movements of retreat and defense.
-- Paul Tillich, *The Protestant Era*

Had he known of the historical origins of voluntary association and its legal form, he would have referred to the nonprofit corporation as the vehicle of choice for the fellowship he envisaged.

The time was right for this sort of thing, a veritable kairos, as Tillich would have called it, the pregnant time, the time fraught with spiritual meaning. There was a fullness of time operating in our midst in search of expression and we were going to be the occasion for it.

How else to explain the success we enjoyed as we watched our nonprofit become a multi-million dollar enterprise in a relatively short period of time.

There is an interesting account of the third way that

includes the notion of the public intellectual who is free from academic confines. This is exactly the experience I shared with Page Smith who spoke openly about our exodus from institutional bondage and how he had been freed up to do the work he wanted to do without the constraints of the academy. His model was his beloved professor—Eugen Rosenstock-Huessy, with whom he had studied at Dartmouth and whose influence on him was total, comparable to Tillich's influence on me.

Eugen had written a wonderful essay about his liberation from the dead works represented by German institutions after the 1st world war: "Metanoia, To think anew." It was the most existential and heart felt account of dropping out and distancing oneself from the dead defeat of a career that was tied to the decay of the major institutions. Instead of resuming his professorship, Eugen took a job at an automobile factory. It took my reading of William Dean's *The Religious Critic in American Culture,* to realize he was describing the role that I and my colleagues, particularly, Herb Schmidt and Page Smith, played as public intellectuals freed from the confines of academia.

I believe voluntary associations of the third sector offer the public intellectual, particularly the religious critic, a better "psychological home" than does the university. I use the metaphor of "home" in recognition of the fact that anyone's, even an intellectual's, most important awareness is more physical and emotional than cognitive and is largely the effect of the social location of the individual. ... Accordingly, if a move between psychological homes is made, it is from one thick and value-laden history of social relations, with physical and emotional dimensions, to another; it usually involves a kind of conversion. My point is, intellectuals interested in becoming

public intellectuals, particularly those interested in becoming
religious critics, would be well advised to adopt some third
sector organization as their psychological home.

After Page Smith and I established the office of the William
James Association in downtown Santa Cruz I remember
wanting to laugh out loud when I saw professors from the
university walking down Pacific Avenue. They stuck out like
sore thumbs.

We came to know the meaning of "free space" as developed
by Evans and Boyte in their book of that title where they speak
of third sector organizations as fostering religious and public
action.

When do ordinary people steeped in lifelong experiences
of humiliation, barred from acquisition of basic skills of
citizenship....gain the courage, the self-confidence, and above
all the hope to take action in their own behalf? What are the
structures of support, the resources, and the experiences that
generate the capacity and the inspiration to challenge 'the way
things are' and imagine a different world?

Dean comments:
And they answer that voluntary associations of the third
sector have provided the historic wellspring of American social
initiative.

It was appropriate that our first affiliate in our nonprofit was
the public restaurant on the campus for the garden to supply
with the best organic produce. We had tried to penetrate
the food system in the colleges but it was run by a national
syndicate and they were resistant. I got myself appointed as a
faculty member of the food committee and forced their hand.

They reluctantly took the produce until they found a snail in one of the heads of lettuce and that was the end of that.

It wasn't very long before someone came to us and wanted to use our nonprofit as a cover for their enterprise and so we took them on as an affiliate. The first was the child day-care center at the university. Then we spilled down the hill of the campus into town. I remember looking at Herb when we were approached by the first inquiry from Santa Cruz realizing that the talk Stewart Brand had given was now coming to fruition. It wasn't long before we had multiple affiliates and had passed the million dollar cash flow mark. We had become spiritual millionaires almost without lifting a finger.

I started to think about money. I wanted to print our own dollar once we had passed the million dollar mark and had diversified to the extent that our own currency could circulate among the various affiliates. I wanted a USA Dollar! I knew that the lumber baron in our summer vacation town— Phelps, Wisconsin, had printed his own scrip, which he paid his employees, only redeemable at his store. I deplored that practice but I thought an alternative dollar would be an interesting economic experiment. There were examples: the Vermont Dollar, etc. I even went so far as to imagine our own Fort Knox where every USA Dollar would be backed up by a gold brick, that is, a brick painted gold.

I found out about the Time Dollar where you are credited with a hypothetical dollar for every hour of service you performed. If you volunteered for this or that you could keep track of your time and be rewarded in an exchange of services based on the number of hours you performed and the Time Dollars you received accordingly. I went to Washington D.C. and met the founder.

It failed to get off the ground.

Eventually, I found out about the Boggs bill, the artist who drew hundred dollar bills and sold them and ran afoul of the US Treasury (they had no sense of humor; he only drew one side). It all started when he was doodling in a restaurant and drew a sort of facsimile of a dollar bill without even thinking about it and the waitress admired it and wanted to buy it. After rejecting the offer he thought it over and sold it to her for a dollar.

I thought he was very clever. I met him in Pittsburgh and asked him to draw a million dollars worth of bills to match my spiritual millionaire success. I would float the issue in Santa Cruz. I offered to give him my experimental electric car in exchange. He jumped at it and agreed. It turned out to be too expensive to print the bills so that never went anywhere, either. Oh well. So much for the alternative currency movement.

There have been a number of times I wished I had gone to Harvard Business School instead of Harvard Divinity School.

We ran USA until 1976 when the affiliates staged a coup and took over the management and turned it into a worker collective called Riptide. They ran into trouble with the IRS over profit making affiliates, such as commercial stores and had to break off the strictly nonprofit entities from the profit ones. Riptide morphed into Democratic Management Services, which carried the ball for a few years and then disbanded. It is no more.

When Herb Schmidt returned to Santa Cruz, after serving at the University of Arizona and Stanford, we decided to resurrect U.S.A. and call it United Services Agency, as we were no longer affiliated with the university. We have had some successful projects, especially used computers, shipped to Cuba, for the medical services there.

I continue to pursue my design vision for Santa Cruz I call Ecotopia and there are currently efforts to pursue the Circle Trail and to include the Chadwick Archive which has gone public.

The William James Association

This nonprofit was born the moment Page Smith walked into our home and sat down at our kitchen table and said: "Let's start the William James Association and re-establish the C.C.C.", by which he meant, of course, the Civilian Conservation Corps. I said, "o.k.", meaning that whatever Page said we had a shot at it because we had a magic wand. We were free to do whatever we wanted and this is what he had in mind. It was a greater adventure than U.S.A., as great as that was, because we intended a specific project that was way beyond our means, as far as I was concerned. What was he thinking? We were just two academics who were out of the game, one by default, denied tenure and one by choice, because he threw in his lot with me. Where were we going to find the means or the wherewithal to start or re-start a national service corps? We weren't Franklin Delano Roosevelt, by any means. But Page was this grand figure in my view and he wouldn't propose something that was impossible.

We incorporated and we went to work. We developed local projects in Santa Cruz, a number of them remarkably successful, like the William James Work Company, which found short term part time employment for the migrant youth that wandered through Santa Cruz in the '70's. The City Fathers called them "the undesirable transient element", also known as UTE's, for short. We found thirty thousand jobs during the tenure of the program before we ran out of gas. We started Community Gardens, which eventually prepared the way for the Homeless Garden Project.

We did a wonderful bicentennial project of broadsides, commemorating the bicentennial of the American Revolution (1976) of which Page was the major historian with the first two volumes of his eight volume Peoples' History of the United States, one of the greatest accomplishments of narrative history of which he was a master. We recruited a group of the finest printers and typographers to contribute to a handsome blue cloth portfolio a broadside of their design and execution. And so on. I can't even remember the number of projects we became involved with. We went to Washington D. C., to lobby for the Corps. We didn't get anywhere. We met with Frank Davidson and Jack Preiss and had lunch at the Cosmos Club. I liked that. We met with Don Eberle who was also lobbying in behalf of voluntary work service and made it clear that under a Republican administration we didn't have a chance.

Voluntary work-service, the CCC, the Peace Corps, etc., was considered a Democrat issue. Therefore, the Republicans would not lend their support or even their interest. Page had been in the C.C.C. in 1940 thanks to his relation to his teacher at Dartmouth College—Eugen Rosenstock-Huessy, who was a proponent of work service in the tradition of William James. Eugen had done organizing work in Germany with German youth and work service camps before Hitler came to power and took them over as Hitler Youth Camps and Eugen had to flee to the U.S. Eugen and Page and Frank Davidson and Jack Preiss and others banded together to open Camp William James in Tunbridge, Vermont, as a leadership training camp for the C.C.C. Then the war drafted them off and the Camp was short-lived. It had made such an impression on Page he wanted to see it reborn because the theme William James spoke about at Stanford, in 1906, entitled: "A Moral Equivalent of War" was such an inspiration it deserved to be pursued. In fact, I came to see it as the theme of the century. The C.C.C., for sure, was the direct outcome .and expression of exactly what William James called for: voluntary work service.

In 1976, Page and I were asked by Governor Jerry Brown to start the California Conservation Corps.

The Citizens' Committee for the Homeless

The year was 1985 and we were worried about a woman named Jane Imler who had announced a fast to the death lest someone open a shelter for the homeless in Santa Cruz. We were forced to recognize that our support for the hippies and our William James Work Company was to be superseded by the homeless. No more UTE's looking for part-time short-term employment, but the need for emergency shelter for those who had no where to sleep had suddenly become the urgent cause as though overnight. In order to save Imler's life we realized it was up to us. No one else was rushing to help. I, for one, could not tolerate the prospect of living in a town where a woman starved to death in behalf of the homeless because no one responded to her challenge.

So we opened the first public shelter and eventually formed a new nonprofit— The Citizens Committee for the Homeless. It was a big success and one of the great adventures of our lives.

Chapter 12
Herb Schmidt: UCSC

Three memoires on my life at UCSC.

Campus Ministry and University Services Agency

Original Plans

Even before the University started, Chancellor Dean Mc Henry encouraged local churches to proceed with plans to build a University Religious Center on Campus and establish a University Interfaith Council. Plans were made for a site for such a center below Stevenson College, but Engineering reports made that impossible. Students came, and Provost Page Smith provided an office for the ministry in the Trailers and it was then moved for a short time to the Health Center and then to Merrill College.

Campus Ministry and the 60s

Being involved in campus ministry during the 60's was exciting, challenging, and life changing. The Civil Rights Movement and the Viet Nam War made it very clear that campus ministry leaders should do more than lead worship, teach, and provide counseling. Faithful ministry must help students realize that faith commitments meant becoming involved in Social Justice and Peace issues of our society. Having a Center was of secondary importance. Those of us in campus ministry became very active in the Civil Rights, Anti War, and Farm Workers Movements. As part of our Anti-War ministry we helped students file for Conscientious Objector status. When the local draft Board refused to grant C.O. Status to all that qualified we helped lead a group of 50 students to protest and close the Draft Board, got arrested, jailed, and sentenced. We then educated the Draft Board members about their responsibilities and most resigned. We helped with the "Teach Ins" at the University. We led marches with Death masks and a coffin through the streets of Santa Cruz to protest the bombing of civilians. At a Joan Baez anti- war rally and concert in the Quarry I received draft cards and burned them. We helped students who could not obtain CO status to make their way to Canada, so they could avoid killing and participating in the war.

A New Possibility

As the University grew space demands meant our office at Merrill would be given to an incoming Faculty member and so we needed an office and meeting place near the center of campus. When the University announced that the Restaurant space in the Redwood building became available for bid, and it included an office we immediately developed a proposal to present to the University. I was on my way to present our proposal when I met my friend and colleague Paul Lee who had just returned from Sabbatical. He had just suffered a painful experience of losing s a dear friend and colleague by suicide and had much uncertainty about himself receiving Tenure. It was a miracle of "syncrebility". We both wanted the same thing. At Prep School, College, and Seminary I had been involved in many service and non- profit student projects. At Harvard Paul had firsthand experience with and knowledge of the Harvard Student Agencies, and so University Services became a reality. It was our response to the 60's. Eisenhower's parting words as he left the

White House about the danger of the military Industrial complex, and the exorbitant profits being made rang in our ears as we reviewed the events of the 60's. The US should be Non-Profit! Any money that was raised in the revenue producing affiliates would go to start other service organizations.

A few Faculty and Community Members provided us with money to get started. (Those included : Dr Floyd and Emily Estes, Manuel and Alice Santana, Norman Lezin, Dr. Ruth Frary, Fr. Gerard Lasko, Dr Burney LeBoeuf, Ed Gaines, Rev. Herb Schmidt, and Dr. Paul Lee.

Our original incorporators were Paul Lee, Herb Schmid Gerard Lasko, Glen Martin, Ron Lau, Burney LeBoeuf, Ian McPhail, Jay Greenberg, and Robert Scott.)

The Beginning

On April Fools Day, 1970 we began. Our first project was the Whole Earth Restaurant. Great organic food was provided through the efforts of Sharon Cadwallader, Carol Teachout and staff. Campus Ministry had a central place to schedule speakers, and we had a counselling office above the Restaurant where we could meet, council, and strategize with students.

Affiliates

Then came several Affiliates with their own Board of Directors. These included the Campus Childcare center, Santa Cruz Community Switchboard, the Santa Cruz Food Project, The Santa Cruz Hostel Society, Camp Joy and the Santa Cruz Horticultural Society, Ecology Action Recycling Center, Group Homes, General Hardware and Feed.

Programs

In addition to Affiliates the USA Board developed a number of special programs such as the woman's media collective, a farm and garden workers training program, briar patch trust, a jail visitation program, a prison reform project, tenants' rights organization, special educational research projects, an alternate energy co-op, a proposal for senior citizens/student housing, and a number of others.

In 1975 perhaps the most important program that USA helped sponsor was the Community Congress which was composed of private non-profit corporations to review the county budget. Margaret Cheap was the Staff Coordinator for the Project. The county administrator had originally recommended $400,000 for nonprofits. After lobbying the county and carefully reviewing the budget $1,500,000 was designated for nonprofits in the county.

Pot, Acid and Parents

Our family came to Santa Cruz in the spring of 1960. As a young pastor who had just taught at one of our prep schools after Seminary I knew very little about marijuana and LSD. Oh yes I have taken a puff or two of weed but never could inhale so it never did me much good. There was a reason for that. When I was in prep school in the 40's the only time we underclassmen could smoke was on Good Friday and then the upperclassman would encourage us to go all out. We made ourselves corncob pipes and when we thought we were smoking the upperclassmen told us it was not smoking unless we inhaled. Of course, we did, and I have never been so sick in my whole life. That really made it impossible for me to receive the wonderful benefits of a hit.

In our parish, Messiah Lutheran Church on High Street we had a very active student group, and of course, they were involved in the beginning of the drug culture. In fact, it was a real problem with their parents who came down heavy on them and often forced many unfortunate alienating separations of parents from children.

Because of this I decided to host a forum entitled "Pot, Acid and Parents" so there could be better communication between parents and kids. I was able to contact the police department and they sent Lieutenant Overton to represent their point of view about the emerging drug culture. I did that to make sure the parents would come. Then I contacted my dear colleague and friend Dr. Paul Lee who had edited the Psychedelic Review at Harvard and had worked closely with Leary. Paul had just returned from a great LSD party in Marin County when LSD was still legal and the great San Francisco "Be In". I thought he might be someone to give a more nuanced view of what was happening in our culture.

At the forum I indicated my concern about the alienation between parents and children and encouraged openness, dialogue, and understanding. You can imagine what Lieutenant Overton had to say. He brought along different kinds of marijuana and other drugs and tried to scare people by telling them terrible horror stories. Then my colleague Dr. Lee presented another view. He shared a description of what happened in San Francisco and even had slides to give a vivid description of the event.

I thought the whole building would come down with the response that the parents made to his presentation. He barely escaped with his life. Young people tried to come to his rescue but to no avail. I realized what a horrible mistake I had made even though I had very good intentions. A few years later when I ran for school board you can imagine the publicity that my opposition developed over this unfortunate incident. Of course, I lost. So much for Pot, Acid and Parents!

Tuition Free

The words were clear, precise, and direct. "Dean, just remember that this University is to remain tuition Free! That's all made very clear in the California Master Plan for Higher Education." The speaker was Governor Pat Brown. Dean was Chancellor Dean McHenry the first UCSC Chancellor. The occasion was the official Site dedication of UCSC, April 17, 1964. The event happened near the present Cowell Courtyard. President Clark Kerr was there, and it had been rumored that President John F. Kennedy had been scheduled to be present. Of course, with his assassination the year before that was impossible. I had the privilege of opening the ceremony with an invocation and closing it with a Benediction. The Cal Berkeley Band was on hand to do the music and we ended the ceremony with the hymn "O God our Help in Ages Past, our Hope for years to come."

Fifty years later on the same date, April 17, 2014, at the anniversary of the event, I was again asked to say a prayer. Then a quick call and email came. Well, we didn't really mean a prayer but rather short reflection. Times certainly had changed and below are some of the words I spoke at that event. Of course, you can imagine the ad libs about the fear of the University hearing a prayer. The following is the end of my remarks:

Provost Crosby, Chancellor Blumenthal, Old Colleagues and friends:
... I'm here to give a short blessing, and I represent many different faith traditions in the University Interfaith Council, including even our secular student alliance, so how does one

pray or bring a blessing? The one spiritual practice that all religious traditions and people of faith without a religious tradition acknowledge and respect is silence. And so, as the gong sounds let us remember in silence, give thanks to God, or just give thanks for all the blessings of these past 50 years and resolve to be a blessing in the years to come. May the dreams of Clark Kerr and McHenry, and implemented by people like Page Smith, Hal Hyde, who is with us today, and so many others over these past 50 years continue to become a beacon for us in the future.

Before we pause for silence, permit me to offer a small "prophetic footnote." When I listened to the audio recording of Pat Brown 50 years ago I was impressed by his insistence on tuition free education. With today's astronomical student loans, it is important that we remember that the California Master Plan for Higher Education hoped to provide "Tuition Free" education for all. As we reflect to remember and celebrate the past 50 years and dream about the next 50 let's add this concern, This University should again be Tuition FREE. A tremendous challenge!

Then the gong and a moment of silence!

Herb Schmidt, Father Gerry Lasko, and Dr. Paul Lee in front of the Whole Earth Restaurant at UCSC which University Services Agency started on April Fools Day, 1970.

Photo courtesy of Herb Schmidt.

UCSC site dedication, April 17, 1964. Second from right: President Clark Kerr, Governor Pat Brown, Reverend Herb Schmidt at podium, Chancelor Dean McHenry.

Photo courtesy of Herb Schmidt.

308   Herb Schmidt

Chapter 13
Harry Noller:
Saxophones, Ribosomes and Santa Cruz

Growing up in the East Bay

My first awareness of hip culture came probably from my uncle, Freeman "Jim" Silva, who had been an art major at UC Berkeley in the 1930s. He was responsible for the invention of the half-time card stunts that involved synchronized participation by hundreds of fans at football games. He was a talented painter who got a job in the animation group at Disney Studios after he returned from the South Pacific after World War II, where he worked on such films as "Fantasia". He was a sort of Bohemian, who added an interesting dimension to conversations at the Thanksgiving dinner table. After he'd had a few beers, his very proper wife would try to shut him up, much to my disappointment. I ended up going to Berkeley (or "Cal", as everyone then called it) in 1956 to major in biochemistry. There seemed to be two dominant cultures - the leftists passing out copies of the Daily Worker at Sather Gate every morning, and the frat rats, grooming themselves to be corporate executives, while draining kegs of beer and vomiting on the front lawns of their fraternity houses. My heroes were the scientists, who had "split the atom" at the Rad Lab (now known as the Lawrence Berkeley National Laboratory) and who had "created life in the test tube" in Wendell Stanley's group at the Biochemistry and Virus Laboratory. I was appalled to watch the first televised congressional hearings, when Joseph McCarthy publicly slandered the nuclear physicist J. Robert Oppenheimer, who had directed the Manhattan Project that had in effect won the war in the Pacific Theater. I watched in horror as the despicable McCarthy attempted to bully the aloof, pipe-smoking Oppenheimer, accusing him of espionage.

But it wasn't long before the House Unamerican Activities Committee set up their hearings in the San Francisco City Hall, which in 1958 was only a leisurely 15-minute drive across the bridge from the Berkeley campus. Many Berkeley students made the drive to attend the hearings to see what they were like in person. They were surprised when they were denied entry to the hearings, discovering that the committee had stacked the audience with a HUAC-friendly crowd. In response, the students sat down in the hall outside the hearings and began singing folk songs. When the committee called for the SFPD to disperse them, they were attacked by the Tactical Squad with nightsticks and high-pressure fire hoses, dragging some of the students, including one pregnant woman, down several flights of marble stairs. The following day, about 200 students gathered in protest in Dwinelle Plaza on the Berkeley campus. Chancellor Clark Kerr ordered the campus police to disperse them, issueing what came to be known as the Kerr Directives, which forbid campus rallies without 24-hour prior approval from the Administration or publication of articles concerning off-campus political matters in the Daily Californian. The next day, deprived by Kerr of their first-amendment rights, the entire staff of the Daily Cal resigned, and the group of protesting students ballooned to more than 2000. Until this time, I had only heard of street protests in remote, exotic places like the Middle East; I was shocked to see massed protesters on my own campus. These events transformed the placid

Berkeley community overnight. A left-wing campus political party was formed, called SLATE, which ran a campaign that resulted in election of Dave Armour to Cal student-body president, displacing the fraternity-house establishment that had run campus politics for as long as anyone could remember. These events transpired at a time when relations between the students and the police, from both UC and Berkeley, had been friendly. (Of course, this all changed dramatically in the early 1960s.)

Off campus, in the surrounding town, Berkeley was complex, mysterious and entertaining. Telegraph Avenue was lined with book stores and cafés. Robinson's Cafeteria ("Robbie's") was one regular hipster hangout, with Horace Silver and the Jazz Messengers and other hard-bop heroes on the jukebox. On Thursday nights, legendary jam sessions took place at George's Northgate on Euclid, half a block from campus. We snuck in carrying our horns, hoping to sit in with some of the top musicians in the Bay Area, exposing ourselves to scary cutting sessions that became a strong motivation to go back home and woodshed. Sessions also sprung up across Euclid, downstairs at La Val's Cantina, where I first played with the tenor saxophonist Pharoah Sanders, recently arrived from Arkansas, known to us at the time as "Little Rock". He later moved to New York City to study with John Coltrane, and soon became Trane's star protegé. Other budding greats like the guitarist Ken Plourde, the brilliant young pianist John Burke, the trumpeter Joe Barrite, the bassist Barre Philips and the Pianist-composer Clare Fisher were regulars at Northgate and La Val's. Our usual drummer was Lawrence Bryggman, who later became a successful Hollywood television ("As The World Turns"), film ("Die

Hard With A Vengeance") and Broadway ("Twelve Angry Men", "RIchard III") actor.

Yet another level to Berkeley was its car culture. But unlike the rest of America, it was all about European sports and racing cars and motorcycles. CJ Motors, on Telegraph, was a major car hangout, a dealership for Triumph, Doretti, Lancia and other exotics, as well as Italian motorcycles. Years later, CJ Motors was transformed into a community market named CJ's Old Garage, where Berkeley hippies bought their brown rice. People like Stephen Griswold and Richard Cory were building and racing race cars fabricated in back yards behind old Victorian houses on Channing Way below Telegraph. We rode our motorcycles on the horse trails off of Grizzly Peak, sometimes riding nearly from Richmond all the way to Hayward, only using the pavement to cross between trails. If we got hungry in the evening, it was not unusual to jump into my TR3 and drive over the bridge to North Beach to the Dante Billiard Parlor (known as "Mike's Place" for some reason) for a bowl of their spectacular Minestrone.

In North Beach, the Beatniks were being chased out by the old Italian families who sensed that their community was being transformed by these people who didn't know how to behave. Many of them moved across the Bay to Berkeley, where they were welcomed as our gurus. Colorful people like Leonard Hull, a methedrine user known informally as Leonard the Locomotive, and his girlfriend Marilyn, could be mistaken for movie stars - Leonard in suit and tie and Marilyn in silk dress and high heels. Hube the Cube Leslie with his beret, beard and sandals had a day gig as an Authentic Beatnik, actually paid to sit in the window of Vesuvio's in North Beach to attract tourists. And Charles Yerby, who pioneered the introduction of peyote to the Berkeley community, visited the all-night supermarket at the corner of Adeline and Ashby to use their coffee-grinding facility to transform his dried peyote buttons into a powder that could be packed into gelatin capsules. Another interesting character was Maury Guy, the 6-foot-8 poet and Sanskrit scholar who introduced us to the Indonesian cult known as Subud (a contraction of *susila bhodi dharma),* which led you through a sort of communal trance called a *latihan.* Endless mysteries were waiting to be revealed in the dark corners of Berkeley neighborhoods.

Eugene, Cambridge, Geneva

In 1960, I was stunned to receive a telegram from the University of Oregon that I had been admitted to the graduate program in Chemistry, and that I would actually be *paid* $1500 per year as a teaching assistant! Eugene, Oregon turned out to be a kind of Northwest Berkeley. I soon began playing with a bebop group called the Jazz Prophets with the trumpeter Keith Johnson, at the Jazz Coffee House. I met Bob Richards, known in Tom Wolfe's book as The Mad Chemist, who drove down from Corvallis on weekends in his 2CV Citroën. I drove to Portland for weekend jam sessions in a basement bar, where I met many of the great Portland musicians. On weekends there were jam sessions at the Union Hall, where I met the guitarist Ralph Towner and the bassist Glen Moore, who later formed their famous group Oregon. I met the neo-Dada artists Jed and Ann Irwin, and the artist-filmmaker Ron Finne, and made experimental films with them that ended up being shown at the San Francisco Film Festival in 1965. And, oh yes, I did find time to work on my research. I did my graduate work in the newly founded Institute of Molecular Biology, where I was introduced to the culture of this rapidly-evolving and exciting new branch of science and got to hang out with some of the Gods of molecular biology. Francis Crick visited our Institute to tell us the latest news about the genetic code that was being unraveled even as he spoke to us. Toward the end of my graduate career, my advisor suggested that I should consider either Harvard or Cambridge for my postdoctoral research. The same week that I received news that I had received a postdoctoral fellowship from the National Institutes of Health to go to the MRC Laboratory of Molecular Biology in Cambridge, Benny Wilson invited me to go on the road with his blues band. I decided that I would probably find musicians to play with in Cambridge, but there would be little chance to do experiments on the road with Benny.

In the week before I left for Cambridge, I ran into Bob Richards in Berkeley, who invited us to join him on a drive to La Honda to visit Ken Kesey and his family. We found Kesey surrounded by a throng of what were starting to be called *hippies* - young longhaired people wearing tie-dyed clothes, seemingly advertising their drug usage. Several dangerous-looking members of the Hells Angels were hanging out in the front yard under the redwood trees surrounding Kesey's cabin. Behind the house was parked a gaudily-painted bus with the destination "Furthur" displayed over the windshield. That evening, raw 16mm film from the bus trip was projected on a sheet tacked to the living room wall, accompanied by non-synchronized tape recordings from the trip. The take-up reel drive on the projector was broken, so someone had to sit on a stool and wind the reel manually to keep the film from piling up on the floor. A small bowlful of amphetamines was thoughtfully provided on a table next to the projector. We slept in a small shed across from the cabin, where I found a diagram showing what must have been the plot line from Kesey's novel *Sometimes a Great Notion,* taped to the wall over a desk. The next morning, we followed Neal Cassady's beat-up Ford sedan up La Honda road to Alice's Restaurant on Skyline. Kerouac had marveled at Cassady's driving skills in *On The Road*; I watched with amazement as he took the corners like a Fangio, setting up the old Ford, with one dangerously wobbling rear wheel, on a smooth racing line, soon leaving Bob Richards's Volvo P122 far behind. We had breakfast with Cassady sitting at the counter, where he carried out multiple simultaneous high-speed conversations - with me, with the person sitting on the other side of him, with the waitress, and with people who were not there.

In Berkeley, I had met Tony Tanner, a British hipster friend of my friend Bob Orlins. Tony told me to be sure to look him up when I got to Cambridge. During my first month there, I remembered that he said he would be in King's College. I found him at King's, where he had become Head of English Studies, and an emerging authority on Saul Bellow. Tony invited me and my wife to a sherry party in his rooms in the 15th-century Gothic Revival building in Front Court at King's College. It was an intimidating event, jammed with brilliant students, Fellows, and faculty. I cowered in a corner with my glass of sherry, hoping not to have to speak to anyone. I realized my strategy had failed when I saw Sydney Brenner approaching. Sydney was generally regarded as the most brilliant of the scientists at the MRC, which included many Nobel laureates, of which Sydney would later become one. He said "I'm Sydney Brenner. *Who* are *you*?" He then asked what I was working on. When I replied, "Glyceraldehyde phosphate dehydrogenase", he said, matter-of-factly, "That's stupid. If you're a protein chemist, why don't you work on something interesting, like the ribosome." I was of course devastated, but couldn't get his words out of my head. I began asking about ribosomes, and learned that Alfred Tissières was starting a group in Geneva to study ribosomes.

By November, 1966, I found myself in Geneva, working with a bunch of mostly American postdocs; learning about ribosomes from them was like drinking from a firehose. Between gigs playing with the Jürg Lenggenhager Quartet, I began working on ribosomes in the supportive and stimulating environment of Alfred's lab. Two years later, I applied for academic positions in the U.S. and was invited for 8 interviews. My first was at the Albert Einstein College of Medicine in New York in April 1968. I had been living in the idyllic Swiss village of Hermance, at the French border on the south shore of Lac Léman, the lake formed by the headwaters of the Rhône and the background for the city of Geneva. I now sat in my host's office at the Einstein, which is located in the South Bronx, taking in the less-than-idyllic vista from his office window, my eyes fixed on two wheel-less cars sitting on a carpet of broken glass. I moved on to my next interviews as I traveled west across the country, accumulating some 6 job offers on my way, at places like Cold Spring Harbor Laboratory, St. Louis University Medical School, University of Chicago and UC San Diego. My final interview was at UC Santa Cruz. My only previous exposure to Santa Cruz had been driving through on my way to the Pebble Beach Road Races while in high school; I had no idea what to expect. I followed the map in my rental car to the UCSC campus and the Natural Sciences building. When I got out of the car, I had no idea even which direction to go; I was standing in a small parking lot completely surrounded by redwood trees.

"This is going to be an easy decision", I thought to myself. I don't think I paid any attention to what they told me about the university, what they would expect of me, or what was going on scientifically at UCSC. I eagerly accepted their offer, and prepared to return to my native land.

On the following weekend, I stopped in Golden Gate Park, where there was supposed to be a free concert. I was stunned by the spectacle, a vivid demonstration of how our culture had become utterly transformed during the brief two and a half years since I had left for Europe. Here were thousands and thousands of people, most of them stoned or getting stoned, as the San Francisco police looked on benignly. In the far distance, I could make out ten-foot-tall stacks of speakers, blasting ear-shattering rock music across the Great Meadow. I was looking forward to re-discovering America.

Santa Cruz
We moved from Hermance to Ben Lomond in November, 1968. We rented a 5-bedroom house, on 3 acres, for $150 per month. I rode my Honda 250 Super Hawk to campus every day over Empire Grade, inhaling the warm pine-scented perfume of the mountains on my way to work. The campus was in its fourth year, and I gradually realized that they were making it up as they went along. As a starting Assistant Professor, I was assigned five 5-unit classes, a teaching load about 5 times what was expected at other UC campuses. I was assigned to 8 faculty committees, and was made Chair of 5 of them, due to a shortage of senior faculty. During all this, I was going through a divorce, which left me with about $400 per month to live on. My lab and office were in a building called Nat Sci I, later to be named Thimann Laboratories. All the science faculty were housed in the same building, with almost all faculty offices on the 3rd floor - biologists, chemists,

physicists, and mathemeticians (including Ralph Abraham, with a huge photo of the headlight of his Norton Commando dominating his office) mixed in together. The house in Ben Lomond became a sort of commune, where I came home each night to discover people I had never seen before, sitting around making themselves at home - the girls combing their hair, the boys rolling joints. Although they were self-described vegetarians, my pathetic lone pork chop would often disappear under mysterious circumstances. There was an aging horse named Ben who grazed in a field above the house; I sometimes offered Ben a fresh carrot in exchange for a bareback ride through the woods just to escape the hippies. When UCSC hosted a film festival in 1971, the Provost of College 5 asked me to host a hipster named Jim Morrison and his girlfriend for dinner. My girlfriend and I accepted this chore, and found Morrison to be an intelligent and interesting dinner companion, more like a thoughtful graduate student than the wildman that he is often portrayed as. On another occasion, we were asked to take Linus Pauling and his wife to dinner. I was terrified to be sitting across from this scientific god, with his Nobel Prizes in both Chemistry and Peace. In fact, it was more like chaperoning a couple of horny teenagers, as these septuagenerians winked at each other, flirting their way through dinner. When the campus was small, there were opportunities to meet and hang out with fascinating artists and writers. A small group of faculty and students met with the science fiction master Robert Heinlein one afternoon in a small conference room in the library, where he discussed his writing, especially his new-age novel "Stranger In A Strange Land". We were surprised to learn that he was a local - a resident of Bonny Doon. Carlos Castaneda spent an afternoon with faculty and students in a classroom in College 5 (now Porter College), talking about his tales of Don Juan, including his books "A Separate Reality" and "Don Juan: A Yaqui Way of Knowledge". At a reception at Cowell College, I was surprised to learn that the gentleman I had been drinking wine with was the composer John Cage.

There was music everywhere in Santa Cruz. I began playing with the guitarist Dave Hollen, who introduced me to the Santa Cruz scene. First stop was the old Catalyst on Front Street, the creation of the wonderful Al di Ludovico. The Catalyst was a sort of café, in a space that had been an old family-style Italian restaurant, with faded murals and a back room set around a little fountain, sunlit by a big skylight. It was the vibrant center of Santa Cruz downtown life. Some of the tables had chessboards embedded in them, and games were often in progress. The legendary Tom Scribner, the retired Wobbly woodsman, would sit down amongst the customers and play some tunes on his saw. The evenings featured different entertainment on different nights, always free of charge. Silent movies were shown on one night, folk music on another. The famous Santa Cruz composer Lou Harrison even presented concerts of Chinese classical music, in costume, featuring his collection of antique Chinese instruments. Thursday nights were for jam sessions, where I met the local jazz musicians. When I first sat in, I was amazed by the virtuosic playing of a Chinese-American trumpet player, who sounded like Dizzy Gillespie. Afterwards, I asked, "Who was that?" One of the musicians replied, "Oh, that was Peter Chang - he's the D.A." Wow, I thought to myself, I have ended up in a town where the District Attorney plays jazz trumpet! Am I dreaming? Sadly, Al di Ludovico eventually sold the Catalyst, which in its subsequent transformation gradually lost its magic. It began to serve hard liquor, accompanied by the arrival of thuggish bouncers. The entertainment was no longer free, and the free-spirited hippie clientele were gradually diluted by the increasing presence of motorcycle gangs and other clashes with the culture of Mellow. Finally, the Catalyst moved to a former bowling alley on Pacific Avenue, where it became a commercial music venue, having finally lost all of its early innocence.

A more remote music venue was a place called Club Zayante, a ramshackle 2-story building tucked far back in the San Lorenzo Valley. You drove under the redwoods through narrow, twisting forest roads for many miles, until a row of parked VW microbuses finally signaled your destination. The music was eclectic and unpredictable. One night I remember arriving at Club Zayante to learn that the evening's headliner was a group featuring the brilliant Zap Comics cartoonist R. Crumb with his Cheap Suit Serenaders. Even more underground was another San Lorenzo Valley venue. On Thursday nights, for several decades, you were welcome to sit in at Max Hartstein's place in Brookdale. You took a right turn about a mile before the Brookdale Lodge, drove over the bridge and there was Max's garage, hanging over the San Lorenzo River. Max presided over what he called Perfect Music, featuring his ever-changing group, the 25th Century Ensemble. Max had been a professional jazz bassist in Europe and in the U.S., eventually gravitating to the Santa Cruz Mountains. Anyone who arrived at Max's garage was invited to join in. There was an astonishing mixture of types - talented professional jazz musicians, hippie guitar players, lost hitchhikers, homeless people, rock musicians, runaway teens, Earth Mothers, bad singers - you name it. Even if you had never played music in your life (and many clearly had not), Max would hand you an instrument. The result was mixed - sometimes amazing, at other times unlistenable. But Max recorded every note of every Thursday night for decades on his reel-to-reel Ampex tape recorder. There were stacks and stacks of tapes which you could find lining the walls of his garage, tip-toeing around the incredible sculpture Max called The Space Bass. Among the favorite downtown jazz venues was the Pearl Alley Bistro, an invitingly warm bar-restaurant, upstairs off the eponymous Alley. And the funky Crossroads in the Sash Mill, where Bradley Dupont's band Griffin made its debut, with the brilliant guitarist Gary Carpenter and the inimitable Willy Durbin on bass. With the pianist-composer Victor Spiegel and his group Dr. Bluejay and the New Mangoids, we played Kuumbwa.

There were many memorable gigs with the talented trumpet player and composer Randy Masters; the pinnacle was probably opening for the Duke Ellington Orchestra at the Del Mar Theater in 1974, only months before Duke passed away. We played at the front of the stage, while the Ellington Orchestra was set up behind the curtain. While we were playing, I vividly remember the excitement (and terror) of glimpsing legends like Johnny Hodges and Harry Carney backstage in their shirtsleeves. When the curtain finally opened, the band blasted "Take the A Train" into the Santa Cruz evening as the immaculate Duke strutted across the stage to a cheering audience. During one ballad, the tenor player Paul Gonsalves wandered into the audience and aimed his patented breathy, liquid sound into the ears of the young ladies. Randy took me backstage when he introduced himself to the Duke, who struck me as a dignified, patient and courteous gentleman. Another memorable concert was at the Civic Auditorium, with Bobby Hutcherson and Eddie Henderson. Randy's charts were musically challenging, written in odd meters like 7/4 and 11/4, in odd key signatures, with lots of sections and complex Latin or African rhythmic figures. On one gig, when Randy left the bandstand for a few minutes, I jumped at the opportunity to call "Body & Soul", just for the relief of playing a standard in 4/4; Randy was *not* amused.

When I started my lab at UCSC, I was approached by Bill Helfman, a 4th-year grad student whose adviser was leaving. He asked if he could finish his work on yeast DNA polymerase in my lab, rather than move in the middle of his thesis work, and so became a founding member of my lab. Bill became famous for his "bare-chest assays" on hot summer days, when he would do his research half-naked while singing in a florid Billy-Eckstein-like voice, ogling the young ladies as they walked past the lab. His buddy Bruce Aidells, another grad student in the Department, opened a restaurant on campus called Fat Albert's Rotunda, and then a deli called Sweet Adeline's in the Sash Mill downtown. During his postdoctoral stay in Europe, he decided that he was a "lousy biochemist, but a good cook", and returned to the Bay Area to make sausages. His sausage company was eventually bought out, whereupon he bought a small mountain in the middle of the Sonoma Valley, where he built a dream home where he now lives with his wife, the celebrity chef Nancy Oakes. My actual first graduate student was George Thomas, who grew up in a Basque family in San Francisco and had done his undergraduate work at UC San Diego. Among our daily adventures was growing bacterial cells in the fermenter on the roof of the lab. When I went to check on one of George's fermentations, he was in deep concentration, carefully adjusting the aeration and temperature. Lying across the floor, I noticed a rubber hose about 3 inches in diameter that I didn't remember us using. "George, what's this hose?", I asked. George shook his head "You got me." A few seconds later, the hose, which in fact had been our half-inch diameter air hose, suddenly exploded, sending us running for cover. Another student was Jim Hogan, who worked on cars and motorcycles, taught SCUBA diving and played City League softball, while occasionally working in the lab. He threw abelone barbecue parties at his cabin in Felton, where I witnessed the Toyota he had rescued from two identical Toyotas that had been totaled in front-end and rear-end collisions, respectively, by welding them together in his back yard. And William "Poindexter" Kennedy, who was detained with his girlfriend by the Santa Cruz Police for fornicating on someone's front lawn downtown one bright summer afternoon. We later discovered that he had also personally delivered his girlfriend's baby on a faculty member's desk in Thimann Labs in the middle of the night.

Another day, my postdoc Steve Douthwaite, a native of the Isle of Man, talked me into joining him at the California Superbike School at Laguna Seca, where the professional motorcycle racer Keith Code schooled us in the art of road racing. After this harrowing experience on a race-prepared Kawasaki Ninja 600R, my system had generated so much adrenaline that I didn't sleep for the next 48 hours. Another daredevil postdoc was Sarah Gerhardt, an internationally renowned champion surfer, featured in numerous surf movies, and one of the few women to brave Maverick's. More laid-back was my student Chuck Merryman, who literally began sleeping in the lab; one morning, I heard a sudden scream from a student who had discovered Chuck's bare feet and ankles protruding from a small curtain he had hung over the kick-space in his lab bench. Another day in the life of the Ribe Tribe.

Over the years, many foreign postdocs came to work in the lab. The wonderful Alexei Mikhailovich Kopylov came to us from Moscow State University with a fellowship from the then Soviet Union. On the way back from picking him up at SFO, I pointed out some Porsches and Ferraris roaring around us on the highway near Los Gatos. He nodded and announced, "Yes - we have the same." The day after his arrival, an FBI agent knocked on my office door. After my initial shock, he explained that this was just a routine visit, and that I should just let him know if Alexei did anything strange that might suggest that he was a Soviet spy. "Oh, that", I said, and thanked him for the warning. Most notable was Jürgen Brosius, an amazing postdoc whom I had met during my sabbatical at the Max Planck Institute in Berlin. Jürgen was fascinated by our Siamese cat, whom we called Little Cat. Jürgen quickly re-named him Kleine Katze, or K. Katze for short. I was baffled by his adulation of cats, and told him "Let's put it this way, Jürgen: K. Katze is not being nominated for a Nobel Prize anytime soon." Jürgen thereupon insisted that we acknowledge K. Katze "for discussions" in all of our published papers from then on. When Jürgen created the first recombinant DNA plasmid expressing an entire ribosomal RNA operon, he named it "pKK3535", the "KK" for our cat, and "3535" for an X-rated German joke. Jürgen's plasmid has since become internationally famous, used in labs world-wide, but few can appreciate its derivation.

One day, our computer programmer Bryn Weiser came to my office with a request. "The Poi Dogs are short a player for our game tonight at 7:45; can you play outfield for us?" I said "Sure", without thinking it through carefully. I had never played serious softball, let alone City League ball against serious teams of young, aggressive jocks. I borrowed my son Django's baseball glove, and found myself standing under the lights in left field at De Laveaga Park in my tennis shoes on a windy night following a light rain. Sure enough, the first batter hit a high fly ball to left field, nearly disappearing into the dark sky above the lights. As I ran up on it, a gust of wind brought it back toward me, and I soon realized it was now over my head. I slid in my tennis shoes on the wet grass, caught myself and backed up in a panic. At the last instant I reached back and caught the ball in the webbing of my glove. I basked in a wave of love from my new teammates, and became a Poi Dog that night, at age 50. At the next game, the umpire, a compact guy with a huge red beard, stood on the pitcher's mound before the start of the game, pulled out a harmonica, and played a solemn rendition of "The Star Spangled Banner". Our team captain was the amazing Scott Milrod, our gifted long-haired shortstop, a contractor from Bonny Doon. Scott created and enforced the Poi Dog culture: We are there to play hard and have fun. Although the Poi Dogs have indeed won some City League championships, they have also lost many games. At the championship game at the end of one summer season, the Poi Dogs finished second, against a particularly aggressive opponent. After it was all over, Jay, the legendary City League umpire, handed Scott a big cardboard box. Inside were a dozen beer mugs with the engraving "Santa Cruz City League Champions". As he turned away, Jay nodded toward the opposing dugout and muttered, "Those guys are a bunch of jerks."

The Jürg Lenggenhager Quartet, exposing the guests at a society party in Cagne-sur-Mer in the South of France to free jazz, as reported in the Nice-Matin in the summer of 1967.

The author (soprano sax) with Victor Spiegel (piano), circa 1977.

The author in his new lab at UCSC in the winter of 1969.

Above: The author, on sabbatical at the MRC Cambridge in 1976, holding up an autoradiogram of one of the first DNA sequencing gels.

At left: The Poi Dogs after a game at De Laveaga Park.

Part 5
THE SAN LORENZO VALLEY

Chapter 14
Fred McPherson:
The Evolution of Environmental Activism in the San Lorenzo River Watershed from the Late 1960s into the1980s.

Introduction and Return to UCSC

During the tumultuous social and political times of 1969-70, a blessed life-transforming event occurred in my life. In the late evening of July 28, 1970 my daughter was born. With me acting as her support, my wife Roberta gave birth at our home in Boulder Creek with the support of a small group of close friends and family present. The birth experience was such a miracle and the coming of this new life into the our lives and the lives of our family, friends, and community was such a joy that all of the tumultuous affairs swirling around us in the world and my personal life seemed to melt away with the love and hope that her life brought. Those stories of the time before the birth and the birth are told elsewhere in Santa Cruz Hip History I and II. This story is about what came next. That powerful birth energy changed the way that I perceived and experienced the world and awoke my deep desire for a better, safer, survivable life. I can now see, looking back, that this new magical being and life force motivated and inspired me in a new reenergized direction for my life.

It was easier to get by economically in the early 70s. Rent was much cheaper, food was cheaper and there was often surplus food that you could get by gleaning the fields and the backs of markets and fruit stands. A few part-time jobs got us by for the summer, but as fall approached I decided to go back to talk to Carl Tjerandsen, my old Dean at UCSC Extension. A lot of changes had taken place at UCSC over the summer since Earth Day1970. The campus shut downs at UCSC, UC Santa Barbara and UC Berkeley had ended with the summer break. The UCSC Extension offices were moved from their old welcoming community location at the entrance to the Campus in the old Cowell Ranch Cook House to the recently completed cold, cement Applied Science II building in the upper campus, and the Cook House was taken over by the campus police. I was hoping that I could at least get my old job back teaching environmental classes. I was apprehensive to do this, but I thought that the worst that would happen was that he would still see me as a threat of some sort and say no.

I was pleasantly surprised that we had a polite conversation and he was willing to let me teach classes again for Extension on a contract basis, with the provision that I focus on classes that were natural history oriented, and stay out of teaching what he thought of as politically oriented ecology classes. He suggested that I teach about the kinds of natural vegetation and wildlife areas that occur in the UCSC service areas on both the Monterey Bay and San Francisco Bay sides of the Santa Cruz Mountains. This helped begin my lifetime interest and teaching career in the natural history of the Santa Cruz mountain range, that continues to this day.

At the time, there were no real maps or descriptions of the ecosystems of the Santa Cruz Mountains. The closest thing to such an ecological overview perspective were the plant community descriptions provided in Munze's *A California Flora*, John Thomas's book *The Flora of Santa Cruz Mountains,* and Robert Ornduff's

Introduction to California Plant Life. Even though these plant community classification systems included habitat (physical environment) descriptions in their name, like Freshwater Marsh for example, there was then as now some argument as to whether plant communities really exist. I combined this information about the Santa Cruz Mountains plant communities with newer information provided in the latest text book *Fundamentals of Ecology* by Odum that I had used in college and included information about the concept of ecosystem and came up with, or chose to use, the term and phrase "Biotic Communities." Biotic communities are the living part of an ecosystem that also includes the non-living parts of the ecosystem. This term was acceptable to the Dean and the academic community on campus at the time. My first class offering for UCSC Extension that fall of 1970 was "The Biotic Communities of the Santa Cruz Mountains." The class was a success and a lot of fun and the income it provided along with some other part-time odd jobs got us by financially for our first fall and winter with our new daughter.

By the next year my teaching career at Extension had expanded into offering two classes: "Biotic Communities of the Santa Cruz Mountains East Side" and "West Side." I also started teaching a Coastal Redwood Forest Ecology class. As I continued to explore the area and learn more, I was allowed to work as a program coordinator again on a "contract basis" and to set up conferences and many other new classes in the areas of Natural History, Biology, Ecology, Education and Horticulture. Sometimes I would set up classes or conferences for someone else, like a UCSC faculty member or someone in the community who was qualified and wanted to offer programs like Horse

Herd Management, The Undersea World of the Scuba Diver, Birds of the Central Pacific Flyway, The World of Algae, Mammals of the Sea, Introduction to Marine Ecology, The Ocean and Man, Ecology of the Sierra Biotic Communities, Biology of Cancer, The Challenge of the Changing Universe, Guided Tour of the Heavens and many others. Other times I was given a free hand to offer programs that I thought would be of timely interest and value to the community in the areas that I was passionate about (as long as they made money), like Starting the Organic Garden, Winter Care of Fruit Trees, Winter/ Spring Organic Gardening, Plant Propagation Principles and Practices, Death Valley Spring Field Adventure, South San Francisco Baylands Ecosystems, Rivers and Streams of the Santa Cruz Mountains, and many others. These classes were popular and considered a success for the university because they did a little bit better than breaking even economically.

I enjoyed this kind of work because it used my past college background and teaching experience in Biology, Ethology, Ecology and Science education and applied it to the needs and interests of our local community in the form of practical field natural history and ecology classes that I loved to teach. It was not full-time work and there were no benefits, but it was very rewarding, and it paid the bills. Even though it was not ideal, it left me time to be with my new family a lot of the time and play music with the 25th Century Ensemble on Thursday nights and at various community benefits and events.

The Revised Santa Cruz County General Plan for the San Lorenzo Valley

One day, Jim Franks, one of the other program coordinators that worked in the Community Services Dept. of UCSC Extension, took me aside and asked me if I had seen the 1967 adopted Santa Cruz County General Plan for the San Lorenzo Valley. He knew that I was interested in environmental issues and lived in Boulder Creek. Jim showed me an impressive 43-page document that had a very attractive cover with redwoods on it, nice large black and white photos, and fold out maps inside the cover. It seemed very professional and well thought out, until he started going through it with me and explaining what the various proposed changes to the transportation system, housing zoning, sewer systems, water storage facilities, etc. meant and what effects it would have on the San Lorenzo River and our forested mountain landscapes. It turned out to be a very pro-growth plan for the San Lorenzo Valley that called for an expressway to Boulder Creek on the east side of the river, a sewage line along lower San Lorenzo River and Highway 9 down to the Santa Cruz treatment plant, dams on the major tributaries of the San Lorenzo River and large increases in population densities (see *San Lorenzo Valley General Plan Santa Cruz County*, Livingston & Blaney, Dec.1967).

I was overwhelmed with sadness to see these plans for the same kind of devastating, large-scale, urban development for the home that I had found for me and my family in the San Lorenzo Valley, as I had seen engulf the San Fernando Valley in smog and track home sprawl where I had grown up. Jim told me that there was going to be a Citizens Review Committee meeting to review this General Plan in September of 1972 in Felton and suggested that I might like to consider attending. He gave me the plan to review further and some suggestions about how to get involved in the political process of approving or changing it. I began to show everyone I knew the proposed plan and get their help and commitment to coming to the meetings to stop the plan from being approved. Max Hartstein, Sharon Cadwallader, Pat and Nancy Bisconti, Dick and Margaret Smith, and other members of the 25th Century Ensemble like musicians Don McCaslin, Sterling Storm (part of the Humans) were very supportive and helpful in getting organized. People in the San Lorenzo Valley and from other environmental/community groups rallied and came to the public meetings to help prevent the proposed plan from being adopted.

When the Santa Cruz County San Lorenzo Valley General Plan revision meetings were finally held at the San Lorenzo Valley High School in Felton, it turned out to be a large, heated, democratic process. The first large meetings were very tumultuous and required the sheriff's help to maintain order. After some heated discussion, new direction of facilitation and committee structure were adopted and Fred Gordon, one of our local dentists, was elected group facilitator. Citizen committees for various focuses of community interest were formed. The new land-use planning process proposed and adopted by the Citizen's Review Committee is now taken for granted and used routinely throughout our county and elsewhere, but at the time the new process stood in stark contrast to the planned proposals and economic interests described in the report and illustrated on the map.

One of the new committees formed was the

Environmental Quality Control Committee. I was elected the chairperson and Max Hartstein was elected the co- chairperson. There were many well-informed, dedicated people on the committee who took part in the discussions. New comers and old-timers from the community contributed their valuable opinions and information and there were people from all walks of life, including artists, musicians, and dancers who had not been involved in local community politics before. John Stanley, naturalists, other scientists and I contributed many useful perspectives and organizational skills from the newly emerging fields of environmental planning.

After almost a year of research, meetings and discussions, our committee made many recommendations, which were presented to the larger General Plan Group, and eventually incorporated into the final revised Santa Cruz County General Plan for the San Lorenzo Valley (Fifth District) and presented to the Santa Cruz County Board of Supervisors. It was adopted by the Board of Supervisors in October or November 1972. The new plan was a dramatic revision of the older plan and eventually resulted in a plan for the Valley's future that was more realistic, sustainable and survivable.

The following is a summary of the Environmental Quality Control Committee report that was presented.

ENVIRONMENTAL QUALITY CONTROLS SUBCOMMITTEE INTERIM REPORT

Due to time limitations imposed by the deadline put upon the Committee to revise the San Lorenzo Valley Master Plan, we feel it is of primary priority and importance to make a set of standards, guidelines, and recommendations, which will solve the problems we have inherited from the past.

It is for us who live here now and know firsthand these problems to recommend a future pattern, which will not further upset the life-support system of our San Lorenzo Valley. It is of utmost need and importance to solve the problems inherited from the past before we can safely advance into large-scale development of the Valley for the future.

Therefore, these are the recommendations and standards that are most urgently needed to relieve our present spiraling pollution syndrome. Through the implementation of these recommendations, we feel our community will find its way to a survivable natural future, able to enjoy the great natural heritage of our Valley.

Recommendations

I. Moratorium on future development until therecommendations are adopted and implemented.

II. Drinking Water

A. Evaluate the impacts of taking more water out of the San Lorenzo River in the driest times of year on fish and other wildlife populations. Do a river resource management plan.

B. Conserve water by repairing all existing leaks in pipes, tanks, and other reservoirs and replace any facilities contaminated with lead or other contaminates.

C. Use water from Loch Lomond Reservoir primarily for Santa Cruz domestic use.

III. Sewage Report

A. We must repudiate Bowen & Williams Sewage plan for the San Lorenzo Valley for these reasons:

1. It pipes water out of the Valley, subsequently lowering the water table, eventually completely depleting it;

2. The Santa Cruz system is presently insufficient

in handling its own sewage;

    3. It would further pollute the ocean (Monterey Bay).

    B. Instead, we recommend small local sanitation district systems, only where needed and installed on the authority of the Santa Cruz Health Department and community to solve the obvious existing pollution problems and syndrome presently being created (seek Federal, State, and County funds to help finance). Recycle the effluent from all local septic systems back into the water table in appropriate ways in regards to geology, hydrology and sanitation.

  IV. San Lorenzo River Riparian Corridor

    A. Establish wildlife refuge corridor along the San Lorenzo River and its tributaries.

    B. Eleven related recommendations to identify, inventory, protect and monitor the San Lorenzo River riparian corridor ecosystem. (See report a-k for full details.)

  V. Energy

    A. Do not build the proposed Davenport Nuclear Power plant. (See reasons and alternatives mentioned in the report.)

  VI. Land Use Management

    A. Inventory of all lands in terms of their environmental characteristics and natural resource values.

    B. Evaluate which lands are suitable for certain uses and not for others.

    C. Calculate carrying capacities of the various ecosystems present in the Valley based on the social value of the resources and their susceptibility to human impact.

D. Do cost and benefit analysis of any proposed future development in terms of environmental and sociological benefits and impacts.

The Save San Lorenzo River Association

At the conclusion of the presentation of the revised San Lorenzo Valley General Plan to a large public meeting at San Lorenzo Valley High School in Felton, a small group of Environmental Quality Control members were hanging around in the parking lot after the meeting talking about how we could make sure that these recommendations, especially about the river, were adopted and incorporated into county laws and programs. Other groups of General Plan participants were forming to take on projects and political campaigns, like running a candidate for Supervisor and having a group to advocate for clean drinking water, but there was a consensus among our small group that there ought to be an organization that would be an advocate for a clean healthy river. This was the unofficial beginning of "Save San Lorenzo River Association" John Muir style. John Stanley and Max Hartstein each gave $5.00 to me and said, "Fred, you are the Treasurer of our new organization, 'Save San Lorenzo River Association.' " I agreed to be the first Treasurer and John Stanley, "volunteered" to be the first President to get things started.

After many meetings at John and Hillary Stanley's house in Boulder Creek to talk about how we could help protect the river and implement many of the recommendations from the Revised General Plan, we began to clarify our goals and get organized. We designed a logo with the help of Diana Troxell, spread the word about our new group and its purpose, put out a little newsletter, made T-shirts and bumper stickers that said "Save San Lorenzo River." More people became interested and got involved, and with a lot of work by Mary Hammer and others we filed the official papers of incorporation. The Save San Lorenzo River Association was officially started and incorporated in June of 1973. Officers were elected and committees formed.

Many of our first activities were educational, designed to inform people about the ecology and environmental resource management issues confronting the San Lorenzo River. We published and distributed a series of fact sheets about the river with topics such as "Coliform (bacteria) Pollution and Rainfall," "Rainfall in the Santa Cruz Mountains," "Steelhead Fishing," "Siltation Problems and Land Use." We also had an education committee that organized community events and held children's story times and river explores at the river (Judy Robinson [Belden], Nancy Ellis, Anne Gulliver, and Mary Hammer worked on many of these educational programs and issues). Alvin Young, one of our earliest presidents, was an avid trout fisherman who was deeply concerned about the plight of the salmon and steelhead in the river. He got steelhead fishermen involved with our conservation issues not only by helping to write the Steelhead Fact Sheet, but also by distributing it to fishermen along the river, and placing it on their windshields parked along highway 9 and at California Trout meetings.

John Stanley, Al and Su Haynes, Mary Hammer and I helped draft proposed new county ordinances to better address current river conservation problems like riparian corridor habitat destruction, septic pollution and siltation from improper grading and logging operations.

Al Haynes helped to find State Fish and Game funding to create a San Lorenzo River Watershed Management Plan. It was prepared by Santa Cruz County's Watershed Management Office under California State Department of Fish & Game's *Protected Waterways Program*. John Ricker was one of the watershed analysts and lead writer for the plan. John Stanley and I from Save San Lorenzo River Association made many comments and suggestions during the writing process and I contributed some of my photos of the river from various field trips. After a first draft of the plan was written, it was introduced in the spring of 1979 at various public presentations held in the valley. Despite the disfavor of the majority of County Supervisors, the plan was adopted in 1980 because they felt compelled to adopt it because of its large public support. It was the first river watershed management plan of its kind in the State. It still needs on-going updates, but it serves us well to this day.

Some of the other big projects the Save San Lorenzo River Association took on included:

1. Stopping the proposed Zayante Dam. There was a Santa Cruz City proposal to build a dam on Zayante Creek, several miles above the store. It would have created a new reservoir about three times the size of Loch Lomond for the Santa Cruz City water supply. Tom Louagie, the owner and manager of the Zayante Club, my adult school river class, and musicians Jack Bowers and Jill Croston (Lacy J. Dalton) did benefits to raise money to stop the dam project from going forward until we could insist on an Environmental Impact Report (EIR) to asses the actual impacts of the large project. Eventually the project was rejected by the City because of environmental impacts on the fish populations, safety risks associated with the active Zayante Fault that ran through the dam area, and increases in cost estimates. There were also legends of a rare and endangered Zayante Hump Backed Banana Slug in the area that may have had something to do with slowing down the approval process.

2. Nancy Ellis led a campaign to stop the City of Santa Cruz Water Department and Director Morris Allen from over

drafting river water at the newly installed inflatable diversion dam near Henry Cowell Redwoods State Park in Felton. When first installed, it reduced the flow of the river to a small trickle and almost dried it up, which prevented enough water from going back into the river to provide for the survival of fish and other species. Nancy and others went back and forth to the State Water Control Board hearings in Sacramento with our documented evidence that eventually led to new mandated limits on minimal flows.

3. We were advocates for the establishment of a new Santa Cruz County Park, in Ben Lomond at the site of the Nasser Estate that came up for sale (now known as Highlands Park). After the proposal for the park was adopted, our group volunteered to be part of the park planning process and to help design and build an educational River Nature Trail and Interpretive Kiosk along the river and the riparian forest flood plain. We also published an illustrated River Trail Guide for the new trail.

When the park was first opened, we had a fall "Steelhead Festival" to commemorate the founding of the trail. It was one of the small proto-community festivals at the park that later morphed into the bigger Redwood Mountain Faire that was held at Highlands Park for many years

4. Anne and Ralph Gulliver and others began a recycling program twice a month behind the Boulder Creek Burl Theater. Because I was president of the Save San Lorenzo River association in 1978, Anne Gulliver asked me to volunteer to help on Saturdays at the recycling operation and use my truck to take materials down to the Ecology Action recycling center on 17th Avenue in Santa Cruz. At first, I think that we only did recycling every other week, or once a month. The Ecology Action folks gave us large containers and a glass smashing tool. I used my truck. (The yellow and

white "thunder truck" that got wrapped around a redwood tree in the 1982 mud slide in our canyon.) We separated materials, crushed bottles and aluminum cans, and put them into separate containers. Various colored glass went into different round barrels in the back of the truck and then we crushed up the glass with a crushing tool. We wore safety goggles, of course. I remember that my daughter Kusum, who was about 7 or 8 years old and Roberta helped with this sometimes. Kusum enjoyed it, but I would not let her get too close when we were crushing up the glass because it seemed too dangerous. From about 1977-78 it sort of became the president's "job" to recruit volunteers and help coordinate the recycling activities along with Anne and Ralph. Not too long after we started, someone from Ecology Action began coming up to Boulder Creek with a larger flatbed truck and more large containers to take away recycled materials. Even though it was fun to take part in this important community activity, it was a relief to me and my family when Ecology Action took over the trucking because there were so many other family activities that I wanted to take part in on Saturdays. I was very happy when Ecology Action and the Valley Women's Club took over this operation in about 1979.

Save San Lorenzo River Association: Headwaters to Downtown Santa Cruz

In addition to what I was doing at UCSC and with the Save San Lorenzo River Association, I was able to introduce people to the Natural History and Ecology of the San Lorenzo River and its entire watershed by creating River Ecology classes through the San Lorenzo Valley School District Adult School program from about 1974-1976. The adult school classes also helped me earn some part-time income in a right livelihood fashion and brought me into contact with many other people interested in working on river issues upstream and downstream. I taught the adult school classes until the entire adult school program was discontinued in the wake of the passage of Prop.13 that severely cut funds to this kind of adult community education.

These SLV adult school classes consisted of a a small group of about 10-15 interested students who met about once a week nearly year round. We went on local walks in the San Lorenzo Valley to get to know more about the ecology and natural history of the river as well as other biotic communities of the area, exploring and taking photos of representative sections of the length of most of the San Lorenzo River, from the headwaters to the river mouth. Gary Lutteringer, Nancy Ellis, who were members of the class and I built up a nice collective slide show about the San Lorenzo River, and then shared it with each other and the public at a number of community events. Many of these students went on to become dedicated environmental activists.

Around 1978 I also began to work with Page Smith, Paul Lee, Bob Hall and others who were interested in the San Lorenzo River as it passed through the City of Santa Cruz to the Lagoon and then out to sea at the river mouth. Page Smith and Paul Lee had established the William James Association and work company, one of their projects, in Santa Cruz and also held Penny University discussions at the back of the Pergolesi Coffee House in Santa Cruz. There were usually interesting, lively meetings, sometimes yelling over the din of the espresso machines in the background. Bob Hall, a member of the Santa Cruz Chamber of Commerce, also attended the Penny University meetings and had a loosely affiliated down town group of Save San Lorenzo River Association that had a small newsletter and took on various projects about the river. I would meet with that group from time to time for "upstream- downstream" coordination of events and political activities involving the San Lorenzo River. Often some of the past and present UCSC staff including Mary Holmes, Todd Newberry, and others, who had known Page and Paul at UCSC, would drop in to add to the discussion.

Malcolm MacAfee and others from Paideia, a state approved alternative university, also dropped in from time to time to update us on the state-wide activities of their community-based university. A loose affiliation between the William James Association, Paideia and the Penny University became a kind of center for Central Coast activities. There were many others who knew and loved the river who would show up with stories and ideas. I would update the group about what was going on up in the Valley, show slides of what we were learning and doing on our river fieldtrips, and invite those who were interested to join us on some of the fieldtrips. Page joined us at the river in Paradise Park several times.

Eventually, this led to the idea of my pursuing a Ph.D. program with Page through Paideia that focused on the Ecology of the San Lorenzo River. In addition to the dialogue at the Penny University, the project involved making and showing a river watershed slide show and writing a thesis about the whole watershed that compared the community values and perceptions of the river and its problems, between people who lived upstream in the San Lorenzo Valley with downstream Santa Cruz residents. In the winter of 1978, at a statewide meeting at Fort Mason in San Francisco, I received my Ph.D. in General Studies–Human Ecology. I gave a presentation that included a slide show and many of those present as well as back at the Penny University signed my diploma.

There was, and still is, a big difference between the upstream and downstream populations of people in terms of their perceptions of the river and how they relate to and use the river as it runs through their communities. Even though it is one river and one interrelated watershed, it is often used in different every day ways and perceived differently politically. When these two groups are brought together in a common cause, very wonderful, powerful things can happen, especially in political ways. This is particularly true in the Santa Cruz County's 5th District, where these two groups are often separated in people's mind by about 15 miles of mountainous topography and curvy roads.

One of the other events that took place during this time was the Pat Liteky/Ron Lang river walk. Pat Liteky (one of our environmental quality control committee members had decided to run for County Supervisor for the 5th District in the up-coming election against Vince Locatelli. Much has been written elsewhere about this political contest, including in Randal Brown's *History of the San Lorenzo Valley Water District*.

Faithful to the goals of our committee and with the help and support of our local embattled Fish and Game warden Ron Lang (who could officially carry a gun), we embarked on a river walk from about Ben Lomond to Santa Cruz as part of a citizen survey of the river to accompany Ron on his annual survey of conditions in the San Lorenzo River. Some of us had cameras. It turned out to be a pretty demanding, arduous adventure, in and out of the river in some very slippery areas. By the time that we had walked in the river and along the river all the way down through the Gorge, Paradise Park and Sycamore Park, I for one was very tired. When we got to Santa Cruz, we were met by reporters and supporters with refreshments and first aid. We were able to document and talk about many areas of erosion and pipes from washing machines and other drains emptying into the river in the urban areas and note stream-bed conditions and numbers of small fish found on our walk. Fortunately, we also had some good support from Save San Lorenzo River Association downstream and great press coverage in the Sentinel. The results of this survey were included in Ron Lang's official Fish and Game annual report for the San Lorenzo River. Probably more important than the actual report and documentation was the press coverage that was given to the walk that demonstrated the sincerity and commitment to the issues of the river by Pat Liteky, as a candidate. The river walk and other factors contributed to a tremendous political upset and Pat Liteky won the election.

One of the other great downstream events of that time was the River Encampment at San Lorenzo Park. Page, Paul and others planned the event in order to draw attention to the river, its natural beauty as an environmental and cultural resource as well as its problems. It took place on the river flood plain bench lands, just below the County Building in Santa Cruz. It was intended to be a two-day encampment with meetings, discussion groups and fieldtrips about the river as it passed through the City of Santa Cruz under the guidance of various experts familiar with the river's downtown environment. The sharing of a meal at the end of the first day, an overnight campout for those who wanted to spend the night, and then fieldtrips on the following day were all part of the plans.

I attended the first day events with some of my students and family and every thing went well. A substantial number of people accepted the invitation including a number of City and County department heads. Page's wife Eloise Smith and others made a large pot of "Brunswick Chicken Stew" and we had a nice little potluck meal centered around the stew in the picnic area that overlooked the river near the children's playground area. Most people went home as the sun set, but a few wanted to spend the night. I do not know the details of what happened, but the park sprinklers ended up being turned on in the middle of the night, and that ended the sleep over.

The next day a river walk scheduled for 9:30 am attracted some twenty-five people. Its leaders were Leo La Porte who spoke on the topography and people, Gary Griggs on the geological aspects of the river, and Ken Burland, an authority on water quality who had done a chemical analysis of the river with one of his students who was also there. Also on hand was Todd Newberry, a biologist and bird expert with strong environmental interests. Ron Lang of the State Fish and Game Department joined us and made valuable contributions. Much of the discussion centered on the problem of flooding and what could be done to lessen flood hazard without constantly disturbing the delicate ecology of the riverbed.

The encampment raised a lot of interest in the river and drew more people into the discussions and activities at the Penny U. After that event, the focus of the dialogue began to be more and more on what could be done to restore and rejuvenate the San Lorenzo River from an environmental and social point of view as it passed through the man-made levies built by the Corp of Engineers to protect the city of Santa Cruz after the disastrous flood of 1955.

This culminated in the Santa Cruz City Restoration Plan for the San Lorenzo River that was finished around 1979. This is also the same year that Bruce Van Allen was elected to the City Council, running on a political platform that included the adoption and implementation of the River Restoration Plan. Bruce went on to become Mayor of Santa Cruz and a leading advocate for the river. The development and implementation of this plan is a story that goes on to this day and deserves its own telling at another time. There are some posters, newsletters, photos, links, and graphic materials about this era on our Hip History Santa Cruz Website: https://hipsantacruz.org/

This is also about the time that Save San Lorenzo River Association upstream became less active and sort of morphed into a part of the environmental activism of the newly formed Valley Women's Club. Another story about this is included in this book by Nancy Macy.

There were many other issues and projects that came up for the Save San Lorenzo River Association and deserve a whole story unto themselves. Perhaps one day someone will have the time and interest to research this history in more detail. Anne Gulliver was our first secretary and served for many years as such. She kept minutes and other documents and left a large box of these documents with the special collections library at UCSC when she retired as secretary in 1979 or 1980.

Fred in the San Lorenzo river.

Chapter 15
Roberta McPherson:
From Marin County to the San Lorenzo Valley, 1964-1980

In 1964 when I graduated from Tamalpais High School in Mill Valley, California, the biggest concerns I had in life were keeping my grades up, going to high school football and basketball games with my friends, and trying to figure out how to back-comb my baby-fine hair so that it stood up into a "bubble," the popular hairstyle of the day.

Soon after graduation, my family moved to Skyline Boulevard near Skylonda. I found myself wanting to experience life outside the confines of school and opted not to go to college. I enrolled in secretarial courses at College of San Mateo, the local community college (which at that time was referred to as a "junior college") and spent the next year and a half learning short hand, typing, how to use a Dictaphone, and a bunch of other incredibly useful skills that have stood me in good stead to this very day. During summer vacations, I worked in the secretarial pool at Stanford Linear Accelerator Center transcribing long, involved papers written by physicists whom I never met.

When I finished, I was able to get a job as secretary to the president of a small venture capital corporation in Palo Alto and, at the age of 20, moved into a nice little apartment in a small four-plex not far from work. I earned $425 a month and paid $89 a month rent. The cost of living was minimal and most everyone could afford a place to live and food to eat.

Not long after that, I met Fred McPherson, and within

a couple of years, we were living together in a little cabin in the redwoods of Boulder Creek, a sleepy little town a few miles inland from Santa Cruz with no bus service and two small grocery stores. I commuted over the hill to Palo Alto and Fred taught Biology at Pacific High School up on Skyline. It was through Fred's connection with Pacific High that I met a beautiful woman named Patti, an art teacher at the school, who later changed her name to Raven Lang. Fairly well along in her pregnancy, I felt an urge to serve her in some way without really understanding how to do that. She was a vibrant woman of expansive energy and looking back now, it feels like no coincidence that my introduction to pregnancy and birth came through her. Her pioneer work in the field of midwifery and home birth would later help countless women and men over many generations through the transformative mystery of birth.

Soon after moving to Boulder Creek, Fred, who grew up in a musical family, met Max Hartstein, a talented bass player, who opened up his studio once a week to anyone who wanted to come and play "perfect music." Everyone was welcome to participate and there were no wrong notes. I began experiencing new aspects of myself, allowing the music to transport me into the realm of dance. Many of the same people who came to Max's studio would sometimes come together at the home of Mike Walker in Santa Cruz to play music, dance and share delicious potluck feasts, as well as traveling to expansive mountain-top fields off of Empire Grade and elsewhere for full moon festivals.

Fred's job at Pacific High School ended and I stopped commuting over the hill. Back then we could live our lives pretty simply without having to worry too much about money, because it didn't take much to make ends meet. Fred began teaching part-time at UCSC in the winter of 1969 as well as doing part-time gardening work, and I spent a couple of days a week setting type on a Justo Writer for the Mid-County Journal in Aptos. That was enough to meet the mortgage, pay the bills, and buy food.

Our friends began having babies, many of them choosing to have home births, inspired, to a great degree, by Diane Scamzer, a courageous woman, who with little experience of birth, chose to have her baby at home rather than in the hospital, to avoid common heavy-handed practices like drugging women so heavily that their babies were born in a stupor. After her own home birth, Diane answered the call from other women to help them and their families through the journey of giving birth at home.

In the summer of 1969 Diane and her little son Dabe (pronounded _Da_'bay), whose name means guide, came to stay with us while her husband, John, was out at sea working as a salmon fisherman. She was a bright and joyful woman who laughed a lot and lived a rather fluid life without schedules or calendars, which was a great revelation to me. She told many stories of home births and people she had helped. She sometimes mentioned Lew and Estelle, a couple who had recently moved to Boulder Creek and suggested we should meet them.

Sometime in the fall, Fred and I were happy to discover that I was pregnant, beginning a trajectory that would change the course of our lives forever, though we didn't know it at the time. For a short while, everything was flowers and magic and happy little birds singing, and then Diane announced she and John were moving to Oregon.

Though initially it felt like we were left with no support, from somewhere deep inside me, the knowledge grew that everything was okay. As my pregnancy progressed, Fred and I spent a lot of time studying *The Handbook for Rural Midwives* and I learned to trust my body and its connection to the universe in deep ways I had never known. Though Fred and I both felt intuitively that everything would work out well, we still looked for and found a doctor in Santa Cruz who agreed to act as our backup resource if we needed him, which fortunately, as it turned out, we didn't.

With Fred as my support, and in the presence of a few friends, I gave birth to a beautiful baby girl. Though the experience rocked me to my very core, it was nothing compared to the depths I needed to delve to learn how to care for the little being who was now totally dependent on me. Giving birth felt like the easy part. Learning how to care for and raise a little baby seemed beyond me. I felt clueless and alone. Much of the way I had been living my life didn't work any more and it no longer made sense to be dancing on mountaintops during the full moon.

I began to seek a new approach to life, spending long hours walking in the woods with my little daughter and trying to make sense of my new situation. After awhile, as Diane's earlier suggestion had foreshadowed, I had a "chance" encounter with Estelle in the laundromat with her sweet, round little baby boy. We began to share stories of birth and get to know one another. A couple of years later, Estelle and her husband, Lew, had a second child, a daughter. And Nick and Betsy entered our lives. From Betsy, I would learn the importance of honoring menstruation and also the art of blessingway rituals.

One election day, Estelle, went to YMCA Camp Campbell to vote. Ever a woman of vision and insight, she realized that the camp was left standing unused much of the year and saw great potential for its facilities. She and Lew, Nick and Betsy, and Fred and I and our kids were given permission to use the camp in exchange for helping build a trail system under Fred's guidance. We filled out the necessary paperwork to be considered a school and began home schooling our children, swimming in the pool, rowing boats in the river, using the campfire stage for drama, and sharing meals by the fire in the dining room during the winter, sometimes joined by our friends Peter and Diana and their family and Bella and her daughters.

When Diane Scamzer moved away, it left a hole that began to be filled by other women who felt impelled to help people who longed for the experience of giving birth at home. Among them was my friend Raven, who always seemed to me to be filled with a powerful and fearless energy, and was one of the driving forces, along with Kate Boland and a number of brave and beautiful women, in the formation of the Institute of Feminine Arts which began to hold classes and conferences in midwifery and childbirth at Camp Campbell.

Around the same time, Fred was busy working on the County General Plan for the San Lorenzo Valley, helping form the Save San Lorenzo River Association, and teaching ecology field classes through SLV adult school and UCSC Extension.

Throughout all the outer activity in our lives, my inner world continued to be in turmoil, as I had a gnawing feeling that there was something missing. I spent a lot of time looking in the wrong places to fill that gap until finally, I began saying heartfelt, fervent prayers to God for help.

Not long after that, my prayers were answered when the Hanuman Fellowship held a retreat at Camp Campbell with their teacher, Baba Hari Dass, a silent monk from India, who they called Babaji as a term of endearment. There was a deep and palpable peace emanating from him that filled me with a sense of hope.

Though he didn't speak, he could communicate with a look, an intake of breath, or a nod without uttering a word. He taught powerful lessons full of truth and wisdom by writing short, to-the-point messages on a small chalkboard. One of the most powerful ways he taught was through his own example, serving God through serving humanity.

On Sundays, the Hanuman Fellowship held satsang with Babaji, using available multi-purpose rooms in various elementary schools in Santa Cruz. Satsang, meaning "gathering of truth," included chanting of sacred songs (kirtan), meditation, and questions and answers with Babaji writing on his chalkboard which was read aloud by one of his students. A few times a year, there were more yoga retreats at Camp Campbell and later, just over the hill at Camp Swig above Saratoga on Highway 9.

Before long, the Hanuman Fellowship began to build a center on Mount Madonna. With help from dedicated members of the Fellowship, Fred and John Stanley were hired to do a resource inventory and write a management plan for the property to submit to the County. Once the project was begun, I came up to Mount Madonna as often as I could, riding up the mountain in the Fellowship van with my daughter. There were many projects needed to build the beginnings of a center and Babaji showed up every work day conferring about the various projects of the day and working very hard himself on the physical tasks necessary to begin what would become Mount Madonna Center for the Arts and Sciences – building rock walls, dragging brush, raising walls on the buildings, and inspiring many levels of work so that no one was left out.

The work was hard and lasted from early morning until afternoon, when we would break for lunch. During lunch, the children who had been enjoying their own activities, including rehearsals for the children's Ramayana, would gather around Babaji, sitting on his lap, laughing and playing with him. Children loved Babaji and he loved them, often making time to be with them. After lunch, we would all go up the hill to a makeshift volleyball court, where Babaji encouraged everyone to participate.

Over the years inspired by Babaji's energy, Mount Madonna Center grew to include a retreat center, Mount Madonna School serving grades K-12, and Mount Madonna Institute devoted to teaching the ancient art of Ayurvedic healing. There was also the establishment of the Pacific Cultural Center in Santa Cruz, and an orphanage and school in India serving many children whose lives were saved or greatly improved because of its existence.

Babaji taught that the goal of life is peace. His simple but powerful lessons included "Live a virtuous life," "Ego, attachment and desire are the cause of all problems," "Nothing happens before its time," and "Love everyone, including yourself." His personal advice to me was "family first," which I have always taken to heart.

Toward the end of the 70s, the sleepy little community of Boulder Creek began to grow. Small vacation cabins were turned into year-round residences and the population increased fairly rapidly. I got involved in precinct walking to help defend Ed Borovatz, our Fifth District Supervisor representing the San Lorenzo Valley and Scotts Valley, from a recall election. I felt a little intimidated at first, but I came to enjoy having constructive conversations with people who might disagree with me and sometimes actually seeing their opinions change. Ed and Pat Liteky, who had been the Supervisor before him, were the beginning of a change from the good-old-boy network on the Board whose main purpose seemed to be to make "improvements" to infrastructure that supported large growth and development throughout the Valley.

Unfortunately, Ed was recalled and replaced by Pat Liberty, who represented a regression toward over-building and development. Because of the weird way the recall worked, Pat won even though she received fewer votes in her favor than Ed had. Nancy Macy and I went to visit Pat Liberty after her "election" to voice our strong support in favor of protecting our valley from over-building. She was very cordial and gave us the answers she thought we wanted to hear, smiling and nodding at whatever we said, but it was obvious that she had no intention of giving any real consideration to our concerns.

Toward the end of the 70s, Fred and I enrolled our daughter in Evergreen School, a small private school that was just starting up in Ben Lomond. The principal of the school was Sheila Carrillo with whom I would work 20 years later to form a group devoted to reducing prejudice in our valley schools, but that's a story for another millennium.

Two of the parents whose sons were students in Evergreen School were Julie Mackie and Joe Cucchiara. Joe took up the challenge of running against Pat Liberty in the next election for Supervisor and like many other people who didn't want to see her continue in office, I devoted a lot of time and energy working on Joe's campaign, walking door to door throughout many precincts in the Fifth District under the able direction of Joe's campaign manager, Fred Keeley, who would later take Joe's place as Supervisor when Joe's time in office ended due to term limits. It was during their campaigns that I came to realize the value of working in local elections to help make positive changes in my community.

The eighties began quite dramatically with a series of heavy rains, which caused many mudslides, resulting in widespread property damage and many deaths, and highlighting the importance of coming together as a community to help each other. Community heroes like Mary Hammer, Nancy Macy, Annette Marcum and many others formed emergency relief projects to help people in need.

At some point, I joined the board of the Valley Women's Club, later serving as secretary and then as president for two years. I would sometimes take a moment during our meetings to sit back and marvel at how amazing this group of women were in their ability to have long, thoughtful, constructive discussions and come to important decisions with harmony and respect for each other's varying points of view.

The more I spend time consciously recalling the past, the more long-forgotten memories come to the surface of my mind. I remember many things that were really important focuses in my life in the 70's – the beginnings of the natural foods movement and making weekly trips to the Santa Cruz Cooperative which I think later became Community Foods Market to stock up on healthy, organic, whole foods which were not available in valley grocery stores; Mira Haslam and her husband, whose name I don't remember, opening the wonderful People's Market in Felton, making it easier to get healthy food on a regular basis without having to go all the way to Santa Cruz; Mr. Natural's, a small hole-in-the-wall natural foods store in Boulder Creek where I could walk into town with my daughter and get a glass of carrot juice before heading across the street to the rec hall to spend the afternoon; and Charlie and Barbara's fruit stand where I was introduced to the wonder of mangoes and the magic of melons in season before it was shut down to make way for a fancy, new County Bank, which later closed and the space is now occupied by our local Liberty Bank. I also remember the Blue Bird Bakery where Lily the Cat Lady could go in and get warm on a cold winter's day in the middle of her rounds to feed all the stray cats in Boulder Creek, and the Burl Theater, in the place where Boulder Creek Pizza and Pub now stands, which showed old movies and provided a space for local talent sharing.

There were many changes from the end of the 60's through the 80's, both internal and external. The times I spent in deep introspection have proven to be invaluable in setting my life in a more positive direction. Many of my thoughts related to birth and growth have begun to shift and merge with the awareness of death and lessons it has already begun to teach me. At this point in my life, as I begin my seventy-third year, life continues to be a revelation. I still have a fair amount of energy and a will to keep moving forward, but I also am aware that I move more slowly than I used to and I have to let go of some issues and activities that are still important to me, having faith that these things will now be taken up by the next generations as I begin to understand more clearly that the same struggles and issues our community is dealing with today have been going on all over the world for eons, and I am only one tiny cell in a very large organism that is beyond my comprehension.

Chapter 16
Nancy Macy:
Environmental Activism
and the Valley Women's Club in the 1970s and 80s

It was a warm March day, after a rainy winter in 1978. A group of women had gathered in the Boulder Creek home of Mary Hammer, in Boulder Creek. It was a feisty group and the discussion was animated. A few were outspoken about the politics of the School Board and the possibility of the High School losing its accreditation; a couple others discussed new evidence of continuing septic pollution along parts of the San Lorenzo River; a few bemoaned the erosion the rains had caused that muddied the creeks and River; another was active in promoting the Nuclear Safeguards Initiative.

Every woman in the room was already active in the community. From serving on the County's Planning Commission or on the Water Board or Board of Education, to being active behind the scenes in education, women's health, election campaigns and environmental groups. We all cared deeply about the Valley and recognized the need to organize to become a stronger influence by joining forces.

Mary Hammer, Ann Gulliver and Su Haynes had served as officers on the board of the *Save San Lorenzo River Association* and were all seasoned veterans of many earlier political and environmental campaigns to protect and restore the river. Everyone was worried about the mounting pressure on the Water Board to allow ever increasing numbers of new water hook-ups, when the systems couldn't handle it due to many infrastructure issues. Mary's comfortable living room was full, with couches and chairs and ottoman occupied and several seated on the floor. Sipping on cool drinks, tea or coffee, and munching on home-made treats, the group quieted down as Mary asked Bonnie Gee to explain her idea about creating a new women-led community organization. Bonnie talked about the San Lorenzo Valley and what it meant to us – its beauty and its environmental problems. She talked about the SLV community; always a haven for individuals seeking solitude and independence, the Valley had become a draw for masses of people fleeing "over the hill" congestion – bringing many of those problem with them.

First seen as a boon, Silicon Valley commuters stimulated a growing bedroom community and some economic growth. New subdivisions sprang up; summer cabins were occupied full-time. Seen as troublesome, Hippies and other free-thinkers found refuge in the rural coastal mountains too. Many locals worried as traditional values, and sacrosanct private property rights and independence, seemed threatened by the many newcomers and changing values they brought in.

We were all inspired by Bonnie's words, and embraced the need for increased collaboration focused on San Lorenzo Valley issues, embraced Bonnie's vision. No one loved meetings, so it would be an action-oriented organization of women willing to become educated in-depth on the broad-range of quality of life and environmental issues. Then, by consensus, to take appropriate action as needed.

We decided upon the name, *The Valley Women's Club*. (*Of the San Lorenzo Valley* was added as incorporation and a 501-c-3 non-profit). Yes, it was tongue in cheek. We wanted to empower women but the image of a women's club at the time was one of women in dresses, wearing white gloves and hats, sipping tea, and supporting good causes. However, the gloves are work gloves, the hats work hats, the tea often herbal, and the good causes include empowering women, protecting the environment, supporting good education, educating the community, responding in a crisis, and influencing government. Mary later said, "We wanted to break that mold and say, 'Hey, we can be activists so watch out'..." We became very famous for that.' We chose the name to emphasize the power of women, not to exclude men.

In that first afternoon, as someone relatively new to the community, I was elected President. Other officers included Mary, Bonnie, Su and the wonderful Anne Gulliver. I wrote the first Newsletter inviting people to join and listing some of the concerns; it was mimeographed and passed around. The idea spread by word of mouth as well, and people began to join. *The Valley Press* and *The Log* (small local weekly papers) each published an article, with a photograph, about the new group. At first only women joined, but within the first few months, as things began to happen, men wanted to join as well – an indication that our name was a draw, not a drawback.

From the outset, a major focus was land-use issues – already the hot-topic for local activists. There was a lot to learn about many complex issues, and there was enormous economic and political pressure to allow continued growth. That didn't slow this group down.

Plans for additional major roads had already been made; their routes were indicated on the County's General

Plan's maps. An extension of the 280 Freeway was to sweep through to the Coast from San Jose; a second wide road was to parallel Hwy 9 -- on the other side of the River -- hooking up to a major road cutting straight from Felton to Scotts Valley and Hwy 17 (yes – that's Mount Hermon Rd.)

The solutions for our inadequate water supply system needed to sustain the proposed growth was unregulated wells, and multiple dams on SLV creeks. On Newell Creek, Loch Lomond Dam and its reservoir had been constructed in 1960. The next dam scheduled was to be on Zayante Creek (a major Coho and Steelhead habitat) and several more were shown on General Plan maps.

At the coast, PG&E had proposed a nuclear power plant near Davenport, and a massive resort was planned for Lighthouse Point in Santa Cruz. A new University of California campus bloomed. Pressure increased for massive housing subdivisions both along the coast and in the SLV, along with demands to expand commercial development along Hwy 9 beyond town boundaries, threatening scenic vistas and open space. Pressure was on to modify the County's General Plan to allow *all* this development.

We all loved the old-fashioned feel of our small towns, along with the beauty and relative remoteness of SLV communities. We were not alone in this. These were contributing factors to their appeal, as was their relative affordability. Thus, an influx of new residents overflowed into the SLV from the San Francisco South Bay Area, as growth there turned acres of orchards into suburban sprawl and crowded freeways.

In the SLV, seasonal cabins with Spartan amenities were converted to year-round housing; modernized bathrooms and kitchens and laundries with large appliances were added, significantly increasing year-round water demands and revealing septic systems inadequate for the volume of waste water, especially during wet winters. Expansive subdivisions with large family homes contrasted to the many clusters of small seasonal vacation cabins -- subdivisions of earlier decades. This brought significant suburban growth throughout the SLV. The growth benefitted many SLV locals financially, as land and home values rose and businesses grew, but large developers benefitted the most, and pressure grew politically to provide the costly infrastructure demands of thousands of additional homes planned for the area – as reflected in the 1960 General Plan.

Due to this rapid growth, detrimental environmental impacts were inevitably accelerated. Historically the SLV was a center for environmentally destructive extraction industries -- timber, lime, tan bark, sand and oil among them. By this time, some of these no longer existed, and others were reduced in economic value. Forests that had been literally denuded of trees at the turn of the century had a flourishing second growth after fifty years; wildlife had returned. The Watershed was restoring itself. State Parks that had saved the old-growth redwoods were a popular draw for tourists, and summer visitors had brought seasonal income to the community. Lime kilns no longer burned trees for fuel but became historically interesting features. There were fewer quarries eager for sand deposits from ancient oceans (while others remained productive), tan bark was no longer needed for the defunct tannery, and no more oil derricks functioned. New sources of revenue were needed, and residential and commercial development seemed a panacea.

The very things that long-time residents cherished, however, and the very enticements that brought seasonal income to the area, were being destroyed by this growth. Accelerated degradation of riparian corridors from erosion and impermeable surfaces (thanks to more roads and housing construction), increasing water pollution (septic, non-point and solid waste), and traffic, were all affecting wildlife, causing landslides, and threatening waterways and drinking water sources. Fish and wildlife were again reduced, invasive plants spread further into the forests, more threatened and endangered native species were identified, and barely renewed second growth forests were increasingly logged as the State took away local land use control of this crucial resource.

Concern grew to restrain this growth, to protect and restore the environmental resources that had provided a valued quality of life and protected the watershed and its native flora and fauna. Much had been happening, including that the SLV's 1967 General Plan – a developer's dream – was amended due to public pressure. A *Citizen's Review Committee* was created, and land-use planning processes providing guidelines for sustainable growth were instituted. "*Save the San Lorenzo River Association*" was formed, focusing on SLV Water District Board of Directors' elections and supporting the decision to curtail new hook-ups with a moratorium. Supervisorial elections brought in environmentally aware representatives (Pat Liteky in the 5th District, followed by Ed Borovatz).

The push for increasing development did not cease. The demand was too high, and the controversies politically volatile. It was in these circumstances that **The VWC** (soon to be "Association, Incorporated," as a 501-c-3 non-profit) was started. While our community focus resulted in many contributions to health and safety, education, the arts, and more – our reputation was built on environmental action, empowering women, and interaction with local government.

The VWC knew it was imperative to inform the community – to open hearts and minds to the interconnections that we all share – environmental, economic, social, cultural. So much was at stake, and at a crucial tipping-point at the time.

1970's – Recall of Supervisor Impacts Land Use Decisions. General Plan Amendments Proposed to Significantly Increase Housing Developments, including Galleon Heights in Boulder Creek.

Two things happened in short order that would impact land use issues. First, 5th District Supervisor Ed Borovatz was facing a Recall in the June, 1978 election. Ed was a great guy – a teacher. He had been appointed to finish the term of Patrick Liteky in 1975, and was elected in his own right for the term starting in 1977. His opposition said he'd delayed construction of the County Jail and that warranted his Recall. (1st District Supervisor Phil Baldwin was also recalled. Neither had been unethical or done anything illegal.)

Why would a new women's organization seeking to gain 501-c-3 non-profit status, become involved in this? Obviously, the VWC could not be and was not involved in campaigns for or against individuals running for office. Taking stands on issues, however, was important, and The Recall was a bad thing and we all knew it was being unfairly manipulated to remove Ed from office.

The Recall process in Santa Cruz County allowed anyone to be on a simultaneous ballot to replace the affected official, if the recall were successful. The top vote-getter took office, inevitably allowing a small minority of voters to "elect" a Supervisor. This was a total anathema to the principle of election by majority vote, so the VWC took a stance against the recall *process*. A second factor, whether the *reason* for the recall failed to meet recall criteria or not, was also a powerful reason for this stance. It didn't.

However, money talks in a campaign and the Recall was successful (but only by a mere 75 votes). This allowed the top vote-getter, Scotts Valley resident, Pat Liberty, to become Supervisor. This change in leadership brought interesting challenges regarding land use issues as the new majority of Supervisors began to chip away at existing protections, claiming they were time-consuming and expensive for builders, and attempted an overhaul of the General Plan to enable widespread housing and commercial development.

One example was a proposal to modify zoning regulations, to expand the number of parcels considered "developable" in rural areas. It would especially impact the SLV. The plan was to allow the construction of homes with both a septic system and a well *on parcels of less than ½ acre*. With shaking knees, I spoke as VWC President at the Board of Supervisors' meeting when the issue was under consideration, joining other speakers and dozens of residents who wrote letters to object. Carefully painting a vivid picture of the potential for contamination to a home's groundwater water source, my comments helped convince three Supervisors to deny the change in policy. This did not forestall the Board from continuing push for General Plan amendments to expand housing subdivisions, including the Galleon Heights subdivision, originally filed for in November of 1975. However, simply getting the message out there felt good, and made it easier to speak the next time, and the next.

Galleon Heights was a major housing development proposal for more that 350 homes outside Boulder Creek (off Hwy 236 above the Boulder Creek Golf Club). It was mired in controversy for over 12 years. This was a real test of commitment and an opportunity to involve more people as word spread and people became worried. Newly involved women learned the issues and how to speak and write about them. We learned that the impacts of such a huge development, in that location, were untenable. Sandy erosive soils on steep slopes threatened erosion and septic effluent contamination of both surface and groundwater sources, including those of downslope water systems. The critical water supply source for the Bracken Brae neighborhood was faced with severe contamination and degradation. They sued to stop the development. Two stages of building were completed, but it was eventually stopped as opposition mounted, as the VWC and other organizations appealed, arguing that it subverted the General Plan, and Bracken Brae won its lawsuit. Galleon Heights was stalled and no more homes were constructed – and more people were involved.

Our ability to involve people, help them become educated on the issues and providing guidance in how to speak and write on the issues, has been a major achievement and was recognized by the Santa Cruz County Women's Commission. The VWC was presented with an award for empowering women to be effective in their communities at the Commission's first annual awards luncheon.

1980's – Proposals to Amend the County's General Plan Threaten to "Destroy Water-supply Watershed Lands." VWC Initiates Candidates' and Issues' Forums. Precedent-setting Ordinances Put Environmental Protection to the Fore Thanks to the *Watershed Management Plan*. Two Major Disasters Bring People Together, and Town Plans Start.

The 1980's were packed with controversy and discord. Ironically it was through natural disasters that the community was brought together and the VWC gained new respect.

Before the June 3rd, 1980 election of Brookdale resident, Joe Cucchiara, as 5th District Supervisor, the majority Supervisors were leading an attempt to modify the County General Plan's land-use policies in significantly detrimental ways. VWC President Vikki Lee presented a "Statement of Concern" that clearly delineated the potentially disastrous changes. This included amendments to lower the minimum acreage required for housing on various designated protected lands (such as water-supply and groundwater recharge parcels, and resource lands such as timber, quarry and agricultural). She demonstrated unequivocally that doubling and tripling the number of homes, with their attendant roads and out-buildings, would degrade water supply and remove resource lands from production.

The Supervisors wanted more buildable lots, and were willing to take the chance of environmental degradation. Their proposed Plan modifications included plans for importation (via pipeline) of water from outside the county for agricultural use. This pointed to a dependency on outside water that would necessarily be threatened during periods of drought. The new Plan would also allow subdivisions in areas of poor groundwater supply, with obvious potential for problems. Especially significant for the SLV, developments within 100 feet of a perennial stream would be readily permitted, threatening degradation of these important waterways throughout the Watershed.

Reducing the requirement for a geologic hazards assessment from a 15 percent slope to a 30 percent slope, and allowing subdivisions in fault zones, threatened grave consequences due to potential health and safety issues.

Finally, the amended Plan would allow commercial development far beyond town boundaries, undermining viability of town businesses in town. This would destroy small-town atmosphere, and eliminate the scenic roadway's bucolic, forested beauty and sense of open space.

The VWC created a chorus of dissent. Through the VWC's outreach efforts, using election techniques like neighborhood coffees and hanging posters everywhere, more and more residents were convinced of dangers and short-term thinking of these amendments. We all showed up at Supervisor's meetings, speaking with emotion backed by information. We reached out to other organizations.

Serendipity is a real thing, because, in the meantime, **The San Lorenzo River Watershed Management Plan** (prepared by Santa Cruz County's watershed management office under CA State Department of Fish & Game's *Protected Waterways Program*) had been introduced in the Spring of 1979. Despite the disfavor of the Supervisor majority, it would be adopted in 1980, and helped increase understanding of the problems the proposed General Plan modifications would cause.

The Watershed Management Plan's adoption was due to a dozen Valley Women's Club members each devoting many hours to tabling at local markets and enticing local businesses to offer copies on their counters, thus introducing the Plan to hundreds of SLV residents, and distributing official summaries of the Plan for them to review. Within a few weeks, the VWC had distributed almost 3,000 copies of the summary booklets. Support for the Plan jumped, public pressure rose, so the Supervisors approved it.

The Plan was a great teaching tool. It was truly an eye-opener! It described the functions of the San Lorenzo River watershed, and effectively proved that specific human impacts were causing potentially irreversible damage. And, proved that those actions needed to be regulated through County ordinances. The headline announcing publication of the plan, in the May 31, 1979 edition of the San Jose Mercury's Santa Cruz County section, read, "Growth Blamed for Soil Erosion, River Pollution." It quoted the Watershed Management Plan saying, "Past water resources planning has focused entirely on water supply development to the neglect of preserving necessary flows in the streams for fish life, recreation, water quality protections, aesthetics and for down-stream water users." The article pointed to the "major source of the river's problems … the rapid development of the San Lorenzo Valley. Some 33,000 people make their home in the river's 138-square-mile watershed… As homes are built in the valley, hillsides are cut up and vegetation removed, causing erosion, described in the plan as the river's No. 1 problem." The erosion rate was 2-to-4 times the natural rate and was causing a muddy, sediment-choked river, roads and homes weakened by the undermining action of erosion, increased flood danger and a damaged habitat for fish and other river life.

The No. 2 problem was contamination from human waste due to malfunctioning or inadequate septic systems, causing health hazards, "especially where the river is used as a domestic water supply and for recreation."

Solutions seem obvious now. They included an erosion control ordinance, a pre-sale inspection procedure of septic systems to assure proper function, an ordinance requiring that runoff from development be "no greater than it was prior to the development" and, more and better use of groundwater for domestic supplies to reduce River water use. (Regrettably and inevitably, this caused the current groundwater depletion crisis.) Costs were estimated at $1.5 million in capital expenditures for construction and equipment, and $265,000 for administration. A public hearing was scheduled and the proposed solutions would then be brought to the Board of Supervisors.

The proposals would be controversial to the Board majority, but community pressure led to the adoption of the Plan. Implementation, however, would be piecemeal until the 1980 elections brought a new majority into office in January of 1981.

Realizing that the General Plan Amendments, and implementation of the SL River Watershed Management Plan, would be among the issues in the upcoming Supervisorial election, the VWC, in conjunction with the *Environmental Council* and the *League of Women Voters*, provided a **Candidates' Forum** for the community. Pat Liberty would be up for re-election and a new candidate, Joe Cucchiara would be running against her. He supported implementing the mandates in the Watershed Management Plan; she supported modifying the General Plan. The goal was to enable voters to see and hear and question the three Supervisorial candidates running in the June, 1980 election. This was the first in an on-going VWC tradition – bringing candidates for local and regional elections to convenient, local venues, in a format that encouraged open and honest discussion of issues. People showed up with banners and signs, and had challenging questions for the candidates. An exciting tradition was born. (Due to the near-violence and rude interruptions by some of those holding signs and supporting one candidate over another, signs and demonstrations were not allowed in the future, and questions were written on cards, with League of Women Voters' skilled moderators making sure that each candidate was respected and that each was given equal opportunity to present his/her qualifications and priorities.

The forums later included SLV Water Board candidates, analysis of local ballot measures, and then candidates for State elections (State Assembly and State Senator). Always well attended, these Primary and General Election Forums have provided local voters a real opportunity to voice their concerns and to understand issues of personal and general concern, enabling them to make informed choices.

As a result of a better-informed electorate, the newly elected Board of Supervisors would assure passage of a series of ordinances designed to implement protections delineated in the Watershed Management Plan. The ordinances included:

-the **Erosion Control Ordinance** (expanded over time into specific guidelines in every conceivable situation) (http://www.sccoplanning.com/PlanningHome/ Environmental/ErosionStormwaterPollutionControl/ ErosionControlPlanRequirements.aspx),

-the **Riparian Corridor and Wetlands Ordinance** (expanded and refined over time) http://www.codepublishing. com/CA/SantaCruzCounty/html/SantaCruzCounty16/ SantaCruzCounty1630.html

-the **Grading Ordinance** (also expanded and refined since then) (http://www.codepublishing.com/ CA/SantaCruzCounty/html/SantaCruzCounty16/ SantaCruzCounty1620.html, and

-a **Septic System Inspection Ordinance** that later grew into Environmental Health's broader **Sewage Disposal Ordinance** (http://scceh.com/Home/Programs/ LandUse,SewageDisposalWasteWaterManagement/ HowSepticSystemsareRegulated.aspx)

(Note: These ordinances became the model for watershed protection, including the **Fishnet 4C Program**. This Program was a county-based, regional salmonid protection and restoration program. In 2001 the Program published a study on the *Effects of County Land Use Policies and Management Practices on Anadromous Salmonids and Their Habitats*. It pointed out a weakness that undermines the effectiveness of our **Riparian Corridor and Wetlands Ordinance** – that each county allows the buffers to be waived if they make a legal parcel unbuildable. And it clearly defined important steps for counties to undertake, to improve the chances for salmonid survival.)

An exciting side-effect of increasing awareness was the overlap into public education, as our San Lorenzo Valley Unified School District Board of Education agreed that understanding our watershed could be an effective teaching tool for virtually every skill, from art and literature to math and science. The Watershed Academy, and other options, became available to local students due to this forward thinking.

At the beginning of the 1980's, the **Storm of '82**, brought home the enormous repercussions of building residences in our all-too-common slide-prone areas. The most devastating and well-known was *the Love Creek Slide.* It and other mud-flows took lives, caused injuries, destroyed roads and changed the route of perennial creeks. The Valley Women's Club and the **Valley Resource Center** (now **Mountain Community Resources,** or **MCR**), under Mary Hammer and Linda Moore, set up and ran the disaster response center in Boulder Creek. This brought increased respect for the Valley Women's Club. Mary and Linda and others worked virtually non-stop for weeks to organize and assist communications, bring in urgently needed supplies, and guide folks in seeking assistance. (Similar work was undertaken by **Valley Churches United Missions** (**VCUM**) in Ben Lomond.)

In the aftermath, the VWC joined widespread demands for the County to develop improved and streamlined landslide protection regulations, now seen in County code relating to Geologic Hazards. This directly impacts land use throughout our steep mountains.

The VRC and VWC then initiated a Valley-wide disaster

preparedness program, including the *Neighborhood Survival Network*. This program, administered by the VRC and promoted by the VWC, trained neighborhood leaders in disaster response (from the Red Cross), and set up a system where neighborhood residents would be prepared to help one another if isolated in a disaster. The system was honored by FEMA, and became the model for neighborhood disaster preparedness at the time. (This was just a part of the VWC's long-standing effort to inform residents about how to prepare for disaster, from wildfire to storm or earthquake. Such preparations were defined and encouraged in the VWC Newsletter back within its first year, and several preparedness workshops have been held since then.) All three organizations (VWC, VRC and VCUM) continue education and disaster response.

Near the close of the '80s, the Loma Prieta Earthquake provided another reminder about the fragility of our Valley, and people again came together to help one-another. Disaster response was vastly improved due to improved coordination between the County, law-enforcement, transportation agencies, the schools, and non-profit organizations.

When the process to create **Town Plans** in the SLV (as well as other areas of the County) was initiated in the late '80s, dozens of VWC members supported and participated in the process. It was a part of the concept of specifically planning for sustainability in the areas where communities had existed for generations. It was designed to be guided and governed by *local* residents. Each of the Valley towns' plans emphasized the *rural* and *bucolic* nature of their towns, and the importance of maintaining open space, viewsheds, and forested lands in their surroundings. Town Plans brought significant improvements to the town centers, like undergrounding utility wires, and would have a continuing impact on land

use decisions. http://www.sccoplanning.com/PlanningHome/
SustainabilityPlanning/TownVillageSpecificPlans.aspx .

Looking to the Future

After 40 years of involvement in a broad range of concerns
and activities, our goals remain those of the earliest leaders.
The Club's Mission Statement now reads, **"The Valley
Women's Club is dedicated to community action, awareness
and leadership in environmental, educational, social, and
political concerns that affect the health and welfare of the
San Lorenzo Valley and our community."**
We are thus involved with programs and issues that affect
the community involving education, social and economic
equity, and women's rights and empowerment. Incredible
events, such as the first 18 annual Redwood Mountain
Faires, brought the often-divided community together. At
first a one-day fine arts and crafts show that soon became a
magnificent two-day music festival at Highlands Park, under
the loving guidance of Linda Moore for the first five years
-- and continued under the dedicated hands of other creative
Directors for thirteen years more. The Faire is now recreated
at Roaring Camp, and for the past nine years has featured
amazing arts and music and community fun, involving
hundreds of volunteers, and has provided over $350,000 to
local community groups, non-profits and schools. The VWC
sponsored poetry readings and art shows and even rock
concerts in Park Hall, featuring local high school bands.

Of greatest pride is the amazing on-going work for women's
equality. Our members attended the *United Nation's Fourth
World Conference on Women* in Beijing in 1995! And have
served on the County's Women's Commission, achieving
major guarantees for equality of pay and support for women.
All the while the VWC has involved women of all ages to

empower them to leadership roles in their community.

So much more was done, and all the while the focus on the environment was maintained. The first recycling center was founded within the first year and grew into our three, state certified, redemption and recycling centers, with dedicated employees serving the community. Also, during the Watershed Festival of Events – on-going since 2001, hundreds of people were led on hikes through the watershed and participated in workshops. Plus, every resident in the SLV received a series of informative brochures – on septic systems, erosion, and other topics, to help them live respectfully on the land. Amazing traditions were born and continue. We just held the 32nd Annual River & Road Cleanup, removing tons of trash and recyclables from the watershed.

The activities of the Valley Women's Club continue to this present day. It is beyond the scope and time frame of this story to include here. We aren't stopping after 40 years and counting. We are committed to continuing – and know well that it takes coalitions of individuals, organizations, businesses, government agencies, and government leaders working together to meet the challenges.

(The later period in the Valley Women's Club history is included as a chapter in the recently published **History Journal #9,** by the Museum of Art and History (MAH), entitled *Land Scapes: Activism that Shaped Santa Cruz County 1955-2015.*)

Bridge Mountain Foundation

There was a magical place nestled in the redwood forest high atop a mountain in Ben Lomond, California. Traveling way up Alba Road, turning right onto a small wooden bridge, and then onto a road with redwood foliage carpeting the ground beneath the majestic redwood trees. Approaching a large redwood lodge graced with sunlight you felt excitement, like you had arrived home. Originally called Dar Boha, which is a Bohemian phrase meaning "Gift of God". Dar Boha became the center for Bridge Mountain Foundation, which was purchased and incorporated by Ruth and Preston Prescott in 1958. From 1958 to 1975 Bridge Mountain became a spiritual growth center. Probably one of the first in California, as Esalen was not established in Big Sur until 1962. Ruth Prescott was a visionary, sculptor, and watercolor artist and Preston was a wellknown sculptor and a high school art teacher in San Jose. He exhibited his sculptures in many places including the De Young Museum in San Francisco. Ruth's vision was to have a place called The University of Living Arts. Her vision was to have a place where all were equal in a community of wisdom, creativity, and kindness. To radiate bright light out into the world. In 1943 The Prescott's had first purchased 20 acres which included a beautiful Amphitheater and built a home and sculpture studio nearby. The Amphitheater was an ancient Indian Healing Ground, a sacred grove where spirits abide. Dar Boha was originally built in 1940 by a wealthy Czechoslovakian man from Norway, it was used as a guest house to entertain friends in the movie industry and movie stars. The Bridge Mountain lodge could sleep up to 30 guests.

Ruth and Preston's dream was to "create a school where people would learn from their own inner wisdom through deep relaxation and the arts." Kay Ortman, another creative and forceful individual, met Preston in 1955 in Chico at a Camps Farthest Out gathering, which means going further out with Christ. Further out seems to have moved into the more spiritual realm and away from religion. Preston invited Kay to come see how special the land was in Ben Lomond. Kay liked what she saw. Kay had developed her own program of using classical music as a carrier wave to liberate people of blocks and self limitation, which would free them to be their own authentic selves. While in the Amphitheater that first day, of her visit, Kay received a long transmission on how to use music as medicine. She could see how her program would fit in with the Prescott's dream. She bought a home on Alba Road called the Great House and moved her son and husband to the Mountain. Soon Kay Ortman began the morning programs with guided relaxation exercises in the large upstairs room at Bridge Mountain. After the relaxation exercises, classical music would be played. Kay Ortman was a pioneer in the fields of relaxation exercises and movement to music. The classical music was used as a carrier wave to lift blocks out of peoples' bodies, by also combining massage and the arts. She used, writing, colored chalk, clay, and movement with music to free people of these blocks. Also to help them open to greater freedom in their own creative field. As one of the early practitioners of these methods, Kay was in the vanguard of the holistic healing field. She grew up in London where she studied music, dance, and movement to music. She also studied at Rudolph Steiner's schools of Eurythmy. Kay helped Ruth and Preston establish Bridge Mountain and worked with them for two years, until she decided to leave and create a program of her own, which she called Well-Springs. Ruth Prescott passed away in 1964 when she was 72 years old. Papa Wurtzbagh had purchased a cabin near Preston's home. Papa did gardening and maintenance for Bridge Mountain. His wife, Mama Wurtzbagh, was a spiritual women who led meditation groups and worked with young women in the community. They had two creative daughters, Liz, a spiritual young woman and Dena, an accomplished artist. When Liz's husband passed away suddenly, Preston invited Liz and her young son Alan Ashby, to move into his home on the upper floor. Liz helped cook and care for Ruth before she died. A women named Carolyn also shared the upstairs and later married Preston in 1965.

I first arrived at Bridge Mountain with my brother and my parents in1964. I was 13 years old. We lived in San Mateo and from the advice of a marriage counselor, and phychologist, named Dr. Jack Downing, my parents began their travels to Bridge Mountain. I don't believe I ever met Ruth Prescott. Dena did teach me watercolor early on from techniques she had learned from Ruth. Liz Ashby became the director of Bridge Mountain and took over Kay Ortman's responsibilities of leading the morning relaxation exercises. Liz was a clairvoyant and beckoned guests into her private warm sunny room for one on one insight and counseling. Jim Creighton arrived at Bridge Mountain and married Liz. There are so many people involved in the story and the history of the mountain. There were residents living there who were friendly greeters, which made you feel at ease when coming in to this new experience. Paul Snyder is one that stands out in my mind. A loving creative spiritual soul.

The very large upstairs room at Bridge Mountain had a stone fireplace at each end and beautiful smooth, shiny dark wood floors. Wonderful for dancing on in your bare feet or socks. There were moving blankets folded and stacked in one corner, so each person would have a floor matt for the relaxation exercises. The long wall had glass windows and doors all the way across looking out to the southeast was a view of redwood forests across the distant San Lorenzo Valley. If you walked out through the glass doors you would find yourself on a long patio deck with expansive views in 3 directions and old movie star style lounge furniture from the 1940s. On the other side of the large room, on the opposite long redwood wall, there was a door to the art room. There were only two types of medium, clay to sculpt with and large colored chalks to draw with on large sheets of newsprint. The blank newsprint was clipped on to a smooth masonite board. That door was always kept closed and when you were being creative in that sun drenched room you had to remain silent. Another door on the long wall went out to the Inner sunny courtyard where there were beautiful flower gardens. The third door led to the guest quarters. Only donations were accepted at Bridge Mountains to pay for workshops, retreats, spiritual counseling, accommodations, and food.

The early morning programs were invigorating and relaxing. Beginning with the relaxation exercises that went on for about 45 minutes. With some yoga exercises incorporated in to the relaxation exercise program and sometimes with a partner massaging each others shoulders. Group participation was encouraged. Coming from suburbia where no one ever hugged or showed much affection to each other, to Bridge Mountain where every one hugged each other naturally and openly, what a contrast. After the relaxation exercises you would lay down and relax on your matt and go into a deep peaceful place or you may even doze off listening to beautiful classical music. When you awoke and were refreshed you could go into the art room or dance freely to music. As a young teenager I felt very inhibited to come out of my hardened shell, or participate freely. It felt very awkward for me to participate in these programs. Somehow those fears soon melted away and I became eager to explore creative dancing, interacting in role play, learning how to massage and find meaning in my chalk drawings. We would have afternoon critiques of everyone's drawings. It was emotional, insightful and healing.

Breakfast was prepared downstairs for the guests, by the guests and the residents. There was always plenty of food. This was the first time I ever saw granola. We would make large trays of it and toast it in the ovens. Mostly healthy vegetarian food was prepared and served in the dining area, which was the central hub for inspiring conversations. Even though I was only 13 years old I found myself communicating with the guests in their 20s and 30s. I was changing and growing into a young adult. Sometimes there would be afternoon programs, we would walk to the Amphitheater, or sometimes I would head over to the children's camp and get to know the other children whose parents were participating at Bridge Mountain. Friendships I still have today. Lunch and dinner were always deliciously prepared with enthusiasm and appreciated by all. After dinner we would then all head upstairs to the immensely expansive room and have the evening program. This program was always different and not like the morning program. The room was filled with energy, movement, expression of feelings, interaction with the other guests in a free flowing dance movement. Just really fun, imaginative with expressive, creative play acting.

Non judgemental and accepting of every human being as they are. Accepting the true essence of who you are and loving that person, Sometimes there would be a guide to direct us into different aspects of creativity that then may lead into a whole other realm. It is hard to express into words about all of the spontaneous realms we would discover. All rewarding and meaningful in the moment. After this invigorating 2 hour experience we would head back downstairs to the small fireplace living room to reflect on the night and relax by the warm fire and sing American folk songs. Usually accompanied by a acoustic guitar player. One guitar player to mention is Kriyananda playing guitar and singing with the sweetest voice. A desciple of Parmanahanza Yogananda. He would come on the weekends. A wonderful end to a lovely weekend at Bridge Mountain.

We eventually moved to Ben Lomond in 1965 to be near Bridge Mountain. Sold our house in San Mateo and rented a two bedroom cabin on Alba Road. I was beginning my first year in High School. When I was not at school we spent most of our time involved with Bridge Mountain. They all became our very close family of friends. Preston impressed me as a creative sculptor and I loved going to his sculpture studio and learning about the process of creating his sculpture into stone, mold making, and his special stone compounds. Both my mother and I posed for sculptures of women he was creating. His property was beautiful with meadows among the redwoods. My father was very close to Preston and when my parents separated, my father rented a little studio apartment from Preston.

I can honestly say that Bridge Mountain changed my life in so many ways and I am thankful for the rich experiences I had there. They are engrained in the fabric of my being. I can only hope by writing about Bridge Mountain in some detail that someone out there can utilize this knowledge and put some of these practices and programs to work. To be able to continue to spread light out into the world where it is desperately needed in these times. To help individuals to regain their true natures. To carry that beacon of light out to you. How precious that is to me to be able to share this place, Bridge Mountain, with the world.

We moved down to the town of Ben Lomond in 1965 and my mother created the Bridge Mountain School of Living Arts in a large old house. That changed the community for the better. On my birthday, March 15th,

I was awoken at 5 am to find out that Liz Ashby Creighten had died on my birthday. That was such a shock for me. The guidance that she gave me for my life has been with me ever since. Bridge Mountain burned down in 1973 and then again in a final fire in1975. My mother received a phone call to let her know the only thing that survived the fire was a painting she had donated to the lodge, still hanging on the upstairs fireplace wall. My mother was able to sell the painting for $500. The funds could not have come at a better time, for my Mother to move on with her life.

The amphitheater at Bridge Mountain

Photo courtesy of Holly Harman

Chapter 18
Estelle Fein: Lew Fein on Astrology

Lew was a humanitarian, always interested in the internal workings and landscapes of people. When he discovered that astrology could be a helpful tool for these leanings, in 1966, he dove right into it, lock, stock and barrel.

He did not use astrology for fortune telling, but rather as a way to help discover and explore the inside story and to raise consciousness about it.

Lew was a man of the people. He kept compensation for his readings low and bartered when there was no money available. He did readings at the homes of clients or in his funky old trailer that resided at our home.

Lew never advertised or promoted himself. He let the community do that and never lacked for clients

Along the way many others discovered astrology and Lew was mentor to several of them.

Lew Fein began his professional life in NYC, as a design draftsman but his real life was destined to be in California, as an astrologer, a choice that gave him a long, satisfied life.

He authored many articles for newspapers, especially for the Free Spaghetti Dinner. Here is one of them.

ASTROLOGY

VI

The Mandala of the Soul

by Lewis Fein

"Philosophies and scientific systems of psychology have never been able to exercise a dominating influence on the life of humanity—not because there was something wrong with them as systems, nor because they were lacking in truth, but because the truth contained in them was only of theoretical value, born by the brain and not by the heart, thought out by the intellect and not realized in life." —Yogananda

The most constructive use of a natal chart lies in the innate potential it has to transfigure its meanings into our living personalities, to guide us to a closer understanding of our basic natures through the inherent power of the symbolization of the planets, houses, aspects, and signs. The analogy of the planet Venus, for instance, with the feelings of love, beauty, and appreciation is rooted in the very beginnings of man's consciousness. Perhaps it was the need to understand why a particular person or child or beautiful object had such a deep possessive effect on us that primitive man resorted to the symbols system. The need to name in order to understand, and eventually control, was the real root of Astrology.

Astrology has survived these many thousands of years because it is a living evolutionary relationship between our instincts and intellect and the cosmic forces that play around and through them. Our natal chart is our own personal mandala which shows us our own particular path of energy. The inscribed cross, which is the main attribute of a mandala, is the cross of our incarnation on this worldly plane. A mandala means a magic circle and this magic circle is the sacred area where our divine

natures are safe from the intrusion of the world of maya. It is up to us to re-discover our own immortality and sanctify this circle so we can receive back the inner vision that is rightfully ours.

It therefore follows that the chart must be understood as a whole unit and not as just one segment such as a sun sign or a moon sign, etc. It is important to keep this in mind because words tend to destroy wholes, and a certain amount of breaking down is required to effectively explain the inner workings of a chart.

The great cross in a horoscope is formed by the interception of the ascendent-descendent horizontal line, and the mid-heaven (medium coeli) -nadir (imum coelie) meridian. The former is called the line of awareness and the latter the line of concrete experience, or the irrational and rational axises respectively. A great many important correspondences are derived from the intersection of these two lines, which I have tried to illustrate in the accompanying diagram.

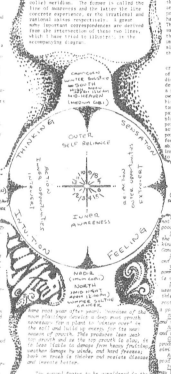

The importance of this division in the interpretation of a natal chart lies in the personality-temperment clues it gives, symbolized by the position of the planets in their relationship to these lines. A majority of planets (at least seven) above the ascendence-descendence horizon indicates that which can be perceived by our senses. It is our self reliance aspect, our ability to objectify our experiences, a consciousness of our selves and our need to see through the material plane. A majority of planets below the ascendent-descendent line indicates our ability to use our inner awareness, or our intuition. It is a pattern that seeks foundations in itself. Since the mandala always seeks unity it is important for the person having the majority of planets above the horizon to marshall his powers of outer self reliance and to seek out and recognize his inner potential to bring his life into the mandala. The same holds true for those with a majority of planets below the horizon, as their dharma is to use their intuition to understand what this earth experience is all about, to sharpen their feelings on the whetstone of consciousness.

The other division produced from this cross is the majority of planets to the east of the Mid-heaven-Nadir meridian. This indicates a person who is strongly influencing destiny through his own decisions. Here is a person who feels the need to control his own fate through the awareness of himself, his personality. It usually takes a important external event to make him realize his particular pattern of energy. A majority of planets to the west of this meridian finds a person who is cast in the role of a re-actor, someone struggling in a world of opportunities and circumstance, someone whose feelings and sensations are his most dependable guides. It will usually take a strong inner development to make him aware of how to best handle the circumstances of life.

Nature is energy--energy in rhythm, energy in cycles--birth**death, expansion**contraction, ebb**flow. Breathing, making love, growing vegetables--all are cyclic events & natural!

These energy cycles are interrelated--the economy, food chains; ecological niches--even life form affects and interacts with every other life form.

Our millions of farmers knew of the effect the cycle of the moon had on their crops. Through observation and experiment they learned that there was greater and healthier yield when seeds were sown during certain phases of the moon.

What follows is a planting guide based on the cycles of the moon and sun. The moon and the sun by their position relative to earth are the most important and dynamic factors affecting all life forms.

The most important factor to be considered when planting by astrology is the phase of the moon. The lunar cycle is divided into four quarters. The first and second occur from the new moon to the full moon (i.e., during the increasing light). The third and fourth quarters occur from the full moon to the new moon (i.e., in the decreasing light).

During the increasing light plant annuals that produce their yield above the ground. (An "annual" is a plant that completes its life cycle within one growing season and has to be seeded anew each year.) The increase of the moon produces a fast tender top growth and tender leaves or fruits.

During the decreasing light plant biennials, perennials, bulb and root plants. (Biennials include crops that are planted one season to winter over and produce crops the next, such as winter wheat. Perennials and bulb and root plants include all plants that grow from the

same root year after year). During one of the moon plantings develop a deep root growth necessary for a plant to 'winter over' in the soil and build up energy for its next season of growth. This produces less sap for growth and as the top growth is slow, it is less liable to damage from heavy frost, weather damage by winds, and hard freezes; bark or trunk is thicker and resists disease and insects better.

The second factor to be considered is the position of the moon by sign. In each of the twelve signs the moon reflects the special characteristics associated with that sign, and ideally your activities should be coordinated to take advantage of this natural cycle.

In Aries, the moon tends to dryness, barrenness and not very good results. It is not a good sign for general planting, but fairly good for pulling weeds and cultivating.

Taurus, being fairly reproductive and earthy, is a good sign for planting many crops, more particularly potatoes and root crops of quick growth.

Gemini, being dry, cold, and barren, is not good for any kind of planting but is good for pulling weeds and cultivating.

Cancer, being moist and very fruitful is the most productive sign in the zodiac; all kinds of seeds planted when the moon is in Cancer should produce good results.

Leo is the most barren sign in the zodiac and should be used only for killing weeds, etc.

Virgo is moist but barren, and is not recommended for planting or transplanting, but is very good for cultivating and weeding.

Libra is moist and semi-fruitful and is used for seeding hay, etc. Seeds planted at this time produce vigorous pulp growth and roots; and a reasonable amount of grain. It's a good sign for flowers and vines.

Scorpio is next to Cancer in productiveness and is used for the same purposes.

Sagittarius is generally considered barren, and will not give good results.

Capricorn is earthy in nature and quite productive. Good for potatoes, tubers, etc.; similar to Taurus, but perhaps a little drier. Aquarius is inclined to be barren and only good for cultivation.

Pisces, like Cancer, is very productive and may be used for the same purposes. It is moist and fruitful.

To summarize: Use Cancer, Scorpio, and Pisces for planting (and transplanting) whenever you can; Taurus and Capricorn are next in order of preference; then, Libra, Sagittarius, and Aquarius, in that order.

Don't forget that it is crucial to combine both sign and phase of the moon to insure maximum productiveness.

'to everything there is a season, and a
time to every purpose under heaven; a
time to be born, and a time to die; a
time to plant, and a time to pluck up
that which is planted.'

—Gwat

ASTROLOGY, *The Mandala of the Soul*
by Lewis Fein

Philosophies and scientific systems of psychology have never been able to exercise a dominating influence on the life of humanity -- not because there was something wrong with them as systems, nor because they were lacking in truth, but because the truth contained in them was only of theoretical value, born by brain and not by the heart, thought out by the intellect and not realized in life.
-- Govinda

The most constructive use of a natal chart lies in the innate potential it has to transfigure its meanings into our living personalities, to guide us to a closer understanding of our basic natures through the inherent power of the symbolization of the planets, houses, aspects, and signs. The analogy of the planet Venus, for instance, with the feelings of love, beauty, and appreciation is rooted in the very beginnings of man's consciousness. Perhaps it was the need to understand why a particular person or child or beautiful object had such a deep possessive effect on him that primitive man resorted to the symbols system. The need to name in order to understand, and eventually control, was the real root of astrology.

Astrology has survived these many thousands of years because it is a living evolutionary relationship between our instincts and intellect and the cosmic forces that play around and through them. Our natal chart is our personal mandala which shows us our own particular path of energy. The inscribed cross, which is the main attribute of a mandala, is the cross of our incarnation on this worldly plane, A mandala means a magic circle and this magic circle is the sacred area where our divine natures are safe from the intrusion of the world of maya. It is up to us to re-discover our own immortality and sanctify this circle so we can receive back the inner vision that is rightfully ours.

It therefore follows that the chart must be understood as a whole unit and not as just one segment such as a sun sign or a moon sign, etc. It is important to keep this in mind because words tend to destroy wholes, and a certain amount of breaking down is required to effectively explain the inner workings of a chart.

The great cross in a horoscope is formed by the intersection of the ascendent-descendent horizontal line, and the mid-heaven (medium coli) -nadir (imum coli) meridian. The former is called the line of awareness and the latter the line of concrete experience, or the irrational and rational axes respectively. A great many important correspondences are derived from the intersection of these two lines, which I have tried to illustrate in the accompanying diagram. [The mandala in the center of the image shown.]

The importance of this division in the interpretation of a natal chart lies in the personality-temperament clues it gives, symbolized by the position of the planets in their relationship to these lines. A majority of planets (at least seven) above the ascendent-descendent horizon indicates that which can be perceived by our senses. It is our self reliance aspect, our ability to objectify our experiences, a consciousness of our selves and our need to see through the material plane. A majority of planets below the ascendent-descendent line indicates our ability to use our inner awareness, or our intuition. It is a pattern that seeks foundations in itself. Since the mandala always seeks unity it is important for the person having the majority of planets above the horizon to marshal his powers of outer self reliance and to seek out and recognize his inner potential to bring his life into the harmony and balance implied in the mandala. The same holds true for those with a majority of planets below the horizon, as their dharma is to use their intuition to understand what this earth experience is all about, to sharpen their feelings on the whetstone of consciousness.

The other division produced from this cross is the majority of planets to the east of the Mid-heaven-Nadir meridian. This indicates a person who is strongly influencing destiny through his own decisions. Here is a person who feels the need to control his own fate through the awareness of himself; his personality. It usually takes an important external event to make him realize his particular pattern of energy. A majority of planets to the west of this meridian finds a person who is cast in the role of a reactor, someone struggling in a world of opportunities and circumstances, someone whose feelings and sensations are his most dependable guides. It will usually take a strong inner development to make him aware of how to best handle the circumstances of life.

==

Nature is energy -- energy in rhythm, energy in cycles -- birth**death, expansion**contraction, ebb**flow. Breathing, making love, growing vegetables -- all are cyclic events (& natural!)

These energy cycles are interrelated -- the sessions; food chains; ecological niches -- every life form affects and interacts with every other life form.

For millennia farmers knew of the affect the cycle of the moon had on their crops. Through observation and experiment they learned that there was greater and healthier yield when seeds were sown during certain phases of the moon.

What follows is a planting guide based on the cycles of the moon and sun. The moon and the sun by their position relative to earth are the most important and dynamic factors affecting its life forms.

The most important factor to be considered when planting by astrology is the phase of the moon. The lunar cycle is divided into four quarters. The first and second occur from the new moon to the full moon (i.e., during the **increasing** light.) The third and the fourth quarters occur from the full moon to the new moon (i.e., in the **decreasing** light.)

During the increasing light plant annuals produce their yield above the ground (An **annual** is a plant that completes its life cycle within one growing season and has to be seeded anew each year.) The increase of the moon produces a fast tender top growth and tender leaves or fruits.

During the decreasing light plane biennials perennials, bulb and root plants. (Biennials include crops that are planted one season to winter over and produced crops the next, such as winter wheat. Perennials and blue and root plants include all plans that grow from the same root year after year.) Decrease of the moon plantings develop a deep root growth necessary for a plant to **winter over** in the soil and build up energy for its next season of growth. This produces less weak top growth and as the top growth is slow, it is less liable to damage from heavy fruiting, weather damage by winds, and hard freezes; bark on trees is thicker and resists disease and insects better.

The second factor to be considered is the position of the moon by sign. In each of the twelve signs the moon reflects the special characteristics associated with that sign and ideally your activities should be coordinated to take advantage of this natural cycle.

In Aries, the moon tends to dryness, barrenness and not very good results. It is not a good sign for general planting, but fairly good for pulling weeds and cultivating.

Taurus, being fairly reproductive and earthy, is a good sign for planting many crops, more particularly potatoes and root crops of quick growth.

Gemini, being dry, cold, and baron, is not good for any kind of planting but is good for pulling weeds and cultivating.

Cancer, being moist and very fruitful is the most productive sign in the zodiac; all kinds of seeds planted when the moon is in Cancer should produce good results.

Leo is the most barren sign in the zodiac and should be used only for killing weeds, etc.

Virgo is moist but barren, and is not recommended for planting or transplanting, but is very good for cultivating and weeding.

Libra is moist and semi-fruitful and is used for seeding hay, etc. Seeds planted at this time produce vigorous pulp growth and roots; and a reasonable amount of grain. It's a good sign for flowers and vines.

Scorpio is next to Cancer in productiveness and is used for the same purposes.

Sagittarius is generally considered barren, and will not give good results.

Capricorn is earthy in nature and quite productive. Good for potatoes, tubers, etc.; similar to Taurus, but perhaps a little drier.

Aquarius is inclined to be barren and only good for cultivation.

Pisces, like Cancer, is very productive and may be used for the same purposes. It is moist and fruitful.

To summarize: Use Cancer, Scorpio, and Pisces for planting (and transplanting) whenever you can; Taurus and Capricorn are next in order of preference; then, Libra, Sagittarius, and Aquarius, in that order.

Don't forget that is is crucial to combine both sign and phase of the moon to insure maximum productiveness.

'to everything there is a season, and a
time to every purpose under heaven; a
time to be born, and a
time to die; a
time to plant, and a time to pluck up t
hat which is planted.'
-- Great88
[Actually, Pete Seeger 1962, The Birds 1965, from Ecclesiastes 3:1-8]

Ralph Abraham:
CONCLUSION

My first LSD trip resulted in my move from Princeton University to UCSC, as I recounted in our first volume. Hence this series of books. Another consequence is my interest in the psychedelic hypothesis, aka the stoned ape theory.

Definition.
The psychedelic hypothesis proposes that the ingestion of psychedelics by humans in history and prehistory has triggered our major cultural transformations.

In 2002, I created the Santa Cruz Hip History Project, with its website *www.ralph-abraham.org/1960s* to document the psychedelic hypothesis in connection with the birth of the Hip Santa Cruz subculture in the 1960s.

Proposition.
LSD catalyzed the formation of Hip Santa Cruz.

Proof.
1. The first volume of this series showed that
    * The Hip Pocket Bookstore (September 13, 1964),
    * The first Acid Test (November 27, 1965)
    * The Barn (Summer, 1966)
    * The Catalyst (Fall, 1966), and
    * The 25th Century Ensemble (1967)
-- all overtly psychedelic and crucial to the emerging Hip movement.
2. The second volume traced the extension of Hip

culture into the 1970's with the growth of the commune movement, alternative education, the women's movement and home births, full moon festivals, organic farming, occult books, and new directions in R&R music.

3. And in this volume, we follow further evolution of all of the threads of the second volume, as well as the emergence of environmental and civic movements, jazz, world music, Eastern spirituality. and astrology.

QED

INDEX
Hip Santa Cruz #1

INDEX
Hip Santa Cruz #2

Index

Symbols

A

C

W

CPSIA information can be obtained
at www.ICGtesting.com
Printed in the USA
FSHW010736081218
54256FS